HEALING WATERS

Veterans' Stories
of Recovery in
Their Own Words

Tight Lines!

Beau Beasley

2-20-24

HEALING WATERS

Veterans' Stories
of Recovery in
Their Own Words

BEAU BEASLEY

Foreword by Capt. Edwin P. Nicholson, USN (Ret.)

NO NONSENSE
FLY FISHING GUIDEBOOKS

Tucson, Arizona

Members of Project Healing Waters Fly Fishing from New York City sit along the Farmington River getting a briefing prior to their outing. Photo by Richard Franklin.

Healing Waters: Veterans' Stories of Recovery in Their Own Words

© 2023 Beau Beasley

ISBNs
Print: 978-1-892469-30-4
Ebook: 978-1-61881-245-2

Published by:
No Nonsense Fly Fishing Guidebooks
P.O. Box 91858
Tucson, AZ 85752-1858
www.nononsenseguides.com

No Nonsense Fly Fishing Guidebooks is an independent publisher and is not affiliated with Project Healing Waters Fly Fishing, Inc. These stories are provided in the interest of honoring and supporting veterans through the therapeutic approach of fly fishing and the friendships created as a result.

Printed in USA

Publisher: Howard Fisher
Editor: Cover to Cover LLC
Designer: Vicky Vaughn Shea, Ponderosa Pine Design

All interior photography by Beau Beasley, except as otherwise credited.

Front Cover Photo
J.R. Salzman, Sergeant (retired) U.S. Army National Guard, setting the hook on a nice rainbow. Photo by Beau Beasley.

Back Cover Photos
Top: Brian Trow has donated untold hours helping PHWFF and has served in a variety of roles. While he is seen here guiding at the Mossy Creek Invitational, he has also served as Vice Chairman on the Board of Directors. His quiet, behind-the-scenes leadership makes him a great role model for veterans and non-veterans alike. Photo by Beau Beasley.

Side: Author Beau Beasley trout fishing on Virginia's Beaver Creek. Photo by Kyle LaFerriere.

TABLE OF CONTENTS

Foreword..9

About Project Healing Waters 12

Acknowledgments..13

About This Book 19

Brian's Rock 23

Introduction 29

    Robert Bartlett..40

    Jessica Callihan (Dial).....................................51

    Alvin Shell..58

    Jerry Miron..68

    Ronald Dean Rudy 80

    Tamar Franklin 86

    Keith Gilbert 91

    John Bass 96

    Willis "Duke" Davis..99

    George Gaines..108

Alaska Fish Therapy...111

    Healing Towers..120

    Elizabeth Springer..121

Casting in the Rain 126

    Eivind Olav Forseth II.....................................132

    Jesse Garza 139

    Lally Laksbergs 142

Andrew Laffey 147

David Curtis Folkerts 156

Curtis Boatman 165

Cake at the Pope Ranch 170

Chris Thompson 179

Jim Bensinger 192

Harry Yates 199

Julie Keene 206

An Angler Is Born 211

John Paramore 219

Ceamus C. McDermott 224

Walter Oliver Cary 228

George Draper 238

Kyle McAdams 246

Joshua Dale Williams 249

Rose River Farm 252

Charles Trawick 257

Bubba Holt 261

Don Lee 267

Carole Katz 270

Jonathan Mozingo 276

Coming Home to Harman's 280

FOREWORD

CAPT Edwin (Ed) P. Nicholson, USN (Ret.)
Founder, Project Healing Waters Fly Fishing, Inc.

Little did I know in 2004, when I began exploring the possibility of using fly fishing to help our recovering wounded service members at the Walter Reed Army Medical Center in Washington, DC, and ultimately other disabled veterans within the Veterans Affairs system, that I would eventually write a foreword to a book dedicated to those individuals.

After having spent a career in the US Navy, and later retiring again from private industry, I found myself as a patient at Walter Reed. While recovering, I came face-to-face with wounded service members returning from the conflict in Iraq; they were there for the treatment of their traumatic injuries, both physical and emotional. This profound experience led me to wonder if, somehow, I could help heal their bodies and minds through the sport of fly fishing, a pursuit I had long enjoyed myself. Originally, I conceived of just offering to take these individuals fly fishing, but fortunately the chief of the Occupational Therapy Clinic at that time, Colonel Bill Howard, USA, had a more far-reaching vision of how to provide a therapy involving a long-term programmatic approach. With his support, the genesis of what would become Project Healing Waters Fly Fishing began.

As it evolved, the programmatic approach to occupational and recreational therapy utilized local volunteers and Trout Unlimited members to teach all aspects of fly fishing, including casting, fly tying, and other associated skills. Participants met weekly at the clinic for instruction and casting lessons on Walter Reed's front lawn. Periodically, fly fishing outings would occur on local waters. By 2007, this highly successful approach was formalized by the incorporation of Project Healing Waters Fly Fishing as a nonprofit, dedicated to rehabilitation of disabled service members and veterans, and recognizing that in addition to providing recreational opportunities, we were witnessing the powers of personal relationship building and the camaraderie of shared experiences. Simultaneously, the organization began to serve in the national VA healthcare system,

Ed Nicholson's goal of helping fellow service members developed into the founding of Project Healing Waters.

using the same programmatic approach and volunteers from Trout Unlimited and Fly Fishers International chapters across the country.

I subsequently met Beau Beasley at one of our local outings, and he became an instant advocate for our mission. As a fly-fishing writer, he graciously used his pen to further our reach across the country, through articles in various fly-fishing media. As we got to know each other, he proposed writing a book that would explore the trauma and challenges of individuals within our participant base. At first, his idea to provide interviews, to capture the intimate details of their experiences, concerned me, because one of the major premises on which our project operated precluded requiring any participant to reveal those personal recollections. Beau assured me that his goal in this endeavor would be a respectful description of these individuals and their experiences, and they would unequivocally provide final approval of anything he presented in his book. To that end, Beau has been scrupulously attentive to this objective.

I have often said that Project Healing Waters Fly Fishing is the bridge from the dark side of the river to the light on the other side, and that the real success of our project is not in creating fly fishers, but rather in integrating traumatized individuals back into society. In this regard, the greatest success is witnessing that this in fact happens. Beau's book illuminates just how dark the far side of the river can be for these individuals while also capturing the restorative efforts of Project Healing Waters Fly Fishing. I am confident that this book will provide a unique opportunity for people to learn about the stories of these special individuals.

ABOUT PROJECT HEALING WATERS

For some, doing nothing isn't an option.

In 2005, while recovering from surgery at what is now Walter Reed National Military Medical Center, retired USN Captain Ed Nicholson came face-to-face with his fellow patients: combat veterans who'd come home from Iraq and Afghanistan with profound, life-altering injuries. A longtime fly angler, Nicholson wondered if the quiet sport might provide both solace and therapy to these wounded warriors.

Indeed it has.

Nicholson's brainchild became Project Healing Waters Fly Fishing, Inc., a nationwide nonprofit with more than two hundred programs in hospitals and clinics in all fifty states, on military bases across the country, and a variety of other locations, including veterans' service organizations, churches, and privately owned buildings. Its motto is "Healing those who serve." PHWFF's tireless volunteers, passionate about the healing power of the outdoors, connect with veterans of all stripes at weekly program meetings, through fly-tying and fly-rod-building opportunities, and on fly-fishing trips, all of which are provided at no cost to veterans.

"We don't just take people fishing," explains Nicholson. "We build relationships, and that takes time. These friendships are where people find healing."

ACKNOWLEDGMENTS

This book began with a call from my friend Alan Folger, an artist who had illustrated my second book, *Fly Fishing the Mid-Atlantic: A No Nonsense Guide to Top Waters*. Folger suggested that I write a book capturing the experiences of the many veterans I knew through Project Healing Waters Fly Fishing. Now, my writing has been about fly fishing, fisheries conservation, and land and water access and usage. Frankly, I didn't feel qualified to write a book about service veterans.

I still don't.

But Folger wouldn't let the idea go. Every few months he would call me out of the blue with the same question: "Have you started the book yet?" No, I'd say each time, reiterating all the reasons I didn't have the time, inclination, or expertise to write the book.

On a day like any other, near the end of my thirty-year career with Fairfax County Fire and Rescue, I was on duty at Fire Station 27 when Folger called again. "Have you started the book yet?" he asked, and I launched into my well-rehearsed litany of excuses.

"Listen, Beau: One of these days we're going to stop fighting in places like Afghanistan and Iraq. And when we do, the American people will forget these folks and what they've done. They'll simply fade away. We can't let that happen."

Folger knew what he was talking about. This was a man who'd been spat upon when he came home from Vietnam. The military had been so demonized that servicemen were instructed to change out of uniform in the airport restroom to avoid being accosted.

"American people will forget these folks." The words haunted me.

My wife's reaction to Folger's words surprised me: "He's right," she said. "It would be your tribute to the veterans you so admire. Perhaps you could bring a fresh perspective to the narratives. And our kids could look back with pride on a book like this." My wife edits everything I write, so with her support secured, I ran the idea past my publisher, Howard Fisher. What I didn't know was that Fisher was already volunteering with PHWFF in Arizona; naturally he was on board from day one. Fisher and his daughter Miriam Warren have helped me immeasurably; without their steadfast support I could not have written the book.

My friend Mark Williams, a firefighter on my shift, saw combat in Kosovo. I'll never forget his response when I mentioned the book: "When you go to war, Cap'n, you get dirty—even if you don't want to. It's not about what you want to do. It's about the circumstances thrust on you, the dreadful decisions you're forced to make. Problem is you come home dirty, and there's no way to get the dirt off you. You gotta figure out a way to live with yourself. Maybe the book could help some veterans do that." Williams's incisive and insightful words will stick with me forever.

Not long after I began the book, PHWFF founder Ed Nicholson invited me to join a group trip to Idaho's Salmon River: "You really need to come along," he said, because "this is often where the magic happens." On the first full day of the trip, we mustered on the riverbank and introduced ourselves. As I listened to each vet state his name and branch of service, I grew increasingly self-conscious. Why was I there? What should I say?

"It's okay, man," said the vet standing beside me, apparently sensing my anxiety. "You're just like one of us, except you serve at home."

I was cut to the heart. "No," I replied, "I'm not like you guys at all. I get to go home to my wife and kids after each shift, and no one is shooting at me at work."

On that trip—and on every occasion since—veterans have accepted me with open arms, warts and all. On that Idaho trip, I was honored to meet Air Force veteran Jim Williams. Little did I know then that Williams would go on to play a crucial role in this project.

Slowly the book began to take shape—and then to stall, over and over again. I was overwhelmed by the raw, gut-wrenching stories I heard and unable to turn them into coherent narratives. Ever faithful, Alan Folger and Jim Williams continued to encourage me; Williams doggedly sent emails checking on my progress even when I made none, eventually sending me one single-line email at a time: "You know the drill."

Paul Norman would occasionally come to Warrenton, Virginia, during the fall hunting season to visit his friend and fellow retired Marine Corps Gunnery Sergeant Jon Rasmussen, along with a handful of other retired Marines. I live nearby, so Rasmussen and his lovely wife, Liza, invited me over for dinner during these gatherings. The meals were great, and the company was even better. One evening Norman and I were the final two holdouts on the Rasmussens' back porch, still sipping bourbon and smoking cigars. He had always been guarded about his time in the service, sharing little more than the comment "I still miss my kids"—those he'd served with who made the ultimate sacrifice—"and I think about them every day."

On this evening, in the deep quiet of the back porch, he said something I'll never forget: "When the shit hits the fan and bullets are flying and everything is going to hell, no one gives a rat's ass about the Constitution or the flag or any of that other happy horseshit. You only care about the guys beside you. You fight for them and they fight for you and everything else is total bullshit." I asked him for advice on moving forward with the narratives I'd collected. "Listen," he said earnestly, "you just be honest. You write what they're willing to share and not another goddamn word. You just tell it like they tell you, and keep all the political bullshit out of it."

My mother, author Nancy Wright Beasley, helped me find my way to an introduction that made sense. She also suggested that I hand over my interview recordings to her friend Allison Daniel, a transcriptionist, which saved me hundreds of hours of work. On her own initiative, Daniel actually did a little research while transcribing; I would often find notes on specific time periods or battles interlaced with the narrative, which provided much clarity. More than once I came across a personal note in the transcription that said something like, "Tape stopped—had to cry a little and gather my composure before going on," or "How do they *do* this for months at a time? I couldn't do this for a single day!" Allison Daniel is the only other person in the world to hear the unfiltered stories of those I interviewed. Her superior work ethic and her commitment to detail were invaluable to me, and I'll always owe her a debt of gratitude.

Finally, I must acknowledge the veterans who shared their stories with me. It's worth noting that *not one* of the veterans featured in this book asked to be included. In fact, in most cases I had to beg them to open up. Some of the narratives are fairly short; others are long and complex. This is because each story has its own cadence and rhythm, unique to the veteran. I can't share all of the interviews I did; some veterans' stories can't be told right now, or perhaps ever. Whether included here or not, I sincerely appreciate the candor and selflessness of every veteran I interviewed. Each and every one changed my life.

One quiet morning on the back deck of the South Holston River Lodge in Tennessee, the most famous fly angler in the world helped me bring this book in for a landing. Over coffee, Lefty Kreh, a longtime journalist who fought in World War II and saw action at the Battle of the Bulge, recounted some of his war stories to me: how he wondered if, after trudging through so much snow, his feet would ever be warm again; what the pitched firefights were like; and the horror of discovering a Nazi concentration camp. "We had no idea such camps existed," he said. "It's hard to imagine such cruelty and evil exists, but I *saw* it."

Kreh was in his late eighties, and still those demons lurked just beneath the surface—demons that had begun to look familiar to me now, after numerous interviews with veterans of all ages and walks of life. There were too many stories to tell, I realized—and too many demons to purge. When and where would it ever end?

"Beau," he said softly, his pale blue eyes looking out toward the river, "this book is going to be very tough to write. I won't tell you what to do, but I know it won't be easy. There will always be more folks to add—more stories you'll want to tell. But sooner or later you have to make peace with yourself and bring the tale to a close so you can share the stories you've collected." Lefty Kreh offered to write the foreword for this book. Sadly, he passed before he could do so. I knew it was time to finish the book before I lost anyone else.

Kreh's service to our country cost him a great deal. Every veteran highlighted here paid a high price—and that's why we call military service a sacrifice. And they aren't the only ones who paid: Their families sacrificed also, enduring long months, or even lifetimes, of separation. When duty called, Lefty Kreh, Alan Folger, Jim Williams, Paul Norman, Mark Williams, Jon Rasmussen, and many, many others raised their hands. They sacrificed everything that matters. For *me*. For *you*. This book is my feeble attempt to honor that sacrifice—to ensure that we Americans never "forget these folks."

Jim Williams served in the Air Force and retired as Lieutenant Colonel. He has volunteered with the PHWFF Fort Carson program in Colorado for many years.

One of the finest people I met while writing this book was veteran Jim Williams. He and I crossed paths while fishing on a weeklong outing on the Middle Fork of Idaho's famed Salmon River. Williams, who retired as a Lt. Colonel from the Air Force, exudes a quiet confidence that draws you in. He's as affable as he is witty—the sort of accomplished angler who lands the largest fish of the day and chalks it up to dumb luck rather than skill. In short, Williams is about as close as one can get to the perfect fishing companion.

By the time our Idaho fishing trip ended, Williams and I had developed a solid friendship. Once home, he would call me from time to time to check on my progress on the book. He'd listen patiently to my updates. He began emailing me regularly and peppering me with the questions that had occurred to him since our last communication. As the enormous project took shape, I occasionally became discouraged—but not Williams: He dutifully kept me to task with regular emails that exhorted simply, "Okay, you know the deal." This was the swift kick I often needed. In this way he held me accountable to move forward, because I knew I'd catch hell if I didn't.

I'm not sure I'd have finished this book had it not been for Jim's stalwart support. I am forever indebted to him.

ABOUT THIS BOOK

I spent just over eight years shadowing members of the Project Healing Waters Fly Fishing programs at Virginia's Marine Corps Base Quantico and Fort Belvoir.

This book is the result of that experience.

Quantico program lead Marty Laksbergs, retired from the Marine Corps, and Fort Belvoir program lead Bob Gartner, retired from the Bureau of Indian Affairs, are both entirely dedicated to their programs—models of selfless leadership. They exemplify all the habits of good leaders, not the least of which is the willingness to put one's own shoulder to the wheel of any task that needs doing, no matter how mundane.

I'd been collecting the interviews for this book for a while already, and I needed a sounding board for something that was troubling me. I didn't know Marty or Bob at all well; nevertheless, I asked them to meet me for dinner to discuss the project. I confessed to them that my wife, Leila, a professional editor, had read several of my early drafts and found that they lacked vitality. I was, she said, capturing veterans' stories "from ten thousand feet"—too far removed from the real lives of these real people. From her standpoint, I hadn't conveyed a close-up, intimate sense of how the program worked. She suggested a radical fix: stop writing for a while and just be with the veterans, embedded with them at their meetings, as they experienced the program.

Laksbergs and Gartner both agreed to help. I would be allowed to fully participate in both programs and even attend events if they had room for me. The veterans would always come first, of course, and ultimately those program members themselves would decide just how much a part of the group I'd become.

I would discover that this "warrior first" attitude was Laksbergs and Gartner's signature leadership style.

About the Interviews

The gracious men and women of the Quantico and Fort Belvoir PHWFF programs did indeed welcome me with open arms; today they are my extended family. Their openness enabled me to drop out of ten thousand feet—to get close to them and try to tell their stories from their own points of view. The stories recorded here were compiled over a period of years and were done with the complete cooperation of the veterans and the leaders of PHWFF. Some of the interviews are brief and leave readers yearning for more. Others are long and vivid and occasionally excruciatingly painful to read. If a particular story hits a little too close to home, then skip it for now. It will be there for you when you're ready.

Most of the interviewees are program participants and volunteers from the Fort Belvoir and Quantico programs, but not all of them. I met some interviewees when I participated in PHWFF events in their region of the country.

In many cases, I have indicated the ranks of the veterans who shared their stories. I hope this provides readers with some context for their military service. But it is important to note that rank has no meaning at all within PHWFF; you'll see a Private First Class and a Colonel sitting side by side tying flies. No participant receives preferential treatment as a result of rank; indeed, many seem reluctant even to mention it when asked. The only thing they're more reluctant to disclose? Any recognition they've received for their valor.

The program participants I interviewed shared as much or as little as they felt comfortable disclosing. Some interviews revolve around combat, but many do not because PHWFF doesn't limit its outreach efforts to combat veterans. The organization exists to rehabilitate and

reconnect all veterans, of any age, any conflict, any branch of service, any length of service, from all walks of life.

Chris Matthews USMC fishes at Rose River Farm while guide Harold Harsch USMC looks on. Photo by Matt Romano.

I conducted nearly all the interviews in person using a small handheld tape recorder or my phone; these recordings were then transcribed by my good friend Allison Daniel. This technique allowed me to concentrate entirely on the veterans—to listen intently to their stories—rather than on taking handwritten notes. I interviewed some veterans long-distance over the phone with the help of a questionnaire I sent before the interview.

Each interviewee was the first person to read their own edited story—and no story went to print without the interviewee's consent. As you will discover, several participants either suffered traumatic brain injuries or experienced some other trauma that has affected their physical, mental, and emotional state—and their memory. The "fog of war" is a very real phenomenon. On behalf of all those who have told me the truth as best they can remember it, any and all errors contained in these pages are now my own and entirely unintentional.

I collected stories that made me laugh out loud. I collected stories that compelled me to put my head on my desk and cry. I collected stories I wasn't able to share. I collected stories that participants told me they had never shared with anyone else, including spouses. Whether or not a story made its way into this book, each and every story—and the veteran who shared it with me—is written on my heart.

Perhaps the most difficult stories came from women who were sexually assaulted. Some had been accosted by enemy soldiers, but most were assaulted by someone in their own ranks—and more than one endured multiple assailants. None had reported the attacks to a superior officer. Why not? Some feared they would not be believed, others that they would be blamed. Some kept quiet for fear that their harrowing experience would be used to discredit the military more generally.

Violations like these rarely leave visible scars, but make no mistake: The trauma is real. The scars are deep. The consequences may last a lifetime. One of the veteran-victims I interviewed was so traumatized and isolated by her experience that she didn't venture outside her home for a decade.

In the end, not one of these assaulted veterans would allow me to include her profile in this book. I am disappointed to have to omit them by their own request, but as far as I'm capable, I do understand, and I respect their decision. I've alluded to them and their experiences here in this introduction, anonymously, as a tribute to their fortitude and to acknowledge that I see them, hear them, and bow my head before their courage and sacrifice.

In a *perfect* world, this book would not exist because perpetual peace had eliminated the need for anyone to fight and bleed and die on a distant shore. We'd all live peaceful and prosperous lives, whole and happy, and die surrounded by those who love us. In a *just* world, this book would be a work ever in progress—because it is filled with the stories of a mere fraction of the honorable men and women in uniform with stories worth telling. In *this* world—neither perfect nor just—this is the story I have been given, by men and women infinitely more courageous and selfless than I am. It is my great honor to pass it on to you.

Author with good friend Staff Sergeant Jason Baker, who served in the Army's 75th Regiment.

BRIAN'S ROCK

A bout an hour west of Washington, DC, among the bucolic rolling hills of Madison County, Virginia, there is a rock. Perhaps at one time this rock was wedged securely alongside others; perhaps it was buried somewhere deep in the earth's crust. Chances are better than fair that it's a chip off of the nearby mountains, which command a breathtaking view of the serene valley below. At first blush it looks like any other rock—but this rock is different.

Surrounded by an open field, it has but one companion: the Rose River flows quietly a few steps away, winding its way across the valley floor. The Rose itself begins in the mountains, a few miles upstream in the Shenandoah National Park. It tumbles from there, picking up speed as it rushes off the backside of the mountains, occasionally stopping to create plunge pools before pushing its way downward. Sometimes the river is delayed by fallen tree limbs that act as miniature wooden dams, but only for a while. In the repeating river-versus-tree contest, the river always wins in the end. It rushes on, turning and weaving, ultimately surmounting all barriers. In time it leaves the mountainous park altogether to traverse fields and old homesteads. Here, cows look on the

Brian Mancini was a combat medic who served with honor and distinction in Iraq. Photo courtesy of the Mancini family.

river with indifference, except occasionally when they slip into it for a drink or a quick dip to escape Virginia's summer heat.

Eventually the Rose makes its way to Rose River Farm, owned by one Douglas Dear, where it widens (just a bit) and deepens (considerably), its cold waters providing comfort to colorful rainbows, browns, and even the occasional native brook trout. And although their noses break the surface of the river periodically to take a struggling fly, the hapless fly angler who carelessly casts a shadow across the river's surface quickly learns that these wary trout are always on guard.

About five hundred yards downstream from the farm entrance the river finally meets and then passes our solitary rock. It keeps a stationary, silent vigil alongside the water, day and night and in all kinds of weather. The rock marks the place where Sergeant First Class Brian

This monument at Rose River Farm is a silent tribute to the true warrior, who is loved and remembered fondly by all who knew him.

Mancini cast a fly rod in the Rose River for the very first time, hoping to land one of its skittish trout. Brian had served as a combat medic until an IED left him without the use of his left eye and with other profound head injuries. He spent months recovering from the blast, and it was during this recovery, at Walter Reed in DC, that he discovered Project Healing Waters Fly Fishing.

Working through severe injuries, Brian learned to cast—a small miracle, considering that initially he needed assistance just to stand. He also dealt with blinding headaches. Bouts of dizziness came upon him without warning. Nausea was induced by his doctor-prescribed medication cocktail. And always pain—nagging, ceaseless, penetrating, often debilitating pain. Nevertheless, Brian, determined to put his newfound skills to the test against the Rose's finicky trout, had a great day on the water during his first visit to Rose River Farm. Since that day, hundreds and perhaps thousands of servicemen and women have followed in his footsteps and found solace on the farm along the banks of the Rose.

On April 29, 2017, Staff Sergeant Robert Bartlett, himself a wounded combat veteran of the Iraq War and the first person to participate in Project Healing Waters, dedicated this rock in memory of Brian Mancini. Flanking Bartlett was the founder of Project Healing Waters, retired Navy Captain Ed Nicholson, and longtime supporter and board member Loralee West. They each spoke fondly of Brian—how they had come to know him personally and just how much he would be missed. We all want to love and be loved, they reminded us; we all yearn to be a part of something bigger than ourselves, to belong and to have a sense of purpose. Developing connections is tough; remaining connected in the face of pain and doubt and despondency is even tougher. When we lose touch with those we love and who love us—when we isolate ourselves from the relationships that give our lives meaning—we walk into a prison cell, the door of which slams shut firmly behind us.

Isolating oneself is relatively easy; reaching out of that agonizing loneliness, beating with both fists on that prison door, is very, very difficult.

During the dedication, I reflected on the Brian Mancini I had known—his sense of humor, his infectious smile—and how his all-too-brief life had intersected my own. I first met Brian on a fishing trip in Idaho, along the South Fork of the Salmon River. Initially I knew no one except Ed Nicholson, and Nicholson, in his inscrutable wisdom, had chosen Brian Mancini to be my roommate the night before we headed out to the river. Not surprisingly, Mancini the veteran Army medic and Beasley the veteran paramedic spoke a sort of common language. So we talked shop. I retired with thirty years on the job as a firefighter and paramedic on an advanced life support unit, and I have seen much, much more than my fair share of horror and trauma, but my experience paled in comparison to Brian's. The things he'd seen—the things he'd had to *do* to save his fellow soldiers—set him apart even from someone as intimately acquainted with death as I am. He became more comfortable with me as we spoke; we quickly developed a bond that first responders share with one another. And yet I knew that Brian was hurting. Beyond the constant, nagging physical pain of his injuries, he had a deep emotional pain that isolated him—imprisoned him—even in the midst of others.

"How much more do I have to sacrifice in the service of my country?" The question hung heavy in the room. I could not answer him. "I've lost my health, I've lost my career, and I've lost my marriage," Brian continued. "What else is there?" I had no answers for him, then or now.

Brian knew as well as anyone that many wounded vets struggle to transition successfully from hospital stay to civilian life. They leave a life of meaning and belonging to enter the unknown, sometimes all alone. Brian eventually moved to Arizona to open the nonprofit Honor House to ease this transition. He worked closely with local first responders,

Brian Mancini with a rainbow trout caught in the pool that would later bear his name.

training them to interact effectively with veterans in emergencies. Brian gained some notoriety for his efforts; I recall watching him being interviewed by Oprah Winfrey and thinking how well he looked. He had gotten a therapy dog. He seemed, I thought, to be well on his way to a full recovery.

I thought wrong.

Instead, Brian took his own life. The *how* doesn't really matter; the *why* is all that matters now. Brian became isolated and alone. He could see no way out of his prison. Tragically, thousands of servicemen and women have felt the same, dying by suicide after returning from their deployments. The civilian wonders how someone can survive a war zone only to come home and end their own life. The civilian doesn't understand that many vets cannot get home, even when they're home. The civilian doesn't understand the seemingly impenetrable prison of isolation and despair that too many vets exist in, right here "at home."

I don't know—I will never know—why Brian took his own life that day. What I do know is Brian's Rock: a silent, stark reminder that our blessed freedom comes at a terribly high price, paid for by a few for the rest of their lives. We civilians, born into freedom, have a solemn obligation to remember the sacrifices of those men and women who have defended that freedom with the last full measure of devotion.

Brian's Rock was dedicated to a hero who was also a real live person. We will never forget his courage and dedication to duty, and we will also never forget his sense of humor or his smile. This book is my attempt to honor Brian Mancini and those men and women like him—heroic and also human—who have served and continue to serve every day to keep us free. You are real. You are not alone. You are not forgotten.

INTRODUCTION

"What's the matter with you?"

My lieutenant's stern face, set like granite, was mere inches from mine. It was midmorning, but a hint of soot from the fire we'd just fought gave him a sort of five o'clock shadow, the helmet that had been strapped tight had left his hair matted and sweat still ran in rivulets down his cheeks.

"Afraid to do your job, son? Is that it?"

Once again he didn't wait for my response. "If you can't do the job when it comes time, you might want to consider another line of work. Because *this is what we do*."

The author trout fishing on Virginia's Beaver Creek.
Photo by Kyle LaFerriere.

I couldn't bear to look him in the face. I couldn't respond. Instead I swallowed hard and looked down at the ground. I was a rookie with very little practical experience; I knew how to get my gear on, but this was my first real house fire. Still, I knew enough to keep my mouth shut.

The other firefighters on the scene remained carefully focused on their task of overhauling the townhouse fire we'd just extinguished; they negotiated their way around us as easily as if we had been inconveniently placed garden gnomes. They heard every word, of course: my public dressing down wasn't quiet, and it had commenced as soon as I'd emerged from the smoldering townhouse.

Lieutenant Art Varnau, officer in charge of Fairfax County's Engine Company 27-B in West Springfield, Virginia, was not a man to trifle with. A highly trained fire officer with decades of experience, Lieutenant Varnau had been more or less everywhere and done more or less everything and did not suffer fools—that is, snot-nosed rookies—gladly. Still relatively new to the shift, I didn't know much about Varnau except that he'd been a Marine and seen action in Vietnam, where rumor had it he'd taken a round in the leg. Was this true? I still don't know; I simply couldn't bring myself to ask him about it, and Lieutenant Varnau never discussed the war with the shift. The only comment I ever heard him make about Vietnam he made almost in passing: "We didn't *lose* the Vietnam War—we simply weren't allowed to win." Occasionally he wore to work a worn yellow T-shirt that read "Asian World Games: USA Second Place." I assumed this was his way of expressing contempt for those who had sent our troops to Vietnam but hadn't supported them there. All I know for certain is that when the crew sat down together to watch a war movie, the Lieutenant remained in his office.

In some small ways the fire service is like the military. First, it's a kind of family. Our calendars may be marked with holidays just like everyone else's, but "holiday" rarely means "day off." The fire service never closes, and the firefighter is never—but *never*—late to work. If the weather service predicts a half a foot of snow will fall overnight, then firefighters plan to sleep at the station the night before their shift begins. Being late means keeping a brother or sister firefighter who has already worked for twenty-four hours straight at work a little longer. Perhaps this is why so many firefighters come from families of firefighters, as I did.

Just like a military unit, a shift of firefighters is greater than the sum of its parts. Firefighters refer to those outside the fire service as civilians; when you graduate from rookie school you realize that you've ceased to be one of "them" and have become one of "us"—a member of a team. We eat, sleep, train, and work together. I had dreamed for years of being a firefighter like my father was, of being a part of something bigger than myself.

Fire departments are also rigidly hierarchical paramilitary organizations with a rank structure—sergeant, lieutenant, captain, and chief—unabashedly borrowed from the military. In fact, many of the

The author at Fire Station 27 with his wife Leila and children Maggie and Jeremiah.

country's first firefighters were Union soldiers. Emergency scenes are chaotic and stressful, and a clear chain of command is crucial to success.

Of course there is a dark side to this fire-forged collegiality. Sometimes firefighters become contemptuous of those outside the service and have trouble developing and maintaining "civilian" relationships. They are consumed with the job—and the job, with its urgency and stress, eventually consumes their other human connections. A standing joke at the fire academy is, "If the Department had wanted you to have a wife, it would have issued you one."

Just as in a family, nicknames are common among shift members. Likening Lieutenant Varnau to the carved-from-marble John Wayne, my shift dubbed him the Duke. With his broad shoulders, thick, coal-black hair, knowing black eyes, and intimidating swagger borne of years of real-world experience, Varnau was a tower of strength, stoic and unflappable in the face of even the most intense emergency situations. He was a larger-than-life quasi-father figure to me: cool, confident, and decisive, Varnau exhibited a deep respect for the citizens we served. And in return I respected him deeply—and perhaps even feared him a little. Yes, the Duke was an appropriate nickname for Varnau, but you may be sure we never called him anything but "sir" to his face.

I had graduated from the fire academy just six months before Lieutenant Varnau had arrived at our station to replace a retiring officer, and in that brief time I had served under a different officer nearly every week. My father had been a career firefighter in Chesapeake, so I knew that successful rookies did as they were told: they arrived at the station early for every shift, volunteered for unlovely station duties like cleaning bathrooms and mopping kitchen floors, willingly grabbed a bucket or a brush to wash the equipment, and gave more seasoned shift members proper respect and a wide berth. As the rookie on the shift, I was lower than a whale's belly, and I knew it.

Before the townhouse fire and my ignominious dressing down, the worst call I'd run had been a car fire in the middle of the night in which a young man, driving drunk, had run off the road and hit a tree. His car flipped over on its hood, bursting into flames. The young driver never made it out. Was he wearing a seat belt? Did he strike his head in the collision? Was he conscious but pinned in the vehicle? I'll never know.

The night sky was lit by two-story-high flames when we arrived, and I'll never forget the doomed driver's pale arm sticking out of the driver's-side window—or the screams of his girlfriend, who had been following him home in a second car and witnessed the horrific wreck. "Paul, get out of the car!" she cried. "Paul, get out of the car! You're dying! You're dying!"

It was Paul's twenty-first birthday.

We put the fire out, but a sickeningly sweet, pungent odor like burnt peppermint hung in the night air. I stood mutely beside the charred remains of victim and vehicle. "Do you smell that, son?" asked Lieutenant Varnau, who had quietly appeared beside me. "That's what death smells like."

I tried to process the chaos of the scene, the tortured cries of the driver's girlfriend, the carnage and horror of the wreck. It was about 3:30 that morning when Lieutenant Varnau told me something I've reflected on frequently over a thirty-year career: "If you're going to stay on this job, son," he said gently, "you're gonna have to get used to seeing a lot of death."

Truer words have rarely been spoken.

I went on to spend nearly two decades on first a Basic Life Support Unit—essentially an ambulance that responds to urgent but not necessarily life-threatening emergencies—and then an Advanced Life Support Unit, which nearly always responds to life-threatening injuries or illnesses. I have worked many thousands of calls, from car wrecks to drug overdoses to domestic disputes. I've seen what nearly every bone looks like when it's broken. I have experienced hundreds (maybe thousands) of heart attacks, strokes, and allergic reactions. I've responded to shootings, stabbings, burns, hangings, and electrocutions. I've delivered babies, helped rape victims, dealt with amputations, witnessed seizures, and treated snakebites. Worst of all have been the children who didn't make it: A medic never forgets the sound of a mourning mother, weeping for her child who will never come home again.

I served another ten years as a fire officer. Obviously firefighting can be a very dangerous job; even with the best gear, proper training, and effective leadership, there's no getting around the fact that the *firefighter is entering a burning building.* As a fire officer I responded to domicile fires and collapses, car fires, shopping center fires, garden apartment fires, high-rise fires, downed power lines, chemical spills, natural gas leaks, swift water rescues, medevac rescues—and, yes, occasionally a call for a cat stuck in a tree. On 9/11 I was on leave; I still feel a twinge of guilt that I wasn't on duty to respond at the Pentagon that day.

One of the worst calls of my entire career involved a life-threatening head injury sustained by a fellow firefighter in the performance of his duties. By the time I arrived on the scene, blood was pouring out of his ear as though it were a garden hose; I honestly thought he was going to die right in front of me. He became terrifically combative—relatively common for such a serious head injury—and it required four of us to subdue him long enough to get him in my medic unit and then transport him to the hospital. I can still see the county seal atop the pale blue spinal immobilization board on which we placed him; seared into my memory is the image of his blood smeared across that seal and running off that backboard. He screamed and fought us all the way to the hospital, pulling out the single IV I was able to place in him. It was the longest trip to the hospital that I can ever remember, and I was certain that despite my best efforts he would not survive.

Upon delivering this critically injured firefighter to the hospital, I was immediately relieved of duty. So was a coworker, a retired Marine who had driven us to the hospital and who I found, half an hour after we'd arrived, still sitting in the cab of the medic unit with his hands on the steering wheel, essentially catatonic, emotionally unable to go on.

I wish I could say that I was back on the job the next day. In fact I was tormented with anxiety, replaying the call over and over and over in my head and imagining what I could have done differently. I was afraid to return to work: Could I still face critical calls and make the necessary split-second, life-and-death decisions? I couldn't sleep, and when I did I had nightmares in which I relived the many traumatic calls I'd run over the course of my long career. The dreams had no particular pattern. Some incidents were decades old, returning to me at night in graphic detail.

I was ashamed. Surely I could have done more. I could have performed better. Somehow I could have changed the course of that traumatic experience. At least *I should have been able to go back to work the next day*. But I couldn't and I didn't.

I was sent to Chip Theodore, a retired firefighter and the county's behavioral health counselor, who convinced me that I needed to see a psychiatrist. I was angry, heartbroken, and ashamed. This was the low watermark in a long career, and I considered taking early retirement to avoid seeing a "shrink." I was too embarrassed to go by the station; after all, everyone knew why I wasn't at work. No one wants or needs a frightened firefighter. When we dial 911, we want someone who will step into the breach. We want someone who is unflappable and can make the hard decisions. We want someone like Lieutenant Varnau.

On the twentieth anniversary of the day I joined the fire service, I found myself at the psychiatrist's office. He asked me a few softball questions before moving in for the kill: "Do you know why you're here, Lieutenant?"

"Yes, sir," I murmured. "I'm not sure I can take it anymore. The last call was . . . pretty bad. And I'm having trouble dealing with it."

He asked me to tell him about the call that had pushed me over the edge, and I did so. Then he asked me something that surprised me: "Tell me about the *first* bad call you ran."

Immediately my mind brought me back to the car fire I'd responded to as a rookie. Paul had died on his twenty-first birthday. The memory came flooding back to me in vivid detail: the twisted, overturned car, the pale arm at the window, the flames leaping into the night sky, and Paul's girlfriend desperately pleading with him: "Paul, get out of the car! You're dying!"

"How long have you been on the job, Lieutenant?"

"Twenty years, sir," I responded. "Twenty years today."

"And how many of these calls—you know, the really serious calls like this last one—how many do you think you might see in the course of a year?"

"In a good year," I responded after a moment's reflection, "you might only have one, but other years you might have a couple or even three. It's hard to say."

"So you can remember the first really bad call with the car on fire," said the psychiatrist, hands clasped in front of him, fingers interlocked as though in prayer. "And you remember this last really bad call with your injured coworker. Can you tell me about the seventeenth call?"

"I don't know what you mean," I responded, nonplussed. He repeated his question. Exasperated, I said, "Sir, I really don't have a damn clue what you're asking me."

"That's precisely my point, Lieutenant," he said, unruffled. "You can remember the first call, and you certainly remember the last call.

You have twenty years on this job. The problem with all you public-service types is that you see one hellish call after another—they just keep coming in year after year after year—and you stuff them down in the back of your mind and do your best to suppress them. Another one comes in, and another, and another, and you just keep cramming them down. You've seen so many horrors. The truth is that you can't recall them all now, but they're still in there. And then one day, *bam*!" He wrenched open his clasped fingers in an explosive motion.

I think that explosion was supposed to be my head.

It was oddly comforting to be understood.

I'd like to say it was smooth sailing from there, but that wouldn't be true. The truth is that I went back to the shrink many times, and I began to improve. Slowly. I still had nightmares that came to me like lost children trying to find their way home. I took those little lost children to the psychiatrist; maybe he could help them. I told him about the amputation I ran in which a trucker lost his leg. I told him about the tragic car wreck and the little boy I couldn't save and the pleading look on his mother's face that still haunts me.

"Did you save anyone, Lieutenant?" he asked me once.

"Yes, sir—quite a few, in fact!" I responded immediately. "I quit counting after about a dozen or so."

"Can you at least take credit for the ones you saved?" he asked.

I considered his comment. "But—Doc, if I take credit for the ones I save, then I'm also responsible for the ones who don't make it. And the math isn't so good the longer you're on the job."

Eventually I did return to full duty. The firefighter whose massive head injury had sent me over the brink made a complete—even *miraculous*—recovery and returned to work. Al, the driver on that call, kept in touch with me throughout the recovery process. He and I became close friends as a result of the trauma we experienced together. Tragically

Al died of cancer a few years ago. Chip Theodore also succumbed to cancer. Chip's compassion and empathy went a long way toward saving my sanity, and I will never forget him. Chip even arranged for me to be sent back to the fire academy as an instructor rather than into the field, but I refused the offer. I knew if I didn't get back in the saddle when I was cleared for duty, I might not ever go back.

Chip's wife, Maia, herself a professional counselor, took his place in the department helping firefighters and medics fight their demons. She gave me one of Chip's old coffee cups as a memento; it's sitting on my desk as I write this. There's never a time I see it that I don't think of Chip and all he did to help me when I needed him most.

I would eventually retire as a captain from Engine 27-B shift—the same shift and station where my career began. I had the honor and privilege of following in Lieutenant Varnau's footsteps, acting in the same position as the officer I had admired so much. I only hope I did my duty and took care of those who worked for me as well as he and others took care of me.

When you're on duty at a fire station, your job is to remain calm no matter what life throws at you. Put out the fire. Reassure the citizen. Bring order to chaos. Make the rescue. You do the best job you can do with the tools and training you have. You hope for the best. This is yet another way that being a firefighter and medic is a little bit like being in the military. There are no "normal hours": You work until the job is done. Sometimes things go sideways—tragically wrong despite your very best efforts. Sometimes *nothing you can do* will help. If you're not careful, your job can become your life. When that happens, the job will chew you up and spit you out, leaving a trail of destruction and broken relationships in your wake. This helps explain how and why a unit is a family, and why that bond is so keenly missed when it's broken.

Every veteran I spoke to mourns the loss of his or her career and the forced separation from military life—mourns it like an actual death. From those who served in Korea to our most recent wounded veterans, all loved and still miss their comrades in arms. Relationships forged in the crucible of armed combat are unique and cannot be replicated in civilian life. This is why Project Healing Waters Fly Fishing is imbued with what Ed Nicholson calls "magic": The organization is by veterans for veterans, reuniting wounded vets with their forever family. Like meets like over the tying bench or on the water, and the results can be transformational.

I have not lived—I will *never* live—the lives of the heroic men and women whose stories are in this book. I have lived my own story. I hope and believe that something in my own story prepared me to hear and retell theirs compellingly. I desire nothing more than to honor their many, countless, ongoing sacrifices by sharing their own stories in their own words. I simultaneously walk in their shadows and on their shoulders. We all do.

Lefty Kreh was a great supporter of this book and often met with Beau.

Robert Bartlett was trained as a sniper. Photo courtesy Robert Bartlett.

Robert Bartlett looked back across the front yard at the footsteps, etched in morning dew, that led from his brother's front door to the car he was sitting in. Those were *his* footsteps—his first steps toward a radically new life.

A few short months ago, Bartlett had been tending bar at McCaffrey's Irish Pub in downtown Phoenix. Owner Seamus McCaffrey, who had fled Belfast in the 1970s to escape anti-Catholic persecution, had embraced his adoptive country with gusto. So when Bartlett told McCaffrey that he'd decided to enlist in the Army, McCaffrey's response was personal. "I'm so proud of ya," he said in his thick Irish brogue, choking back tears. "This country has given me so much—it's worth fighting for. I'm so proud of you, lad, so proud. Go with my blessings."

Bartlett, whose father had served in Vietnam, enlisted because the war in Afghanistan was roaring and he sensed the country was on the brink of war in Iraq as well. After all, he reasoned, brutal dictator Saddam Hussein wouldn't willingly give up power without a fight. "I was an able-bodied man with no wife or children," Bartlett says, "so I figured I should follow my father and go to war. I joined under the delayed-entry program. I was thirty years old when I enlisted, so I had thirty years of debt and belongings to deal with. I sold off as much stuff as I could and moved in with my brother for a few weeks before heading off."

Trained at Kentucky's Fort Knox as a cavalry scout, Bartlett was the oldest person in the platoon. "I was called everything from Papa Smurf to Old Man," he says. "The next-closest guy was twenty-five years old." When sniper training became available, "I immediately volunteered and found that I loved it." Nevertheless, Bartlett was plagued by a nagging anxiety that he would die young: "I turned thirty-one in sniper school, and—it sounds crazy, but over and over in my head I kept hearing the numbers thirty-one, thirty-two . . . thirty-one, thirty-two . . . thirty-one, thirty-two . . ."

While Bartlett was stationed at Georgia's Fort Stewart, a twenty-one-year-old Soldier died in his sleep of a brain aneurysm. Bartlett's scout platoon was selected to perform the service. At the time he had never given religion or faith much thought. "Our platoon chaplain, Captain Mike Spikes, a Baptist, was a great guy," he says. "We all liked him and trusted him as a faith leader. Around the time of the funeral I talked to Chaplain Spikes about premonitions of my own death. I told him I knew that I was going to die at the age of thirty-two—that even before joining the military the number thirty-two had entered my mind over and over through the years. Now these numbers—'thirty-one, thirty-two . . . thirty-one, thirty-two'—ran over and over again in my head and I just *knew* what it meant. Chaplain Spikes assured me that thoughts of dying young were normal but that I should pray about them if they really bothered me. I trusted him. And he left the door open to come in and talk." Bartlett took comfort in knowing that a man of the cloth would be praying for him. But he still couldn't shake the feeling that he would die sooner rather than later.

On leave over Thanksgiving, Bartlett flew home to Phoenix and was visiting his old stomping grounds at Dubliner Irish Pub when he spotted a familiar face he'd seen once or twice while tending bar. A friend introduced them. "I couldn't help but notice Jordan because she's so pretty," says Bartlett, who sheepishly admits that he stole a kiss that evening. "Her lips were the softest things I've ever felt. I couldn't get over her and thought of her often. To me she became known as 'soft lips.'" Bartlett got her phone number and called the next day. "She didn't call me back. I found out later that she didn't want to get involved with a guy who was about to be deployed overseas."

A mere few weeks later, Bartlett had traded Irish pubs in Phoenix for Camp Rustamiyah near Baghdad. "We provided a lot of humanitarian aid while we were there, trying to win the hearts and minds of the locals," Bartlett explains. "Still, I'd be deployed on a sniper mission every now and then. Sometimes I provided overwatch from a hidden location for our guys on patrol; sometimes we'd go do other sniper operations. There were lots of enemy snipers in Iraq trying to take out our guys: Iranians, Palestinians, and Chechens. We'd go out with a .50-caliber or a suppressed .308, both excellent weapons and very effective. A good sniper can take out a bad guy a thousand yards away; a great sniper with a .50-cal can take out a target more than a *mile* away."

By March 2005 the area around Baghdad where Bartlett was deployed had become a hotspot for Iranian terrorists to detonate improvised explosive devices, or IEDs. "As the summer heated up, so did the IEDs. We'd go out on patrol in our Humvees; sometimes the vehicle in front of you would get hit, and you'd just have to push on through." Vehicle-borne IEDs, placed in dump trucks or old cars, were even deadlier. "The enemy would put the bombs in almost anything: buckets, used propane tanks. . . . They'd mix them in with daily trash items and just leave them on the side of the road."

The depravity Bartlett witnessed defies description. "Sometimes these Iranian-backed terrorists would set off a bomb just as kids were coming home from school. They didn't care, just as long as they caused maximum carnage. The idea was to intimidate folks into submission." Similarly, when terrorists identified a village in which they wanted to set up shop, they would kidnap children from other neighboring villages and execute them in public. Their message? *This is what will happen to all of your children if you tell the Americans we're here.* "Once when I was on guard duty," says Bartlett, "a poor farmer came to me with a picture of his kid. He said he'd been kidnapped. There was nothing we could do but refer him to Missing Persons in Baghdad. It was simply heartbreaking. I remember thinking, *Chances this father gets his son back alive are next to zero.*"

On May 3, 2005, twenty-two days before his thirty-second birthday, Bartlett was driving the lead vehicle—an armored Humvee—in a three-vehicle patrol when a device detonated as he drove past. It was an EFP (explosive force penetrator): a bomb with a copper bowl on one end and an explosives-stuffed length of pipe on the other. When the metal bowl that faces the bomb is superheated it can reach almost unimaginable temperatures and "tear through metal, a passing vehicle, a tank—just about anything."

The bomb tore through Bartlett's door and into him and his gunner, Corporal Todd Bishop, as well as Staff Sergeant William Brooks in the passenger seat and Staff Sergeant Edwin Greer, who had volunteered for the patrol because his own vehicle was in maintenance. "The explosion tore off about a third of my face from the top left quarter of my temple down to my jaw and shredded Corporal Bishop's legs, nearly amputating them. It took off the top of Staff Sergeant Brooks's head from his eyebrows up. It was so powerful, it continued tearing through the passenger door. I felt like someone had hit me in the face with a molten sledgehammer. The inside of the vehicle was covered in soot and smoke. I couldn't see anything at all. I later found out that Greer was blown out of the vehicle. Fortunately, he had a brace on his knee from a previous injury; that knee brace got caught in the door. And that's how the Humvee, which was still moving after the explosion, didn't roll over him."

Remarkably Bartlett neither lost consciousness nor bled to death. In an ironic twist of fate, the searing heat of the blast actually cauterized Bartlett's extensive facial injury. "I vaguely remember hearing some-one screaming—just screaming. Took me a few minutes to realize the screaming was coming from me. I was the one doing the screaming, crying out in incredible pain."

He began to die. "My lung collapsed with internal bleeding, and every time I took a breath, less air filled my lungs. Then Bishop fell on top of me, and pain stimuli woke me up enough to straighten out his damaged legs as he laid his back to the windshield. I knew I was dying, and Todd felt it too—so without a word I just laid my head down on his chest. We were going to die together. At that moment Greer yanked three times on the door, which finally opened. Blood came from his eyes, ears, and nose as a result of the concussion; he was a mess, covered in soot."

Greer moved Bartlett to the back seat. "By the grace of God," says Bartlett, "the vehicle was still running, and Greer managed to drive it out of the way so others could rescue the guys in the last two Humvees."

Bartlett's nose and nearly half his face were damaged or had third-degree burns. His left eye was gone. He had lost a few teeth and an inch of his jawbone. His bulletproof plates and vest probably saved his life, protecting him from devastating internal injuries. Even with the vest, however, the blast collapsed one of his lungs and caused internal bleeding. Now back at the camp on a stretcher, Bartlett believed his worst fears had materialized: he would surely die. Captain Spikes, the chaplain, began to pray.

Bartlett went into respiratory and cardiac arrest and was resuscitated before being flown by helicopter to the Eighty-Sixth Combat Support Hospital at Balad Air Base. Later that day he went into cardiac arrest again and was once again resuscitated. He was stabilized and flown to Walter Reed in Washington, where he died yet again and was once more resuscitated. In fact, Robert Bartlett died three times in five days, just twenty-two days shy of his thirty-second birthday.

"When I died," Bartlett reflects, "I woke up and was naked and on my knees on a marble floor. Before me were four columns, two of which were broken and lying in a pool. Marble steps led down into the pool—a giant pool of blood. I could see this drip coming from above—from eternity—and filling the pool. I knew then that I was kneeling before the Blood of Christ. You can't be more vulnerable and helpless than when you are naked and on your knees. I don't fear much, but there I was so afraid. So very afraid.

"Over my left shoulder, on the same floor on which I was kneeling, I saw Satan on a pillar. He looked just like a dragon. He had no wings, but he did have long claws and horns on his head that grew backwards like a goat's. He was scaly and scorched and looked as though he'd been burning for thousands of years in the eternal fire. He came off the pillar, reached out, and tore into me with his claws, causing agonizing pain—an intense and deeper pain than the bomb I had just experienced. I can't express how much it hurt.

"Writhing in pain, I cried out for God: *Help me!* Instantly I was whisked away. I'd no sooner called out for God than I was pulled away and saved from the grips of the dragon. I felt an indescribable peace, joy, and love. I felt I was the only Robert God had ever created. I knew I'd been meant for

After suffering from an IED explosion, Robert was hospitalized for about four years. Photo courtesy Robert Bartlett.

this place. It was home. I didn't want to go back to earth and time. I desperately wanted to stay where I was. But my buddy SSG Brooks told me to *go back.* I heard him plain as day. I didn't see him, but I could hear him.

"Did I see God? It's hard to say. The simple answer is yes, but this is beyond most people's understanding. Also, I could *hear* Sergeant Brooks clearly—as clearly as if he were standing beside me in formation. He told me I had to go back—that I had to get married and have kids. That I couldn't stay. I wanted to stay. I had *no desire* to go back among the living. But Brooks was very clear. I have an image in my head of sitting next to Jesus and looking out into the valley from a hill and under a tree. We talked, and I was part of His body, and the next thing I remember it was like I was being torn from His flesh. This was the most painful part: leaving Him. Every ounce of my being screamed in pain as I was torn away. We who follow Him are part of His body—one flesh.

"Greer visited me at Walter Reed. I thanked him for saving me, but he brushed it off, saying, 'Don't thank me; I had almost nothing to do with it. When I woke from the blast all I could hear was Brooks's voice telling me to get up. He told me as clearly as I'm talking to you right now: *Get up, Greer. Greer, get up! You gotta move this Humvee. You gotta get Bartlett out of here. Greer, get up. Get moving!*'

"Brooks had a wife and kids of his own," concludes Bartlett, his voice thick with emotion. "I don't know why I lived and he didn't. It was God's plan, but I know as sure as I'm standing here that had it not been for Brooks, none of us would have survived."

Bartlett's severe facial and internal injuries and extensive third-degree burns left him in constant pain. "Some patients might receive a quarter of a Fentanyl patch," he explains. "I was getting two complete patches when I reached Walter Reed.

"I remember the blast, and being in Iraq—and the next thing I know, I'm waking up at Walter Reed. I was really disoriented and didn't trust anyone, including the nurse giving me a sponge bath. All I could think about was getting back to my guys, back to the battle. That's how far out of touch with reality I was: I thought I would go back to fighting." Instead, Bartlett would fight an entirely different battle at Walter Reed as his life became an endless cycle of surgeries and physical therapy sessions. A bone graft would be followed by a skin graft and then an implant surgery—and on and on it went. "I had at least fourteen major surgeries, one of which lasted nearly thirteen hours. I've had nearly forty total procedures to correct various injuries or to provide materials to recreate bone structures. My lips, for example, came from the inside of my mouth and both arms."

His family visited regularly, carefully keeping Bartlett from seeing his own reflection. "I distinctly remember the first time I looked into a mirror. I burst into tears at the sight of my face. I remember thinking, *What* woman would want a man with only half a face?" A few years later after hunting in Virginia he would be asked by a waitress in a restaurant if he'd been mauled by a bear. "No, a bomb in Iraq," Bartlett replied, laughing.

Back home his old bosses and a host of others had heard about Bartlett's injuries and raised nearly $40,000 to help his family take time off of work and travel east to be with him. "When you consider that it all came from blue-collar folks—from bartenders and cops and firefighters and other locals—I was simply blown away."

In late July 2005, Bartlett left Walter Reed with his dad for the

Robert and his wife Jordan, who supported him through thick and thin. Photo courtesy Robert Bartlett.

first time to go home to Phoenix between surgeries. "I was still a mess," Bartlett remembers. "I couldn't walk well, and my memory was spotty, but I wanted to get to the pubs and thank everyone in person. Imagine my surprise when a buddy at the Dubliner told me that Jordan was at the other end of the bar and I should come over and say hello. I made a beeline for her and told her that in a month when the swelling went down on my face, I was going to kiss her again."

Back "home" at Walter Reed, Bartlett trudged the slow, painful road to recovery. "In Iraq I weighed in at a solid 215 pounds; two weeks after my injury I was down to 175." Bartlett would spend just over four and a half years at Walter Reed before being discharged for good.

Bartlett's recovery process included occupational therapy to improve the fine motor skills in his badly damaged fingers—and that's where he met retired Navy Captain Ed Nicholson, when Project Healing Waters Fly Fishing was not quite an idea yet. Nicholson just wanted to share his passion for fly fishing. "He asked me to stay for a presentation about helping wounded veterans through fly fishing. I said, 'I'm all in—I don't need to see your presentation.' But he was an officer in the Navy," Bartlett says, laughing, "so of course he had a pretty extensive plan, video, and presentation. 'Oh no,' he says, 'you need to see my program.' He had a talk, slides, a video, and a three-ring binder. . . . I didn't need to see any of that stuff. I was in as soon as he said he was going to take me fly fishing! As far as I know, I'm the first person who said yes to what would become Project Healing Waters."

As good as his word, Nicholson had Bartlett out on the water, fly fishing a pond on the Old Soldiers Home in the District of Columbia soon after their meeting. "Colonel Howard was there—a great guy who was then the head of occupational therapy at Walter Reed. Retired Soldier John Colburn gave me pointers," Bartlett remembers. "He was a great encouragement to me and taught some of the other guys how to tie flies. Yes, that first time at the pond—I really can't describe how good it felt to be out of the hospital and outdoors. My buddy from my platoon was visiting from Iraq, so he learned about fly fishing as well. It was a good day.

"Just being around moving water does something to you. I remember thinking once while fishing in a river that the current pushes the sand over the stones, making them smooth. That same water has

Oivind Moldestad, Captain, Norwegian Airforce, acting as a guide for Robert Bartlett, Staff Sergeant (SSG) US Army, at a PHWFF fundraiser. Photo by Matt Romano.

washed over me, too. It's helped wash away the harsh places on my soul and scars on my body. Thank the Lord for folks like Ed Nicholson—folks who really care."

When Bartlett reflects on his long and painful journey, he's surprisingly sanguine. "It takes a long time to heal; I know I'll be recovering for the rest of my life. I also know that you have to be patient with yourself and get over your anger. I've forgiven the men who tried to kill me. I've learned that you can't let yourself become isolated. You can't refuse to let others help you. In the end, you have to make peace with yourself and your past. I could have more and more corrective surgeries—but why? I love my beautiful wife, and she doesn't care how I look. I'm good with her, and I'm good with God. Honestly: What else is there?"

Robert Bartlett is a devout Roman Catholic. He speaks often about his near-death experience and supports veteran nonprofits aimed to stop veteran suicide and save marriages.

Jessica Callihan landed her first fish on a fly rod on Tennessee's South Holston River. A mere eleven inches long, what the spunky rainbow lacked in size it more than made up for in vibrant beauty. What Callihan calls her "trophy fish" marked a turning point in her life: the point at which she refused to view herself as a victim any longer or allow her injuries to continue to sideline her. When she returned her trout back to its river, Callihan returned herself to the world.

Jessica Callihan (Dial) loved serving her country in the Navy and had planned on making it a lifelong career prior to being injured. Photo courtesy Jessica Callihan.

Callihan grew up on a family-owned-and-operated dairy farm before heading to Western Michigan University on a full academic scholarship. The 9/11 terror attacks changed her life, weighing heavily on her mind until finally, turning her back on her scholarship, she defied expectations and enlisted in the United States Navy.

After boot camp and her initial advanced training, Callihan became an Airman qualified to work on electrical systems aboard Navy aircraft. As a result of a fall during a training event, however, Callihan shattered her right knee, tore her right shoulder, and misaligned her lower back and hips. Initially she believed that she would recover from the accident within a few months; instead she began a seemingly endless cycle of operations. Though her first three procedures caused more harm than healing, Callihan eventually underwent a total of ten surgeries in five years. At just twenty years old, she found herself unfit for duty, ejected from a career she had come to love, and in need of a wheelchair to get around because her shoulder injury made using crutches unbearably painful. Jessica Callihan was broken.

Because she complained of excruciating pain, Callihan became convinced that her doctors thought her mentally unstable. She admits that for a time, she almost wished for a missing limb—something obvious to explain the pain that plagued her. She might have appeared healthy and whole, but for the first time in her life, her thoughts turned to suicide. "At times, I felt as though my legs were on fire," says Callihan, "and I couldn't even tolerate the sheets they tried to put on me. I spent most of my time wearing shorts while in and out of the hospital. I remember once they placed ice on me to help with my swollen leg, and instead of feeling relief all I felt was an intense burning sensation."

Eventually a specialist diagnosed Callihan with a severe case of complex regional pain syndrome; doctors implanted a neurostimulator in her spine to block pain signals. She found her pain much more manageable after treatment, although being plugged in twice a week to recharge the device's batteries certainly took some getting used to.

One cold December day, Callihan made a friend who changed her life. At the Western North Carolina Fly Fishing Expo in Asheville, Callihan met retired Coast Guard Captain John Miko at the Project Healing Waters Fly Fishing booth. "I remember distinctly," she says, "that John Miko looked right at me, like I was a real person, and treated me like an equal. He didn't judge me. He didn't make me feel like I was some sort of faker—or anything less than a Navy veteran. I knew nothing about fly fishing at the time, but he invited me to attend the Mossy Creek Invitational in Virginia. This is how I became involved with the program, and it not only changed my life but literally saved it."

∞

Since 2008 the Mossy Creek Invitational (MCI), Project Healing Waters Fly Fishing's inaugural fundraising tournament, has been held annually on riverfront property owned by Bob Fitch and his wife Robin. Fitch is a retired US Army Lieutenant Colonel who saw combat in Vietnam, served eleven years on active duty, and spent the rest of his career with the Army Reserve. Eventually he moved into the defense contracting industry where he met John Miko, now the director of the MCI, who steers the event with ruthless efficiency. Miko is easy to spot on the tournament grounds: he's the man holding a bullhorn. Like so many other veterans, both Fitch and Miko shun the limelight, prefer to operate behind the scenes, and steer conversation away from their military service and accomplishments; when pressed about that service, Miko comments that he's merely a "washed-up old helicopter pilot." Between them the two men have volunteered countless hours to the event; of course, they haven't done it alone: Fitch, Miko, and all of the veterans who participate in the event are indebted to Brian and Colby Trow, owners of Mossy Creek Fly Fishing in Harrisonburg, which provides all the tournament guides. The original goal of the MCI was to raise $1 million dollars in ten years. The tournament team did it in seven and to date has raised $2.5 million.

The MCI is generally held the first weekend in June, by which time Mossy Creek's fish are quite active—though spring rains can raise the water level and make the fishing conditions tough. On the Friday afternoon before the tournament gets underway, participants, sponsors, stream monitors, and guides meet and greet at O'Neill's Grill in Harrisonburg, which feeds all the participating warriors at no cost. "I wouldn't miss this afternoon's gathering for the world," says O'Neill's general manager Andy Anderson, whose brother, Specialist Brian Anderson, died in 2010 fighting in Afghanistan with the Tenth Mountain Division. "We are honored to have the warriors here as our special guests. Seeing them here together, enjoying themselves, making new friends—we're just happy to be a part of it all." The restaurant's patio fills to capacity with veterans and their guides and fishing partners, many of whom are meeting for the first time. Often participants spill into the parking lot to cast their fly rods while they enjoy burgers and conversation.

On Saturday morning, participants—both locals and those from as far away as the West Coast and even Europe—are driven through nearby Bridgewater in a PHWFF van with a motorcycle escort. American flags dot both sides of the street into Bridgewater, and a welcome banner stretches across Dingle Avenue and Main Street. Should bad weather require the event's awards ceremony to be moved, Arey Hall, the municipal meeting area, is available at no cost. Here in humble Bridgewater it is clear that small-town America is firmly behind its veterans.

∞

Arriving at the tournament grounds for the 2013 Mossy Creek Invitational, Jessica Callihan and her fellow veterans proceed to a large white tent packed with tables and chairs and sitting only a few yards from the creek itself. John Miko, clipboard in one hand and bullhorn in the other, begins calling names and pairing vets with their guides and fishing partners. "Introduce yourselves to each other, and formulate your plan on how you'll win this tournament," suggests Miko. "Win or lose, you're going to have an excellent time, because this place is beautiful, the trout are hungry, and we're so pleased you're here."

Callihan is introduced to Elizabeth Trenary, her tournament

fishing partner, and it is immediately obvious to all right from the start that the women are a perfect fit. They confer upon a strategy to take turns casting into likely spots along their designated stretch of river; their guide suggests which flies to use and where to cast. Initially anxious and intimidated, Callihan snags several patterns in streamside trees, the branches of which hover just above the water's surface and provide both shade and cover for Mossy's fish.

Jessica uses nature to inspire her various works of art. Her pieces are sold all over the country. Photo courtesy Jessica Callihan.

Directly across from where Callihan stands is a perfect trout lie; the trick, however, is casting the pattern below the low-hanging tree branches, landing it perfectly, and then managing a casual and natural-looking drift. And even then there are no guarantees: Mossy Creek trout are notoriously wary and often produce strong takes, sometimes biting off a pattern on their initial strike. Manage to set the hook, and these wily trout love to dive into undercut banks or wrap themselves around underwater structure. Mossy Creek is famed for its fishing, and not because its trout are easy.

Trenary, just as driven as her partner, casts to and quickly lands a nice rainbow. The fishing heats up as both women continue to take turns at the trout. Late in the day, Callihan is up and casts to a likely looking spot, but it appears that no one is home. Casting is becoming more difficult now because her shoulder aches and her knee throbs. Her face is set in a grimace. Pain is Callihan's constant companion, of course, but few know that she has only just been cleared to attend the

MCI—and that her physician admonished her to take it easy and not pick up anything heavier than five pounds. Fortunately for Callihan, the Mossy Creek trout don't get the memo: she and Trenary land several fish that day, and Callihan brings two to hand that are just over five pounds apiece. She and Trenary go on to win the Mossy Creek Invitational.

Callihan is asked to speak at the award ceremony, where she shares her story—her injury and her long, painful road to recovery—with those gathered under the big tent. She tells them of the anger she felt at being injured at such a young age, the frustration that injury closed the door on a promising career in the Navy. She tells them of surgeries, depression, and being a wheelchair user at twenty. She tells them of isolation, shame, and feeling like a burden to others. Here, finally, is an audience who understands.

All eyes are on Callihan when she says, "Then one day I met John Miko, and he didn't look down on me. He saw me for who I was, and he believed in me—and that had a huge impact on me. Since then I have met so many great people in this organization and I know that I'm not alone. I know I'll never be 'normal,' but I did discover I wasn't alone. I didn't have to stay in the very dark place where I'd found myself. I could get on with my life. All sorts of people wanted to help me. I just had to find them and find my own path. I know fundraisers like the MCI are important, but to be honest, it's not the money that's raised here that makes the difference. It's the relationships you build and the time you spend with special people that make the difference."

There are few dry eyes in the tent when Callihan quietly sets down her microphone to make her way back to her chair. Thunderous applause erupts in the tent when an old, washed-up helicopter pilot steps up to envelop her in a bear hug.

Today Jessica Callihan faces severe, daily pain—and the withering looks of strangers when she pulls into a handicapped parking space.

Jessica Callihan started fly fishing locally, but her passion as taken her all over the world. She is seen here fishing in Scotland. Photo courtesy Wesley Grant-Parke.

Still, she is at peace with her life and her circumstances and feels a strong bond with fellow injured veterans. On May 17, 2015, Callihan graduated from Maryville College in Tennessee with a fine arts degree. She's since become an accomplished artist and fished from Montana to Scotland. She insists, however, that that first South Holston River rainbow remains her trophy fish because of what it awakened in her.

Jessica Callihan lives in Sweetwater, Tennessee, and remains close friends with Elizabeth Trenary.

Alvin Shell with a dandy snook he landed at a PHWFF-sponsored tournament in the Florida Keys. This fish helped Shell secure second place in the tournament. Photo courtesy Alvin Shell.

Ask Alvin Shell who he is, and he'll tell you plainly: "I'm a child of God, son of Alvin and Mabel Shell, husband of Danielle Shell, father of Sean, Tre', and Jachin Shell. I'm nothing special; I'm just an ordinary Soldier." Shell's calm voice, mild manner, and easygoing smile belie an inner strength that has seen him through years of emotional and physical torment.

Alvin Shell graduated from Virginia State University in 1998 with a bachelor's degree in sociology, eventually following in his father's footsteps and pursuing a career in law enforcement. He became a deputy sheriff in Richmond, Virginia, until paying off outstanding college loan debt and meeting the financial needs of a growing family became increasingly difficult. Shell's wife, Danielle, hit upon an idea: Why not consider a career in the Army?

"She grew up an Army brat," Shell explains. "Both of her parents were Army, so she had a sense of what Army life was like and thought it would be a good environment for me. Turns out she was right." Despite the flexibility his college education afforded him, Shell knew he wanted to serve among the enlisted ranks: "I just thought in order to be a good leader, you need to learn how to follow first. So, I decided to go the enlisted route."

In 2002, Shell, who had been serving in Germany, was chosen for Officer Candidate School in Fort Benning, Georgia, where he also attended Airborne School. Shell jokes, "I learned how to fall out of planes safely." Paratroopers are highly trained Soldiers who parachute or "jump" into battlefield environs, often behind enemy lines. After completing his paratrooper training, Shell became part of the Twenty-First Military Police Company (Airborne) at Fort Bragg, North Carolina.

His orders to deploy to Iraq came just after Danielle gave birth to Shell's third son in 2003. "It was the only time I wanted to tell the Army no," he recalls. Jachin's delivery had been particularly difficult, and the baby had been released from neonatal intensive care just the week before his scheduled deployment. "My wife was a tower of strength," Shell says, "and told me she'd be just fine. There wasn't even a hint of reservation about how she'd manage three young children all by herself, and one of those a newborn. She's always been there for me and continues to be a tower of strength in our family, and to me in particular."

In Iraq, Shell and his company of military police struggled to establish order amidst the chaos. He experienced multiple firefights in places like Fallujah and Baghdad, but it was interacting with civilians that proved especially challenging. "It was hard to see kids literally eating garbage or searching for food in what passes as a dump in Iraq. We would go on patrol day after day trying to instill some sense of order and normalcy, which was really difficult in a war zone. When you go to war, you can't just drop a few bombs, engage in a few firefights, and then call it good. You have to connect with the population if you want things to change. You have to be seen as the good guys—but

Alvin Shell and his son Jachin were awarded a trip through Project Healing Waters to sail and fish in Ketchikan, Alaska. The trip helped bring Shell and his youngest son together through a once-in-a-lifetime fishing experience. Photo courtesy Alvin Shell.

this is extremely difficult in places like Iraq. How do you explain to folks that you want to bring them freedom? They live in a world where only the meanest and most brutal people are respected. How do you explain freedom or liberty to people who, up until a few months ago, lived in a country where if you criticized Saddam publicly, you might not ever be seen again?"

Shell reserves his harshest criticism for soldiers in the Iraqi Army. "Those spineless cowards would abandon their position, then tell the locals as they fled, 'The Americans are coming to rape your women and children and take your land!' You can imagine the response we often received when met by local farmers who didn't know any better and only knew what they'd been told about us. They would often dig in deep and lie in wait for us to arrive. We had terrific firefights, I mean really pitched battles, and I'm sad to say that sometimes it was with women and kids. But what can you do? You can't speak their language, and when they open up on you with their weapons, you have to defend yourself. It was often a no-win situation, but you have to survive. You have to take care of your folks."

Moments of light pierce Shell's otherwise dark recollections: "My mom is a schoolteacher, and she and my dad would often ship me school supplies to give away to the kids. It was wonderful to be able to give some of those kids just a little bit of help, just a little bit of hope. Still," Shell says with a sigh of resignation, "you had to maintain a posture of being a real badass. They need to understand that while you might be nice to them when on peaceful terms, if things change you're going to be the toughest guy walking the streets. They only understand strength over there, and you have to project a strong posture and be ready for anything."

On August 31, 2004, Alvin Shell's life changed course. "I'd taken another Lieutenant's slot on convoy protection duty that night. Seemed like a typical mission: we would watch trucks as they moved food, water, and other supplies for the troops. I happened to be working with another squad that night, and a top-shelf paratrooper, Sergeant Spaid, asked if I wanted to ride with him in his jeep. I agreed, and we were watching this convoy when all of a sudden one of the trucks hit an IED, and all hell broke loose. We ran to the scene to try to help out the driver of the truck that had struck the IED when the enemy opened fire on us. We managed to get the driver out, but the enemy's guns had us in a pretty tough spot. To make matters worse, shrapnel from the IED explosion had ruptured the fuel tank of the lead truck, and fuel was running down the road. The convoy was at a complete standstill because we couldn't move the disabled lead vehicle out of the way. We were in the process of trying to winch it out of position when a rocket propelled grenade struck and blew me into a ditch a few feet away. I remember seeing the RPG come over my shoulder like some clip out of the movie *The Matrix*. The explosion knocked me unconscious briefly, and when I came around, I could hear people screaming and the night was lit up in flames."

When Shell regained consciousness he was lying in a watery, putrid-smelling roadside ditch. He immediately realized his squad was in terrible danger, simultaneously exchanging gunfire with the enemy and trying to aid the convoy victims amidst the flames. Shell rushed to assist Sergeant Spaid, who was himself on fire, rolling him on the ground and pushing him out of the flames. "What I didn't realize was that my clothes were soaked with diesel fuel that had spilled out of the truck," so that when Shell rushed to the flames to assist his injured comrade, "I lit up like a Christmas tree. I looked around, but all I could see was flames. All I could feel, tremendous heat and pain. My skin was burning. I didn't know what to do, so I tucked my face into my right arm and ran through the flames as best I could."

Somehow Shell made it through the wall of flames and back to his colleagues, who tried unsuccessfully to extinguish him as the firefight continued. In the end, Shell jumped right back into the same ditch the original blast had blown him into and rolled around in the putrid water and dirt until the flames either burned out or were extinguished.

The firefight was over almost as quickly as it had begun; Shell believes the enemy soldiers were either killed or decided they had had enough of tussling with US Army paratroopers. A medic hurried to him, eyes as big as saucers, and asked, "Are you okay, Lieutenant? Are you okay?" Shell responded that he was fine and wanted to account for all the wounded and the team's equipment, especially their weapons. More Soldiers now coalesced around their injured leader, encouraging Shell to seek immediate care and to call in a medevac helicopter for himself and others. Shell assessed the situation and determined that they could get to help faster if they simply headed back the way they came, to Camp Victory.

His Soldiers pleaded with him to leave right away and receive care for his life-threatening injuries, insisting that they would take care of the ancillary equipment. "I told them I wasn't taking a vote, and I wasn't going to move one damn inch until all my people were accounted for—and that included all their gear. I told them, 'I'm the tail here, do you

Alvin and his wife Danielle Shell were invited to President Obama's Inauguration. Photo courtesy Alvin Shell.

understand me? I'm the tail,'" which is a Soldier's way of saying that he is the last to leave—that he won't move until everyone else is out. Shell was going to complete this mission in charge and by the book—and that included retrieving his own weapon, which he had lost control of in the midst of the chaos and trauma. His weapon located, Shell and his Soldiers headed back to Camp Victory, with Shell in the last vehicle in his column.

When Shell finally arrived at camp by jeep over two miles of broken road, he was in excruciating pain. He would later find out that about 70 percent of his body had been burned, nearly half of which were third-degree burns that in some cases went to the bone. Upon reaching Camp Victory, Shell exited the jeep and collapsed in agony. When he regained consciousness on base, his burns were being treated, but the pain was unlike anything he'd ever experienced. He asked for so much morphine that the medic told him, "Lieutenant, I can't give you any more for the pain; if I do, I could kill you myself." Shell remembers his Captain patting him on his chest and yelling into his ear over the prop wash of the medical chopper, "You're a hero, Alvin—an honest-to-God hero!" "No, sir," countered Shell. "A hero is a sandwich. I'm a damn paratrooper!"

"When I woke up in the hospital," recounts Shell, "the first thing I saw was my wife in scrubs. She pulled down her mask and kissed me. My father was there too, and I remember thinking that the Army had lost its mind. Why in heaven's sakes had the Army flown my wife and father to a war zone?" In fact, nearly a week had passed. "I'd been placed in a drug-induced coma, and when I woke up I found I'd been flown to Germany and then to Brooke Army Medical Center in Texas—but I didn't remember any of it. One minute I was on the battlefield; the next moment I was in a hospital, and I could hardly move. I've never felt pain like that in my entire life. It was excruciating, and I felt it all over my body, nearly all the time."

When Shell finally became lucid, he discovered to his horror that he was only able to move his left hand. He couldn't move his legs, turn over, move his right arm, or assist himself in any way. And there was constant, excruciating pain. "Did you know the average hospital ceiling tile has 3,654 tiny holes in it? I know that because I'd count the holes in the ceiling tile to just keep my mind off the pain." But the pain was just one facet of an odyssey toward recovery that included thirty surgeries in eighteen months. Eventually Shell would discover that he'd lost part of his vision. Entire muscle groups were completely burned. At one point in his recovery, severe smoke inhalation left him completely speechless. Countless hours of physical therapy kept his multiple skin grafts from becoming too inflexible. "You have to move your joints so they don't become fixed in one place," he explains, "and that skin has to be pliable or it's nearly useless as far as movement goes."

Sometimes Shell's skin grafts would tear from the physical therapy, and he'd have to start all over again. "I can't do this anymore," he would say. "I can't take the pain. I'm not going through this anymore. Just leave me alone." But his wife and family refused to listen, refused to leave him alone, and instead rallied around him. Shell's brother and sister pitched

While on patrol, Shell and his platoon discovered desperate Iraqis scouring a dump for food. Moved by their plight, Shell and his comrades immediately offered them their own MREs and water. Photo courtesy Alvin Shell.

in to help, as did his neighbors. Danielle's father, mother, and sister also played pivotal roles in Alvin's recovery and in supporting Danielle. "My mom teaches disabled children and works in speech therapy, and she's the one who taught me how to talk again. My dad practically moved in with my wife to take care of our kids so she could be with me in the hospital nearly all the time."

Still, inside, Shell struggled alone. "I went from ten months in a war zone where I was one of the toughest son-of-a-guns on earth—with the toughest fighting men on the planet—to not even being able to feed myself. I couldn't even wipe my own rear end when I went to the bathroom. That does something to you; it makes you feel helpless, and all you can do is hurt, and lie in bed and think, and then hurt some more."

Recognizing that her husband was in dire physical and emotional straits, Danielle Shell issued him a challenge: "I'm going to need help. I need you to be able to walk before Jachin does." Shell met his wife's challenge and learned how to walk again just before his youngest son. Though the pain continued, he gradually became accustomed to what seemed like endless physical therapy.

His visible wounds healed, Shell left the Army in July 2006 and went to work for the Department of Homeland Security. Because he'd been critically injured while in the service, he'd been enrolled in the Fort Belvoir–based Army Wounded Warrior Program (AW2), established in 2004 to help wounded Soldiers either return to service or transition to civilian life. Shell's injuries prevented him from returning to service, but he maintained his relationship with Ayandria Barry, his advocate in the AW2 program. Barry also advocated for David Folkerts, another severely injured Soldier who told her about Project Healing Waters Fly Fishing. It struck Barry that the quiet sport could be therapeutic for Alvin Shell. "While Alvin was healing well on the outside," says Barry, "I felt he had some unresolved issues and would really benefit from Project Healing Waters." Barry emailed Bob Gartner, PHWFF's Fort Belvoir program lead, to make the connection.

Shell went to his first meeting and loved it. "I'd been trying for years to teach myself how to fly fish," he says, "but I had no idea what I was doing. I mean, you can watch stuff on YouTube, but you really need someone to show you the ropes. I was afraid at first that they would baby me, but that didn't happen. Bob Gartner really made me feel a part of the group and was supportive from the very first meeting. They'd encourage me and give me tips on how to make better casts, how to tie the right knots, and even how to tie flies—but they didn't treat me differently. In the end," he says, "they helped me help myself, by encouraging me to get out more and enjoy the outdoors. It has helped me a lot with my PTSD and allowed me to connect and enjoy being with my family even more."

Since that first meeting, Shell has become quite an accomplished fly angler. In fact, *twice* he has won first place in the renowned Project Healing Waters 2-Fly Tournament, held each year at Virginia's Rose River Farm.

"People think I'm tough," says Shell. "They think I'm some sort of special person because I learned how to walk again after being severely burned, and now I'm able to compete in triathlons. I was speechless, but now I talk just fine. They think I'm special because I was right-handed prior to my burns, but due to my injuries I had to learn how to shoot with my left. Sure, I'm an expert shot, and I'm back to working full-time in a job I love, but I didn't do any of this on my own. I had an unfair advantage that many other folks don't have. I had a family who wouldn't stop loving me; they are the reason I made it. I had Project Healing Waters, which gave me a great outlet and a way to get out of my head and away from my problems while on the stream. I'm a very blessed man."

For his heroic actions on the battlefield in protecting his team and saving the life of a fellow Soldier, Captain Alvin Shell was awarded the Bronze Star with Valor. Shell was also awarded a Purple Heart and earned another Bronze Star for exceptional achievements during battle while deployed in Iraq. He's reluctant to speak about his battlefield actions and even more reluctant to mention his meritorious conduct. If pressed, however, Shell will say simply, "I'm a child of God, son of Alvin and Mabel Shell, husband of Danielle Shell, father of Sean, Tre', and Jachin Shell. I'm nothing special; I'm just an ordinary Soldier." Anyone who knows Alvin Shell, however, knows he is anything but ordinary.

Alvin Shell continues to enjoy fly fishing and is an active member of the Project Healing Waters Fly Fishing program at Fort Belvoir, Virginia.

Jerry Miron was only nineteen years old when he was drafted to serve in Vietnam. Photo courtesy Jerry Miron.

I'd seen at least one brief, ominous flash of lightning—a pale, slender arm reaching toward us across an increasingly gray sky. The foreboding clouds were moving our way quickly and would certainly overtake us soon.

The day had been a pleasant one for me: I'd managed to land a few nice trout. My new friend Jerry Miron hadn't been so lucky. A veteran from Minnesota, Miron was with a group of vets who had flown to Colorado to take part in a Project Healing Waters Fly Fishing fundraiser called the Battle at Boxwood. The day after the event, our group had scored a shot at some private water owned by a local rancher, who warmly welcomed us and even provided us with fishing guides. As the day drew to a close, however, a dejected Miron mentioned that he'd not had any luck hooking up. Not a surprise, really: Miron's fly-angling career had begun precisely . . . yesterday, at Boxwood.

One of our guides, Mike Tayloe, was a fellow paramedic. "Hey, brother," I said to Tayloe, "my buddy is new to fly fishing. He's been fishing most of the day and hasn't landed squat. We don't have much time left—even I can see a storm's headed our way." I hitched a thumb over my shoulder at the menacing clouds. "Any chance you can get him hooked up on his first wild fish before we call it a day?"

Tayloe sized up Miron with a glance before casting an experienced eye toward the darkening horizon. He stoically gazed downstream for a moment before unceremoniously spitting out some dip he'd been holding in his lower lip. Wiping the spittle off his red-whiskered chin with the back of his hand, Tayloe turned back to me. "Well, hell yes, I can. Get your buddy over here."

I waved Miron over, and he gingerly made his way toward us, still a bit awkward in his waders. Stepping downstream, Tayloe changed Miron's pattern and told him to cast toward the edge of the stream. Though his casts were a bit clumsy at first, with some quick pointers from Tayloe, Miron's presentation improved. A few minutes passed. Nothing. I noticed the wind was picking up, and the sky was growing even darker. Still nothing. Things weren't looking good. I began to feel anxious for my friend. Though Miron seemed to be having the time of his life, there was no hint of a trout. "It's okay. Try again," said Tayloe easily, as though he and Miron had all the time in the world. "Just stay focused and be ready to react." Miron continued with an intensity rarely seen in beginners; he seemed to pour his entire being into watching his pattern. As it turns out, Miron has had plenty of practice focusing—not as a sportsman but as a Soldier.

At Home

On July 4, 1967, Miron had just returned from a leisurely walk home with his mother from Murphy's, a local department store back in Minnesota. The Miron family was quite close, and Rita Miron, Jerry's mother, was the undisputed head of the household. Her husband of nine years had died unexpectedly when she was only three weeks pregnant, and with five other children at home. "My mother was a true saint," Miron recalls. "I loved her an awful lot. I recall teasing my Mom once," he says with a smile. "I told her, 'You and Dad were married for nine years, and two of those years he served in World War II. I think if you guys had been married long enough, you'd have had at least thirty kids!'" Rita Miron's retort was as pithy as it was succinct. "Your father and I loved each other very much, and that's all I'm going to say about that." After their walk home on that day in 1967, Rita Miron checked the mailbox and brought back a letter addressed to her son from the United States Army. "Greetings," it began.

Jerry Miron had just been drafted.

Walking Point with Rebel

Within a few short months Miron was an infantryman, though he'd applied to go to Airborne school. "I was turned down for Airborne training, and was instead selected to be a scout dog handler," recalls Miron. "Funny thing is, who do you think led the Airborne guys in Vietnam?"

As a scout dog handler, Miron's primary responsibility was to walk point with his dog, Rebel, for various companies of Soldiers, sometimes numbering well over 185. A dog team—consisting of one handler and one dog, almost always a German shepherd—was inseparable, even when once a month the dogs were sent to the rear to be examined by an Army veterinarian technician. Here the dogs' paws and faces were checked for lacerations from working in thick bamboo, and they were monitored for parasites. Malnutrition was also a concern: Between their long hair and mandatory work harnesses and temperatures that often exceeded 115 degrees, these loyal dogs could literally work themselves to death for their masters. No matter how harsh the conditions, scout dogs stopped working when their masters told them to and not a moment before.

Rebel prior to a patrol. Photo courtesy Jerry Miron.

Miron and Rebel were charged with locating enemy positions and preventing the patrols they led from falling victim to enemy ambushes. Miron carried a weapon, an M16, as all scout dog handlers did; in reality he was entirely focused on Rebel's every move, alert, and indication. Indeed, because Miron's focus was fixed so completely on Rebel, a Soldier acted as his bodyguard while on patrol. This position was called working "shotgun" because early in the war, such weapons were carried by these Soldiers. This weapon was soon discarded because the jungle generally required more firepower to penetrate dense cover, but the nickname stuck.

Though an integral member of the fighting force, Rebel was strictly off limits to everyone but Miron: "They'd all been told, 'Don't touch the dog, don't speak to the dog; do nothing—simply ignore him,'" Miron remembers. "When I held Rebel on his choke chain, no one approached me. And I mean no one. He hadn't been trained to be my personal guard dog, but he certainly acted like he was. When I put him in his work harness, however, he knew his job was to look for other threats. Guys could approach me easily when Rebel was in his harness, but if he was on his choke chain, they were better off keeping their distance."

On most mornings Miron and Rebel rose before dawn. "We'd get up about 5:00 a.m. if we hadn't been out on ambush duty or a night patrol," he says. "I'd eat cold C rations and then spend time with Rebel getting him excited about the day. I'd hold him close to me and get him all amped, and he'd be so excited about going out on patrol. Obviously dogs aren't like people: You can't tell them, 'I'm asking you to do more today because if you don't, somebody is likely to die.' They simply can't communicate on that level. And yet you can build such a strong relationship with them that they'll do absolutely anything you tell them to do without question. They want to please you that much."

Most people, argues Miron, have no idea just how smart dogs really are and how effectively they can be trained. Rebel, for example, had three primary tools with which to search for the enemy. The first and most sensitive was his nose. "When you or I walk into a kitchen," explains Miron, "we might smell chicken soup cooking on the stove. Rebel could smell not just the chicken but the carrots, celery, potatoes—even the salt. His nose was unbelievably accurate; he could pick up the slightest scent, even in windy conditions.

Rebel was so good at detecting the enemy and signaling danger that he is credited with saving hundreds of lives, including Miron's own during his service in Vietnam. Photo courtesy Jerry Miron.

Next up in Rebel's canine toolbox was his ears. "Sometimes," says Miron, "Rebel would simply stand still and listen for the slightest sound that seemed out of place. If he heard anything that didn't belong, he'd throw an alert to let me know there was something out there!"

"Dogs have great vision," concludes Miron, "but this is actually the last sense they rely on unless they're in a confusing environment—down in a valley, for example, in which the wind is blowing and swirling in all different directions. Humans by contrast mostly rely on sight; but of course in the jungle, by the time you see the bad guys, it's simply too late. In fact, if you're waiting to see the bad guys, you'll probably end up dead."

Through hundreds of patrols, multiple enemy contacts, nighttime firefights, and other life-threatening situations—experiences that left emotional scars that, decades later, still have not fully healed—Rebel was by Miron's side. Among the memories that haunt him is that of a patrol that went horribly wrong. What began as a standard patrol began to change when Rebel threw an alert and Miron signaled to his shotgun and radio man to relay to the commanding officer that the column had to stop; moments later his CO signaled the patrol to push ahead. Miron assumed he'd been misunderstood and again signaled to stop; again his CO signaled for him to continue. Making his way back to the officer leading the patrol, Miron said the patrol needed to stop. "I told him," says Miron, "that there was an ambush about two hundred meters ahead on the left and that we needed to call in some artillery or air support to clear out the area. The new officer wasn't having it." He had communicated up the chain of command via radio, the young officer assured Miron, and he had been informed that recon had not reported any enemy threats in the area. They needed to move forward.

"We went back and forth; it got pretty ugly," says Miron. "I told him, 'Rebel is never wrong. You're going to get us killed, sir.'"

Unimpressed and now irritated, the officer threatened Miron with a court-martial on the spot. "There is no way that dog knows there is an ambush two hundred meters ahead on the left," the officer shouted. "That's just bullshit."

"Court-martial me if you want," responded Miron, standing his ground. "At least I'll be alive. Why do you have me and Rebel leading you if you're not going to trust us? I'm telling you we can't go forward; we need to call for support, sir."

The officer relented in frustration, calling up a group of five Soldiers to move ahead while the rest waited behind. "I did everything I could to stop them, but the officer wouldn't listen to me," Miron chokes out. "I begged. 'Guys,' I said, 'take your guns off safety. Spread out and be careful. I'm telling you, Rebel isn't wrong; there *is* an ambush up there.' I can still see the fear in their eyes: They knew they were being ordered to their deaths. Every man sent on that forward patrol was killed in the ambush. I remember yelling at the officer, 'I hope you have to write to every one of those kids' parents! I hope you have to explain why you thought it was a great idea to have their kids killed for nothing!'"

"How the hell is that possible?" responded the dazed officer. "You're just a damn kid, and you're telling me you knew there was an ambush up there? I just couldn't believe it. You're just a damn kid."

"I didn't know," responded Miron in despair. "Rebel did."

When Miron learned that his tour was coming to an end, he found himself torn—eager to get home and reluctant to leave his comrades. One thought plagued him above all others: "What about Rebel?" Wrestling with this question for days, Miron eventually hit upon a solution: Rebel had to die.

First, during Rebel's routine checkup, Miron asked the veterinarian technician if he could surgically remove Rebel's "doggie dog tag," the Army marker embedded in his ear. Yes, he could, confirmed the vet tech. Next, Miron reached out to an officer he and Rebel had led many times and asked him to write a report that said Rebel had been killed during a firefight. Yes, he would, said the officer. Finally, it was time to approach his own commanding officer—the man who oversaw all the dogs and their handlers—and make a personal appeal. "I explained that I couldn't leave Rebel behind," says Miron. "He listened, but I could tell I wasn't really getting anywhere. He said no." In the end Miron was so desperate that he recklessly offered his commanding officer a bribe: "If you let me take Rebel home," he pleaded, "I'll give you a thousand bucks!"

"Miron, you've been here about a year, right?"

"Yes, sir," replied Miron.

"In that year, how many times do you think Rebel has saved your life?"

"I don't rightly know, sir," Miron answered carefully. "A lot of times. Rebel's the best there is. He's fearless! He's smart as they come, sir. He'd work himself to death for me if I asked him."

"And how many other Soldiers lives do you think you and Rebel have saved?" asked Miron's commanding officer patiently.

"I don't rightly know, sir," said Miron again. "A lot of lives."

"Would it be fair to say," he persisted, "that you and Rebel likely kept Soldiers alive nearly every day you were on point?"

Miron nodded.

"Would you say you and Rebel saved hundreds of lives over the course of the past year?"

"I don't know, sir."

"Well I do, Miron. I'm the one who sent you out on all those missions."

"Yes, sir," said Miron with pride in his dog, "I suppose that's accurate."

"Could it be more men than that? Perhaps many more?"

Miron nodded uncomfortably. "To be honest, sir, Rebel does the real work. I just relay what he tells me back down the line. Rebel is so smart, it's as though he's talking to me—and I understand every word. I know every alert he has, and why he's making them. In fact," Miron concluded with a grin, "Rebel's probably smarter than I am."

The officer smiled and then asked quietly, "And how many Soldiers lives will Rebel save back in Minnesota?"

Miron felt the question like a gut punch. He looked away from his commanding officer as tears welled in his eyes. "He was right, of course," Miron admits. "I just couldn't bear the thought of not having Rebel with me."

Not long after this fateful conversation, Miron was sent stateside. Rebel continued to serve.

At War at Home

Miron had left the battlefield, but the battlefield wouldn't leave him. At home in peaceful Minnesota, his thoughts strayed to the fellows he had left behind in the jungle—and to Rebel. "I'd run into people on the street in my hometown, and they'd ask where I'd been. When I'd tell them I'd been fighting overseas, they would ask stupid questions like, 'Did you shoot anyone over there? What's it like to kill someone, Jerry? Did you lose any buddies over there?' It was horrible—and that was just the dumb people. The evil ones would call me a murderer or curse at me when they found out I'd served in Vietnam. My own uncle called me a baby killer to my face when I'd been home less than a week. I'll never forget that. I realized those people didn't give a damn about me; they just wanted me to live out my worst nightmares for their entertainment."

Miron found it particularly difficult to explain to skeptics just what he and Rebel had accomplished overseas. "You're so full of shit, Jerry," he'd hear when he explained that he and Rebel had identified enemy camps and discovered weapons caches and acted as an early-warning system. "There's no way on God's green earth that a dog can tell you all that! If you're not proud of your service, fine—but please don't make shit up. Don't make yourself out to be something you're not." Dumbfounded by this response, Miron says, "Something inside me just died. I simply shut down. I didn't talk about it."

It would be nearly thirty years before Miron would talk about his service to anyone besides his wife—not even to his brothers, who also

Guide Mike Tayloe helps select just the right fly for Jerry Miron's first attempt at catching a fish on a fly rod.

served. "Vietnam wasn't something I wanted to discuss. With anyone. I wanted to put it all behind me and just forget about it. But it was really hard. Sometimes I'd have extremely vivid nightmares that felt like I was back on the line, fighting it out in the jungle. The chaos of battle, men screaming, machine gun fire—I could even smell the jungle. We had some godawful firefights, and scenes like those can play over and over in your mind—scenes you just can't shake. They stay with you, one way or another, for your entire life."

At Peace

The gathering clouds had turned from gunmetal gray to charcoal in a matter of a few minutes. The wind began to whistle and then howl through the nearby birch trees lining the banks, and I zipped up my rain jacket against the dropping temperature. The current began shifting the streamside gravel beneath my feet; I shifted my stance in response. I was ready to pack it in and call it a day. And yet my eyes remained glued on Miron.

Cast after cast, Miron's pattern went unnoticed—until a single dimple finally broke the surface of the water. Tayloe instructed Miron to stop casting as a lone, hungry trout rose. The clouds were closing in; now birch tree leaves occasionally lighted on the river. Still, Tayloe and Miron held their ground. Tayloe repositioned Miron and changed his pattern yet again. Miron resumed casting. And then the magic happened: His pattern alighted on the water and gently floated downstream without a hint of drag. Within seconds the nose of a trout eagerly broke the surface to take Miron's pattern. And the fight was on.

Both men slowly stepped downstream, Tayloe keeping a steady hand on Miron's shoulder as the trout made a desperate bid for freedom. Miron's rod was deeply bent now, and over the buzzing of the reel I could hear Miron squealing like a little kid and Tayloe trying to keep him calm. "Don't lose him, Jerry!" I shouted in encouragement. "Don't lose him! You lose that fish, and I'll never let you live it down!" Miron handily played the trout, and Tayloe carefully slipped the net beneath the fish in a single movement. "I got him!" Miron shouted, grinning from ear to ear. "I got him! I really got him!" Ever the professional, Tayloe just smiled at me with a knowing wink.

"When I was holding that trout," Miron said hours later at the hotel, "I could just feel the life in my hands. I've never felt so connected to something that was wild." When over the course of the night Miron spoke of Rebel, I realized that I was listening to a proud parent brag about his child. "I just wish I could have figured out some way to bring him home with me," he said. "That dog saved my life and the lives of so many other men. There's not a week goes by that I don't think of Rebel. I don't think I'll ever stop missing him."

The United States signed a peace agreement in Paris in 1973 that effectively ended the Vietnam War, but not before just over fifty-eight thousand American Soldiers were lost. Nearly three thousand more

Vietnam veteran Jerry Miron attempts to land his very first fish on a fly rod. Moments later a dandy rainbow trout came to hand.

were classified as missing in action; some will never be found. As combat operations wound down, the Army determined that repatriating American scout dogs would be too expensive. Instead, many of the dogs were simply euthanized.

Miron never learned what became of his beloved Rebel.

Jerry Miron is currently working on a book about his exploits in Vietnam with Rebel. He is featured in the 2016 documentary Iron Will: Veterans' Struggle with PTSD, *narrated by Billy Bob Thornton.*

NAME: RONALD DEAN RUDY
RANK: AIRMAN 1ST CLASS E-3
BRANCH OF SERVICE: US AIR FORCE
YEARS OF SERVICE: 14 MONTHS
HOME BASE: OLATHE, COLORADO

Ron Rudy puts his angling skills to the test on the South Platte River while competing in the Battle at Boxwood. Photo courtesy Ron Rudy.

Climbing into the plane, Ron Rudy looked at the flight nurse and smiled despite the throbbing pain in his arm. "This is my first ride in a medevac," he told her, lying down on the stretcher, "and it'll probably be my last." Indeed, it was a small miracle that Rudy was alive at all. As the plane lifted off he closed his eyes and wondered how a brief afternoon adventure had turned into a death sentence.

Ron Rudy joined the US Air Force on December 7, 1966; he readily admits he did so to avoid being drafted into the Army. He had hoped to be a paramedic or work in a hospital and even managed to deliver a baby while training on an ambulance. Rudy's training would indeed save at least one life: his own.

While on leave visiting his mother in Colby, Kansas, and hiking near Russell Springs, Rudy learned of an old clifftop cave reputed to be Kit Carson's former hideout when on the run from local Indians. What else was a curious nineteen-year-old to do but make the climb and see the hideout for himself?

Rudy was making excellent time scaling the cliff that beautiful morning when he felt a sharp prick on the fourth and fifth knuckles of his left hand. Born and raised in the West, Rudy knew immediately that he'd been bitten by a rattlesnake. He'd not heard its telltale rattles because the reptile's shedding skin was covering them. "I wasn't overly concerned," recalls Rudy. "Instead, I was angry because I knew my leave was going to be blown, and I was going to spend my time off getting treated for a snakebite." Within forty-five minutes Rudy was at a hospital in Oakley. Per military protocol, he gave the attending physician all of his military contact information and expected that he would be out of the hospital and back at his duty station within forty-eight hours.

Unfortunately, he was wrong.

Instead of contacting the military, Rudy says that the attending physician sedated him and put his arm in a tub of ice water above his elbow to within six inches of his shoulder. Three hours later the physician took his arm out of the ice water, gave Rudy the only dose of antivenom he would receive while under his care—in his shoulder and in multiple injections sites around his wrist—and then put his arm back in the ice water.

"On days four, seven, and ten, my arm was taken out of the water and laid on a sterile towel beside my body. I was greatly concerned about infection, but the doctor didn't seem to share my concerns. Despite my protests he continued his ineffective treatment, and at times it took as many as eight people to hold me down to administer painkillers to keep me sedated."

Between the infection and the fact that he couldn't keep anything down, by his eleventh day in the hospital, Rudy had lost fifty-five pounds. Even worse, he could tell that gangrene was setting in. He feared he would die. For nearly two weeks he begged the doctor to call the 1029th Medical Service Training Squadron, but the doctor refused to do so.

His mother was too intimidated by the doctor to intervene on her son's behalf. Even heavily sedated for much of the time, Rudy knew that his doctor was out of his depth—so one afternoon when he surfaced from sedatives and his nurses were distracted, Rudy was finally able to secure a telephone. He called his close friend Army veteran Charles Arnold, who listened to Rudy's desperate plea and called Rudy's uncle Milt, the 1029th Medical Squadron, and then-Congressman Bob Dole's office to inform them of Rudy's plight. Rudy's uncle Milton Rudy, himself a WWII veteran, called what was then Colorado's Fitzsimons Army Hospital and told them how his nephew was being mistreated. "To be honest, I'm still not entirely sure what happened," says Rudy. "I suppose contacting Dole's office really got things going, because within twenty-four hours of that call, a medevac plane was sent to retrieve me."

The closest airport was an hour from the hospital; no ambulances were available for immediate transport, so a hearse was pressed into service to transport Rudy to the medevac plane. He was eventually flown to Buckley Field in Aurora, Colorado, and transported by ambulance to Fitzsimons.

At Fitzsimons doctors took Rudy out of the ice, elevated his arm in traction, and attempted to save whatever healthy tissue remained. Despite their valiant efforts, doctors were concerned gangrene was overwhelming his system. The family was told to prepare themselves: Rudy might not survive. Eventually doctors determined that to save his life, they would have to amputate Rudy's arm at the waterline where the first doctor had submerged it. "They were skeptical that I would even survive, much less keep my arm. Thankfully those doctors did save my life, and Congressman Dole's office took such an interest in my case that they continued to follow up on me for three years after I was discharged."

Though wiry and small of frame, Rudy had been a linebacker, wrestler, gymnast, and swimmer in high school. He had also been a

Ron Rudy with a nice crappie caught while on an outing with the Grand Junction program in Colorado. Photo courtesy Ron Rudy.

swimming instructor and keenly interested in paddle sports such as canoeing and kayaking. "We wanted to work," says Rudy of himself and other wounded veterans he met at Fitzsimons. "We wanted to participate in making a meaningful contribution to society by doing something constructive with our lives. There is only so much recreational therapy you can do. We all wanted more out of our lives than just surviving." In 1968 Rudy and other veterans lobbied for the introduction of "work therapy" at Fitzsimons.

Eventually Rudy married Debbie, the love of his life, and together they raised three children: Hilary, Alicia, and Garth. Their son Garth died tragically at fourteen, on their back porch in Rudy's arms. "I did CPR on my son with one hand. I did the best I could," remembers Rudy.

"But I just couldn't save him. That was the worst day of my life, and I basically stopped hunting and fishing after that."

About twelve years after Garth's death, the Grand Valley Anglers chapter of Trout Unlimited in Grand Junction, Colorado, formed the first PHWFF program at the Grand Junction VA facility. Led by Matt Lucas and Ryan Keyes, the program became very successful, and numerous disabled veterans, including Ron Rudy, began fly fishing, rod building, and tying flies.

In time Rudy took on a leadership role in his program, mentoring other disabled veterans. "Our program at Grand Junction was greatly helped by Charlie Hensel, Kevin Matthews, and others," Rudy says, quick to deflect credit toward his fellow vets. "Hensel eventually got me involved in the Battle at Boxwood, a former fundraiser, and I had a ball. I also was fortunate enough to take a trip on Idaho's Middle Fork of the Salmon River. I had a great time there, met a lot of wonderful veterans— and I even went kayaking on the rapids!"

Rudy has overcome tremendous adversity by facing it head-on. Something as simple as opening a tiny coffee creamer container is a daunting task for an amputee, even with a prosthetic limb. And then there are the stares—and the child who cried out, "Look, Mommy, it's Captain Hook!" Cringing, Rudy says, "Captain Hook was an evil character, consumed with revenge, stuck in the past. And that's not me.

"Project Healing Waters helped me come face-to-face with parts of myself that needed to heal in order to achieve recovery. The water helps you heal because it's always in motion. It's not accidental that people all around the world see rivers as an analogy of life, and how you have to move on and not be caught up in a back eddy of despair," says Rudy. "The gentle direct human contact and encouragement helps you reach your personal goals to do things for yourself. Once you reach the point of doing it for yourself, you can then reach out to help others.

I've found over the years that my skills improve most when I'm helping others."

The words "I can't do it" simply aren't in his vocabulary, says Rudy. "You can do pretty much whatever you want; it usually just comes down to how badly you want to do it."

Ron Rudy also enjoys other sports on the river. Photo courtesy Ron Rudy.

Since beginning with Project Healing Waters, Ron Rudy has become a diehard tenkara angler, as well as a traditional fly-fisher, and remains a committed kayaker. While he owns a variety of fly rods, his favorite was custom-made for him by his mentor Kevin Matthews from the Grand Junction program. It reminds him that good rods are like good friends: they aren't made overnight.

NAME: TAMAR FRANKLIN
PHWFF ROLE: PROGRAM LEAD, REGIONAL COORDINATOR
YEARS OF SERVICE: 10
HOME BASE: NEW YORK CITY

Tamar Franklin has served PHWFF for many years both as a program lead and as a regional coordinator, seen here on a fishing trip in the Bahamas. Photo courtesy Tamar Franklin.

New York City may be the country's cultural capital, Gotham, and the city that never sleeps, but the Big Apple is rarely included on the short list of World's Friendliest Places. Home to skyscrapers and unending streams of tourists, one can easily feel alone in the midst of a very, very large crowd. But if you are a fly-fisher and happen to be walking in Central Park on the second or fourth Friday around noon between April and October, you're apt to find yourself among friends. Even jaded NYC natives tend to stop and stare at the brightly colored fly lines waving in the Central Park breeze.

The intrepid casters are members of the New York City Program (NYCP), which began in 2008. Sometimes more than twenty members will be in the park; on other days only a dozen or so will make it. Right in the middle of this motley crew of Soldiers and vets you may find its founder, Tamar Franklin, whose penetrating dark brown eyes roam over her charges like a mother hen. She knows each member's story—and yet a casual observer is likely to overlook the diminutive Franklin entirely. And that's just how she likes it.

Dr. Tamar (Martin) Franklin, a PhD in counseling psychology with a specialty in rehabilitation and neuropsychology, taught at Hunter College and NYU. In the course of nearly thirty years of professional counseling, she has treated clients facing every conceivable challenge, including trauma, illness, and loss. Not surprisingly she's an excellent listener; she is also, however, ready to offer honest and unvarnished advice to those who ask for it.

Franklin came to the quiet sport through the back door. Her husband, Richard, is a professional outdoor photographer whose work took him across the globe covering fly-fishing events. Occasionally the *New York Times* or a similar publication would send him on assignment to an exotic locale to photograph a fishing venue, and Franklin would tag along. Eventually she decided to try her hand at angling, and the rest is history. Franklin has become an especially adept fresh- and salt-water angler in her own right.

Franklin has spent much of her life in the world's most harried city, so she relishes her quiet time outdoors. She says that releasing her catch to the water often feels as though she's releasing a bit of herself into the wild. Hydrotherapy indeed.

When Franklin stumbled across an article in a fly-fishing magazine about Ed Nicholson and his work with PHWFF at Walter Reed Medical Center, the mental health professional in her was intrigued. Only a few months after reading the article, she attended a professional conference in Washington, DC, which gave her the opportunity to visit Nicholson's fledgling group of vets in person. While his program participants cast their fly lines on the hospital grounds, Nicholson explained his vision of fly-fishing therapy to the seasoned psychologist.

Franklin recalls that some of Nicholson's program volunteers were initially wary of her. "I'm not so sure they knew what to make of me," she says. Though the reception Franklin received was decidedly cool, the professional in her sensed that Nicholson's concept was red hot. Franklin doesn't remember everything about the conference she attended that weekend, but watching wounded veterans casting fly lines on the grounds of Walter Reed left a lasting impression that changed her life.

Franklin returned to the city and began to pull together what would eventually become PHWFF New York City. "As a native New Yorker, I have some trust issues," she says with a laugh. "I wasn't sure what those guys at Walter Reed thought of some woman from NYC they didn't know just dropping in on them, and I was concerned I would be viewed as a complete outsider. I could just see them thinking, 'What does this little woman from New York think she knows about veterans' issues? How could she know what we face when we come home injured, both physically and emotionally?'"

Franklin had reservations of her own. "I have to be honest: I thought Ed Nicholson's idea was just too good to be true. And since I hardly

Tamar Franklin loves fishing anytime she can. She is seen here on the famed Delaware River in New York. Photo courtesy Richard Franklin.

knew Ed and didn't understand his commitment to the program, I decided to start my own group in New York from scratch."

As an avid angler, Franklin knew that members of the NYC fishing clubs—like the Theodore Gordon Fly Fishers, the Federation of Fly Fishers (now Fly Fishers International), Trout Unlimited, and the Juliana's Anglers—would be interested in partnering with her. Rather than align with any one group and risk alienating the others, Franklin formed a brand new organization called Veterans Anglers of New York (VANY). Before long, VANY was drawing a variety of participants and volunteers. "I soon discovered, however," says Franklin, "that Ed Nicholson and his organization are as good as they come, and they want nothing but the best for our veterans." By early 2010, Project Healing Waters' New York City program was established with Franklin as its first program lead. The program has flourished ever since.

Franklin and her volunteers have worked tirelessly to make the program a welcoming place for both participants and volunteers. "Folks really have no idea," she says, "the stress a veteran's family faces. Take for example a guy with a twelve-year-old daughter. If Dad gets back from deployment nearly a year later, that daughter is a different child as a year makes a huge difference in a child's development. Family members have to reorient themselves to new roles—and that often brings conflict, along with the joy of a returning loved one."

Franklin, who has also worked as the regional coordinator for New York, New Jersey, and Pennsylvania, is quick to point to her fellow laborers. Volunteers like West Point graduate Andy Roberts, who served as an Army captain in Iraq, stepped into Franklin's role when she became a regional coordinator, and Craig Buckby, a Fly Fishers International master certified fly casting instructor, helps to train other volunteers.

Central Park is a delightful fly-casting locale from April through October, but as NYC winters can be daunting, Franklin quickly realized that the group needed a more amenable meeting place for the winter months. One of the volunteers, John Enochty, a member of the Jewish Community Center on West Seventy-Sixth and Amsterdam, reached out to secure the gymnasium. "I can't say enough about how they have supported us," says Franklin. "They not only let us use their gym for fly casting and fly tying in the winter, they do this at no charge. As if that weren't enough," she continues, "they allow us to store our rods and other ancillary gear in one of their storage areas. Their generosity has allowed us to focus our attention on our participants rather than stressing over logistics."

Eventually it came time to put participants' newfound casting skills to the test. In stepped program volunteer, certified casting instructor, and professional guide David Blinken, who coordinates at least two trips a year for the group to famed fisheries on the East End—Montauk.

The NYC program, while strong, faces challenges just as its sister programs do. "Once I had someone volunteer and then complain to me about the age of our participants," says Franklin. "It surprises people that we have veterans from the Korean and Vietnam Wars. They aren't all twentysomething-year-olds. The truth is that we have a wide age range in our program, and we'll accept any veteran with a disability who wants to be a part of our program.

"We're simply here to serve the men and women who have done so much for us," she says. "To volunteer, you don't have to be a great casting instructor, or a guide, or even an angler. You just have to want to help. You have to have a willing heart."

Tamar Franklin has served both as a program lead and as a regional coordinator and, while she has stepped down from those roles, she still loves to support veterans in their recovery.

NAME: KEITH GILBERT
RANK: STAFF SERGEANT E-5
BRANCH OF SERVICE: US ARMY
YEARS OF SERVICE: 7
HOME BASE: LULA, GEORGIA

Keith Gilbert sits at the edge of the kitchen table with a Monster energy drink in one hand and an unlit cigarette in the other. Gone is the gentle giant with the breezy Georgia bluster I've come to know so well; in his place is an anxious, scarred, brooding warrior.

"We lost another one last night," says Gilbert in a hoarse whisper as he stares down at the energy drink clutched tightly in his hands. His bloodshot eyes speak of another sleepless night. He struggles to keep his composure. "I got a call late last night about a medic who had returned from serving overseas. He went to his brother's grave, and then afterwards shot himself in the head with his own pistol. I guess he just couldn't take it anymore." We absorb this news together in numbed silence.

Keith Gilbert continues to struggle with chronic back pain as a result of combat injuries and finds great solace in fly fishing.

A former paratrooper assigned to the famed 82nd Airborne, Gilbert served two tours in Iraq. Airborne cavalry scouts locate enemy positions and (if possible) gauge the strength of those positions; they generally carry enough firepower to defend themselves, but they'll avoid an

Enjoying every minute of a foggy day, Keith Gilbert landed this strong rainbow. Photo courtesy Curtis Boatman.

out-and-out firefight because their primary mission is to find the enemy. As one such scout, Gilbert spent a lot of time far from the security of base camp and close to the enemy.

Gilbert's first deployment was to Baghdad in an area well forward of the operating base, where he lived a life inconceivable to most Americans. Each new day was a new mission and a new patrol. He called home four times and took seven showers in fourteen months. Grief had no place here, where a momentary lapse of focus could spell disaster or death. The goals of each day were to complete the mission and survive until tomorrow.

Back home in the land of the living, Gilbert suffers primarily from recurring back pain, headaches, and severe PTSD.

Like most Soldiers, Gilbert desperately wanted to get home to his wife and children and away from the carnage and horror. And yet when he and his men were injured, they often refused medical care. They knew that a certain number of injuries would remove them from service, and none—least of all Gilbert—wanted to leave his platoon. Now that he's home he is frequently wracked with anger and grief, and the special guilt reserved for the Soldier who survives when so many of his comrades did not.

Twice IEDs blew the front end off of his Humvee. He can't count the number of times he was shot at. Once Gilbert miraculously stepped over an IED; the Soldier behind him was less fortunate.

Picking just the right pattern is key to Keith Gilbert's success at landing big fish.

The explosion threw him into a wall more than forty feet away, and he lost consciousness. "When I came around, my lower back was screaming out in pain. I had blurred vision, and I was bleeding from both my ears."

Many of the daily patrols and routine duties of Army life begin to run together, but some days and events stand out. Though Gilbert would prefer to forget those difficult days, he imagines that he never will. On one patrol a high-ranking officer insisted that a certain road be used to move equipment and personnel; he and his officers countered that the road was too dangerous for such an exercise and that the move was unwise. Nevertheless, the superior officer insisted that Gilbert's men use the road. "When it was all over, more than a dozen of the folks from my group died in one day. I can't ever remember a time other than that when I saw nine medevac helicopters all trying to land at the same time." From that day forward, Gilbert is at home on the anniversary of that day remembering his lost comrades.

"I was at Walter Reed from March to November 2010 and then went into a warrior transition unit at Fort Gordon in Georgia," says Gilbert. "While I was at Walter Reed I noticed guys casting fly rods. One day I saw a guy dressed in a kilt casting a fly rod, and *that* really caught me by surprise." The kilted caster was Philip Krista, a popular Maryland fly-fishing guide, casting instructor, and volunteer with the Project Healing Waters Fly Fishing program at Walter Reed. "It was Krista who introduced me to PHWFF and inspired me and many other vets recovering at Walter Reed. I'll never forget him."

Gilbert's homecoming and recovery have been rocky and marred by setbacks. His marriage collapsed soon after his return, and he has struggled with depression, a sense of isolation, and a bone-deep frustration with the byzantine, bureaucratic, and slow-as-molasses medical care wounded veterans face.

Gilbert finds solace in fly fishing. "Project Healing Waters has been a huge part of my getting better—especially the support I've gotten from other vets in the program. When I'm fly fishing I can concentrate. It makes me feel better than any medicine I take."

But fly fishing isn't just therapeutic for Gilbert; as it turns out, it's something he's really, really good at. "Honestly, I always thought trout fishing was spin fishing with a rooster tail," says Gilbert. "I didn't know that fly fishing can be summed up in a single word: intimate. And I have to admit I struggle with intimacy." Gilbert goes on to say, "During the healing process my faith and dependence on Jesus Christ has been the backbone of my recovery. By His grace, I believe fly fishing was used as an important tool in my recovery."

Once Gilbert was offered his "dream job": a chance to guide professionally in Alaska. While many anglers would pull their eyeteeth out for such an offer, he did what many unmarried men wouldn't do and turned it down immediately. "I'm never going to be that far away from my kids again," he vows.

Keith Gilbert continues to struggle with debilitating back pain which at times leaves him unable to walk. He also struggles with intermittent numbness in both arms. While he loves his primary care physician, he believes the Veterans Administration has left him more or less on his own to deal with lingering mental health issues. Keith lives in Lula, Georgia, is happily remarried, and hopes to one day enter seminary training.

Despite being paralyzed at a young age, John Bass was an avid fly angler. His leadership and ability to reach others has left a lasting impression on all who knew him. Photo courtesy John Bass.

It might be his no-nonsense, call-it-as-he-sees-it personality that enables John Bass to connect with seriously injured veterans who are interested in authenticity rather than platitudes. Bass is unfailingly forthright and honest, with an intensity and openness that might be misinterpreted as gruffness to the hypersensitive. In fact, Bass is himself very sensitive to others' difficult experiences, and he has come by his empathy the hard way: living over half his life as a quadriplegic.

In 1974, after "too much Jack Daniels and too much Budweiser," Bass's life changed forever when he jumped into a swimming pool. He came out of that pool with a severed spinal cord. Says Bass, "When you're critically injured like I was, you can either live with it or die—and I thought living was the better option."

During a stay at the famed Greenbrier hotel in West Virginia in the summer of 1994, Bass noticed a fly angler fishing in Howard's Creek, tempting one trout after another onto his line. "I watched this guy land a rainbow trout and, in that moment, I saw an opportunity even for a guy like me." Guide Earl Poe, who worked at the hotel's Orvis shop, was only too happy to take him out on the stream. After nearly eight straight hours on the water, Bass had landed just one fish. He had also developed a brand-new passion: he had become consumed with fly fishing.

Outdoor writers King Montgomery and Lefty Kreh encouraged Bass, suggesting places he might fish from his wheelchair. "Between the two of them, my good friend Harry Sloan, and my computer, I found lots of opportunities to fish. Initially I was only able to fish in some ponds for bluegill and crappie with a fiberglass collapsible pole. Then when that didn't challenge me enough, I had a boat built that looked like a landing craft that I could mount my wheelchair on, and I pulled it with my van." I witnessed Bass's fly-fishing prowess firsthand and saw him land more than a few nice trout while fishing at Rose River Farm. Because he had limited use of both hands, he was forced to roll cast. While his range was quite limited in distance, he more than made up for it in accuracy.

The day after Thanksgiving 2005, Bass went fishing with his good friend and angling partner Bill Nuckels on Big Cedar Creek in Lebanon, Virginia. Just that morning he'd heard on the news that local veteran Lieutenant Ryan McGlothlin, a Marine who'd been awarded the Silver Star, had died serving his country. While traveling to the stream to fish that day Bass actually passed his funeral and saw him being buried. Seeing the funeral of the fallen veteran touched Bass in a way difficult for him to explain. When he returned home that night he called Eric Stroup, a former veteran himself and a fly-fishing guide who'd told him about PHWFF. Stroup, a strong supporter of the program, gave Bass the home phone number of Ed Nicholson. The rest, as they say, is history.

"I made my first trip to Walter Reed in March 2006, where I met Josh Williams and several other veterans. I was just overwhelmed and thought how fortunate we are as a country to have men and women who want to serve for us and are willing to put themselves in harm's way to do so."

John Bass was an avid fly angler and known for his compassion as well as for his habit of not mincing his words. He is seen here streamside at Rose River Farm in Virginia.

"Because I'm handicapped," says Bass, "I can relate to these guys in a different way. If a guy in a wheelchair tells me that he can't fly fish or cast well because he can't get in the water, I ask him this question: Can you use your eyes? Yes? Then you can see that I'm in lousy shape too. But I can fly fish—and so can you!"

Bass readily agrees that he gets as much from Project Healing Waters as he gives. "I've met some of the most incredible people in the world in this program, and those people have made a significant difference in my life. The truth is that you will struggle with your disability. But in the end, if you struggle with it long enough, you're going to conquer it."

Sadly, John died unexpectedly not long after he approved this chapter. A stone marker was placed in his honor near a handicapped casting platform at Rose River Farm. His lifelong friend and traveling companion James Arrington sang "Amazing Grace" a cappella on the day the marker was dedicated. By the time James finished, there were no dry eyes in the crowd.

The memorial marker reads, "John R. Bass: A beautiful soul, a dear friend to his friends, a loving mentor to many, and an inspiration to all. *Aqua Vitam Spirat*: Water Breathes Life."

"On behalf of the president of the United States, the commandant of the Marine Corps, and a grateful nation, please accept this flag as a token of your loved one's sacrifice. Semper Fi."

Duke and Kara Davis are longtime supporters of PHWFF. Photo courtesy Duke Davis.

Decked out in his dress blues and struggling not to cry, Gunnery Sergeant Willis "Duke" Davis handed a flag to the solemn widow grieving for his fallen sniper comrade. Next to her stood another Marine, this one only five years old and wearing a spotless Staff Sergeant's uniform—a tiny, exact replica of the one in which his father was being laid to rest. The Marine Corps Honor Guard stood at attention as the funeral continued and others paid their last respects to a Marine who had been so emotionally devastated by what he'd seen and experienced in combat that he'd taken his own life.

Few relish the daunting task of presenting the flag to a family suffering such a tragic loss. Davis volunteered. "If I didn't do it," he says, "then some other Marine would have to do it. I'd just as soon it be me, since I knew him." Perhaps Davis realizes that if his own life hadn't taken certain turns, his wife Kara might have been the grieving widow accepting the flag.

Gunnery Sergeant Duke Davis grew up in Alabama, which left as its mark on him an accent as heavy as a thick coat of quality paint. Davis had already been to the Army recruiter across the room at the small recruiting station in Albertville, Alabama, when Marine Corps Staff Sergeant Leroy Pate asked him, "Are you ready to be a man, son?"

"Pate walked the walk," says Davis, "and I could see what a Marine was supposed to be." Davis laughs. "The Marine Corps isn't for everyone. I tell folks that we aren't like the other branches of the service. The Air Force, for example, is like a corporation; the Marine Corps is more like a cult. We are all the same, and you never really leave."

Davis became a Marine Corps sniper, part of an elite group of sharpshooters that never officially numbers more than 150, handpicked by the Marine Corps to provide security for other Marines while they're engaged in combat operations. "A Marine sniper," recites Davis, "is a Marine highly skilled, highly trained in field skills and marksmanship, who delivers long-range precision fire from concealed positions in support of combat operations. Period." That "period" is crucial: a Marine sniper's job description is, quite simply, to save Marine lives.

Marine snipers operate in teams of two: one watches through binoculars for enemy movement, and the other fires a variety of lethal weapons. They might find themselves lying in a field for days on end or sitting atop a roof providing "overwatch" for Marines on patrol or engaged in house-to-house searches. In some cases they might be looking for bomb makers who plant their devices along the road or in other seemingly innocuous places hoping to detonate a device by surprise and kill as many Marines as possible. The Marines themselves rarely know the location of their own guardian angels, lest they inadvertently telegraph their location to the enemy.

Davis has been deployed nearly a dozen times overseas, and half of those deployments involved combat tours. He's served in such far-flung places as Haiti and jokes that his team put Sarajevo's infamous "Sniper Alley" under new management. But it would be the multiple deployments to Afghanistan and Iraq where he would see the most combat; those deployments haunt him both physically and emotionally to this day.

He needs no reminders of his combat losses; nevertheless, Davis wears a single metal bracelet with the name of a Marine inscribed upon it as a tribute to those who made the ultimate sacrifice—and to those who made it home but ended their own lives in the aftermath of their service. It has become somewhat common practice to wear such bracelets in support of our troops. At home, Davis has a box of such bracelets—mementos of friends lost to service. "If I wore them all," he says solemnly, "I could cover both arms from my wrists nearly to my shoulders."

Eventually his overseas deployments bled one into another. "There are so few snipers that they tend to rotate us a lot. And sometimes . . . you come back early." Marines "come home early" when they're so badly injured that they can no longer remain in the field to complete their tour. In Davis's garage is a wooden crate with his last name and rank stenciled in black on its side. "There is only one difference in the letters," he says, pointing to the "W.I.A." on the crate's face, "but that one letter means a lot." The crates containing a Marine's personal effects and gear are shipped home when they're badly injured—"wounded in action"—or killed. "Only one letter's difference," he repeats, "but it's a big difference."

While his son Seth was at home celebrating his birthday, Duke Davis was at work half a world away. "I was in a truck with a squad of Marines and we were traveling on our way to a strategically important location in Afghanistan. This particular area we were driving through had a box canyon with plateaus on both sides. Our truck ran over an IED, and that's when it all started going south. I can still remember being thrown from the truck; it was a pretty nasty deal."

When Davis regained consciousness from the explosion, he discovered that the driver and vehicle commander were dead and another Marine had had both legs blown off. The truck behind them had come under heavy fire and was retreating, leaving Davis and his men exposed to withering fire from the plateaus above the canyon. He realized suddenly that he was both the most experienced and highest-ranking Marine in the group. He was in charge. He communicated his position via VHF radio to the truck behind him, which was connected by satellite phone to command.

Their mangled truck in flames, Davis and his Marines were in a desperate position. Some tended to the injuries of their fellow squad members while others returned fire. As shots rained down from enemy positions around them, Davis recognized that his group's only hope was to push forward.

Their motto is *semper fi*—always faithful; Marines don't leave a man behind. He told his men to gather their comrades and prepare to move.

"We fought our way out for nearly two miles while carrying our dead and wounded with us as best we could," Davis says, his voice hoarse with emotion. At times those two miles seemed endless: the Marines could travel only a few yards at a time, taking advantage of any available cover to return fire. "I'll tell you one thing," he says. "My two fire team leaders were true warriors that day, boy. I can't mention their names, but they know who they are. They saved all our lives—mine included. I wouldn't be here today if those guys hadn't returned fire and supported me as I led us out of that canyon." Davis's eyes fill with unshed tears, and his voice breaks. "Those two guys are warriors. True warriors."

After hours of running and fighting, their prayers were answered. "I finally heard the Blackhawks coming, and it was the best thing I've ever heard in my life. They showed up and engaged the enemy, and things took a dramatic turn for the better."

As the Marines placed their dead and wounded on board, the crew chief summoned Davis to get on board the chopper with the rest of the wounded; what he hadn't realized until that moment was that blood was running out of both of his ears. Nevertheless, Davis refused to go. "I couldn't leave my men," Davis says resolutely. "My injuries weren't a big deal. Besides, I was in charge." As for the helicopters, Davis is magnanimous: "I'll have to give it to the Army: it was sure good to see them that day. Those boys saved our lives, and I will always be grateful."

The fight in the canyon was just one battlefield engagement; Davis has lived through countless others and been injured many times. Once, after running over an IED, he awakened in a field hospital and found the patients on either side of him covered in white sheets. "It's a pretty solemn thing," Davis intones, "to wake up and see the guys on both sides of you didn't make it."

Once his sniper team was providing overwatch when a truck full of combat engineers ran over a hidden IED. Combat engineers build all sorts of buildings, bridges, and other structures in hostile territory to support ongoing combat operations; they might be driving a dump truck or leveling out an airfield, but they do it with machine guns in their laps. On this particular day these troops were eager to get back to base early and took a shortcut on a less secure thoroughfare. The truck struck the IED and exploded, killing all the Soldiers. Davis remembers this particular incident vividly because it happened almost directly in front of him. Rushing to the truck to render aid, Davis found that an unsecured saw blade had struck the truck driver's head, cutting it nearly in half. Not even Marines can witness such scenes and walk away unscarred.

Davis eventually returned home, becoming a recruiter like Leroy Pate and encouraging others to join what Davis believes to be the most elite fighting force in the world. The problem was that he couldn't leave the battlefield behind—or more precisely, the battlefield wouldn't leave him.

"I had horrible nightmares. At times I would wake up screaming, holding my wife down in bed and hollering, 'It's okay! It's okay! I got this shit! I got this shit covered!'" He constantly relived firefights and battlefield searches for fallen comrades. One particularly gruesome nightmare recalled the horror of the day when he found what looked like a mass of damaged flesh that turned out to be what was left of the face of a Marine he knew. The memories haunted him to the point where he would come home from work and drink himself to sleep—when he could sleep at all, which wasn't often.

On one particularly difficult day after some serious drinking, Davis decided he'd had enough. He stepped out onto his back porch, pulled out his pistol, placed the barrel in his mouth, and pulled the trigger. Click. Instinctively reverting to his Marine training, despite his drunkenness, Davis tried to chamber another round. He placed the barrel of the gun back in his mouth. Click. At that moment, Davis fell to his knees in tears, wondering how he had come to this point and crying out to God for help. His wife Kara stood by him through everything—even nights in which she'd found him attempting to clear their home with his weapon drawn looking for enemy soldiers. "You'll make it, honey. I know you will," she encouraged him again and again. "I love you. We all love you. You just have to get some help. I'm here for you, babe."

Davis's career eventually lead him to Marine Corps Base Quantico when he was selected for the Corps' elite Gunner School. Marine Corps gunners are weapons experts who wear the emblem of an exploding bomb on the collars of their uniforms. A mere one hundred coveted gunner positions exist within the Marine Corps. Davis, forty, was doing well in the program when he suffered a severe heart attack, which his physicians believe was brought on by the stress of continuous combat duties.

On his first day at Quantico, Davis had met retired Marine Jim Bensinger, at that time an assistant program lead for Project Healing Waters. He and retired top Sergeant Marty Laksbergs held bimonthly meetings at the base, successfully running the only Project Healing Waters Fly Fishing program on a Marine Corps base. "Jim Bensinger really went out of his way to help me from the very first day he met me," says Davis. "I think he saw that I needed help, and that I couldn't help myself." The two soon became good friends, and Davis took Bensinger up on his offer to attend a PHWFF meeting at the base. Later that first day, Davis tied his first fly.

During the last days of Gunner School and right before his promotion, Davis suffered a second heart attack. This one nearly killed him. He was participating in PHWFF, was on his way to becoming an accomplished fly tyer and was scheduled to go on a PHWFF trip to Harman's, a family-owned retreat with rustic cabins along the banks of the Potomac River in Cabins, West Virginia. "I told the doc, 'I'll do whatever you say, but you've got to cut me loose from here, because I can't miss that trip to Harman's with the folks in my Project Healing Waters group.'" The doctor discharged Davis, he went to Harman's, and he had the time of his life. He also landed his very first trout there, on a fly that he had tied. It's a moment he'll never forget.

Fly tying has brought Davis tremendous peace. "There's just something about it that's magical. It takes the pack straps off of the stuff you are carrying around with you. Maybe not the whole day's worth, but for most of the day it gets better. And the more you do it, the more it releases the straps, and the lighter the pack is eventually going to get."

Duke Davis with a beautiful yellow-eyed rockfish caught while fishing in Alaska. Photo courtesy Duke Davis.

Davis was medically retired as a result of complications from the many injuries he sustained on the battlefield. Because of his traumatic brain injuries, he struggles with balance and memory. He has diminished hearing, and he lost much of the dexterity in one of his hands when it was nearly severed after running over yet *another* IED. Is he bitter? No. Instead, he is resolute that he wouldn't trade being a Marine for anything.

Duke Davis divides his time now between his guide service
Tango Down Fishing in Naples, Florida, and Healing Towers
in Ketchikan, Alaska. His philosophy about helping others is

straightforward. "Now that I've retired, I want to take guys from the service fishing and show them how much fun life can be— and in some way give back to this program that has helped me so much." Apparently old snipers don't retire; they continue to watch over their fellow Marines.

George Gaines is a founding member of the leadership team which created PHWFF. He is known for his great kindness and consistent leadership. Photo courtesy George Gaines.

Spend a little time with George Gaines, and you learn quickly that he wears his very, very big heart on his sleeve. His life's goal is to serve hurting people, irrespective of their status. Perhaps because he spent forty-three years at the National Institutes of Health, Gaines understands that a bureaucracy must never lose sight of the human beings it serves.

Gaines is a familiar face to many, many mid-Atlantic fly anglers. He is active in Trout Unlimited, working with youth in the popular Trout Unlimited Tri-State Conservation & Fishing Camp held for years near Shenandoah National Park. Though he recently stepped down as the regional coordinator for the National Capital Region PHWFF, he served as the first PHWFF Treasurer and as a member of the original board of trustees for a decade. Yes, Gaines is well known and beloved, but few know that he's been a part of PHWFF from the very beginning.

Gaines was president of the National Capital Chapter of Trout Unlimited when, in 2005, Ed Nicholson called seeking help for getting a crazy idea off the ground—establishing an organization that assisted wounded active military at Walter Reed by taking them fly fishing. Gaines conferred with his fellow TU chapter members, and they readily agreed to provide help that would prove to be absolutely crucial.

"We provided the new organization with volunteers and its funding for its first eighteen months," recalls Gaines. "I and my fellow chapter members also helped organize the very first outing for participants at Morgan Run in Maryland. All of the first PHWFF participants had obvious physical injuries and disabilities. We came to understand over time, however, that many of the active military and veteran participants in our programs had invisible disabilities that may not in any way be obvious. This could have been viewed as making it more difficult for our volunteers to know how to treat the participants, but in fact it made it easier. The simple and better approach is to treat all participants the same, regardless of whether their injuries or disabilities are obvious or not. This keeps us closer to the objective of treating the participants as though they are—or can be—'normal,' just like the rest of us."

Gaines spent countless hours volunteering at Walter Reed during the early days of Nicholson's pet project. Gaines was himself battling cancer at the time, and after a particularly difficult day at the hospital, he took a break beside a newly constructed fountain. As he sat gazing at and listening to the fountain, he read its inscription: "Healing Waters." What a perfect analogy for Nicholson's fly-fishing therapy. He pitched the name to Nicholson, who added "Project" to the organization's title, and the rest is history.

"PHWFF accomplishes amazing healing and strengthening," argues Gaines. "I have personally seen near-miraculous change and healing in participants who credit PHWFF with their improvement. As the organization has grown from our first local program at Walter Reed to 220 programs in fifty states, we've seen dramatic improvement in

Jim Ottevaere, at left, with George Gaines, at right, at a Rose River Farm event. Photo courtesy George Gaines.

our participants—even in those who served in combat as far back as World War II. The constant, extended commitment of PHWFF to be there for participants, week after week, has made a real difference in real lives."

Whereas Americans routinely think of their active-duty and retired service personnel as heroes, many wounded vets find themselves in a strange place—a place "where they do not think of themselves as heroes and may be relatively insecure and vulnerable," says Gaines. "Their lives have been turned upside down, and they are uncertain or fearful about their future. They're seeking a sense of normalcy and want to be viewed as they were before combat changed their lives. Most of our program participants are just like the guy or gal next door; they want desperately to be treated that way. Offer them care but not pity, respect but not reverence. They need encouragement and instruction by example—they don't need things done for them. They want and need to do things for themselves to see that they can adapt to normal living despite their injuries and disabilities."

In recognition of his selfless service to others, Gaines was recently inducted as a humanitarian into the Fly Fishing Museum of the Southern Appalachians Hall of Fame. He's also received the highest honor PHWFF can bestow, the Patriot Award, for his dedicated leadership and service to the organization.

George Gaines continues to provide selfless, quiet, and humble leadership in the National Capital Region.

ALASKA FISH THERAPY

I peered over the side of the *Hot Ruddered Bum*, into the cold Alaskan waters below, and watched the scene unfold. "Keep the heat on him, brother!" shouted Joel Sinner in encouragement to his fellow angler. With grim determination, Dave Inbody struggled to keep pressure on the reluctant fish and was slowly gaining line—until suddenly the reel screamed and more line began peeling off at a frantic pace. "You can do it, brother, you can do it!" Sinner shouted again as we both made our way to the back of the *HRB*. Inbody was both enjoying himself tremendously and gritting his teeth as he slowly gained back some of the lost

Garry Morfit is the captain of *Hot Ruddered Bum* and also its chief cook. Guests aboard his ship often eat what they catch. Photo courtesy Garry Morfit.

line one agonizingly slow crank at a time. Sinner and I continued to encourage him, and the captain took up his gaff. Who would prevail was anybody's guess.

We didn't doubt that Inbody had an Alaskan halibut on his line, and we were all eager to see it brought aboard. Landing the halibut would be the climax of a voyage none of us would ever forget. The previous week had seen Inbody bring silver, pink, and chum salmon to hand on a fly rod. Sinner landed the same salmon species plus dogfish, several black sea bass, and numerous brightly colored grouper as well. In fact, just one species remained on the bucket list: halibut. Now Inbody was grappling with a halibut that looked like the largest fish of his life. We'd fished nearly all the previous week with fly rods, but the sheer size of this particular species required conventional gear. We stood spellbound as Inbody's epic battle played out.

∞

I'd met Dave Inbody and Joel Sinner, both injured Army veterans, only a few days before at the airport in Ketchikan, Alaska. We knew nothing more about each other than that we were all slated to spend nearly a week in close quarters fishing the Alaskan wild. We picked up fishing licenses and a week's worth of groceries at a local store before making our way to the boat and an obscure and intriguing adventure.

On our first morning on the water, I awakened to the sound of the captain walking the deck overhead. I rolled over and peered out the small port window to the inlet where we'd anchored the night before, stirring as soon as the ship's generator kicked in. Our day had officially begun. I rose, made my way through the larger berths where my two new companions were still sleeping, and walked through to the small galley that doubled as our kitchen and dining area. I carefully climbed up the ladder into the pilothouse, where Captain Garry Morfit sat in his chair.

One hand wrapped around a cup of coffee and the other around the ship's wheel, Morfit took one look at me and said, "Took you long enough to get up," in his characteristically gravelly voice. "I'd have thought a firefighter like you would've been a little faster turning out of the bunk. What do you think this is, a pleasure cruise or something?" I saluted the captain and apologized for taking nearly three full minutes to dress and appear on deck. "Aye aye, sir," I replied. "I'll do better tomorrow, Cap'n." Morfit merely grinned in response before returning to his radar screen and his coffee.

As a way of thanking veterans for their service, Garry Morfit hosted two veterans on his boat in 2007. Since then, he has hosted hundreds. Photo courtesy Garry Morfit.

Walking out of the pilothouse and onto the deck of the *HRB*, I gazed toward the surrounding waters and postcard-worthy tree-lined mountains. The gently lapping waves and humming generator might normally have lulled me back to sleep, but not today. Today we had work to do, and I was bound and determined to pull up the ship's crab traps before my shipmates beat me to it.

Along with pulling up crab traps, my job was to do . . . whatever Captain Morfit told me to do, from swabbing the deck to cooking to washing dishes after meals. I also rotated giant coffee cans full of water, frozen into blocks of ice, from the ship's freezer to coolers on the deck, which acted as extra refrigerator space. I'd then rotate the completely thawed and dripping coffee cans back to the freezer to refreeze.

After just a few tugs on the ropes that held the crab traps far below the water's surface, I surmised that we'd been lucky overnight: The traps felt heavy. Maybe we'd have crabs and shrimp for supper! In the distance I could hear Captain Morfit bellowing, "One of you fellows needs to hurry up and help Beau before he hurts himself. He's not as young as you guys. And if he hurts his back pulling those traps, God only knows how slow he'll be tomorrow morning when it's time to go to work." My shipmates grinned broadly at the captain's remarks and quickly took their places coiling the ropes that were tethered to the traps as they came on board. One set of traps was thick with Dungeness crabs, while the other contained several pounds of fresh shrimp. Yes, it looked like we were in for a feast that night.

∽

In 2006 Captain Garry Morfit, known affectionately to friends as Magoo, read an article in his local paper about fishing with veterans. Since he already operated a boat in some of the most productive fishing waters in Alaska and had been a Lieutenant in the Army in Vietnam, he seemed ideally suited to participate in such a venture. Morfit brushes off his own service; nevertheless, he obviously empathizes with the struggle that many veterans face as they attempt to reintegrate into "normal life" after their service. By 2007, Project Healing Waters Fly Fishing organizers had vetted Morfit, sending two anglers to fish on his boat for a few days. The trip was a success, and before long the *HRB* was hosting several dozen visitors over the course of a season.

Today Morfit operates what may best be described as a floating occupational therapy center. He's hosted more than a hundred service members, all of whom fish in Alaska at no cost. Best of all, since the guests are on a boat, Morfit can simply motor to the most productive fishing areas. Some guests even take the *HRB*'s dinghy out for day trips on some of the remote islands and feeder creeks to fish and watch wildlife such as eagles, whales, and bears.

∽

Inbody was still locked in battle with his halibut, and it looked as though we might be headed for a stalemate. Sinner took the opportunity to land a few blows of his own: "Hey, Inbody, if you don't think you're tough enough to land that fish, I'd be glad to give you a hand." Sinner grinned. "I'm used to helping out officers who've gotten in over their heads—that was part of my job description as a Sergeant First Class." Inbody was preparing his reply when our attention returned to the rod, which was bent double as the fish took off on another run.

∽

Sinner's jab was especially funny to anyone who knows Inbody, a stoic and quietly confident Lieutenant who was badly injured when his patrol vehicle ran over a roadside bomb in Afghanistan's Ghazni province. "To be perfectly honest, I wasn't exactly certain what had happened when our vehicle detonated the bomb. One minute I was on patrol and everything was fine; the next minute I felt like the world had turned upside down." Inbody recalls looking up at his hatch, which had been blown open from the blast, and thinking, "Well, that can't be good." In fact, Inbody was lucky to have survived the explosion. He suffered multiple injuries, the most extensive of which meant that his right foot would eventually have to be amputated.

"I know it sounds strange, but all I could think of right after the blast was if my guys were all right. I just wanted to know they were safe. It took me a while to get my bearings." Inbody's injuries took months to heal—especially because, among other challenges, he had to learn how to walk again. "Crazy as it may seem, I just wanted to get the amputation over with and go on with my life. I told myself that once the operation was over, I was going back to the battlefield and back to my men where I belonged."

∞

Inbody, who can give as good as he gets, got his fish back under control. "I got this, Grandpa," he said wryly. "At your age you might throw your back out or develop chest pains or something, and I don't want that on my conscience." To which Sinner laughed and raised his hands in surrender, backing away with a grin, content to watch the contest between man and fish.

∞

Like Inbody, Sinner is also a combat veteran. He began his career as a medic, eventually becoming an ammunitions handler and serving in multiple operations around the globe, including some drug interdiction work in Puerto Rico.

During the last two weeks of his tour of duty in Kuwait, his wife of seventeen years asked him for a divorce. When he returned home, Sinner recalls, "I hit the booze pretty hard." He was eventually given orders to join the 145th Field Artillery, Charlie Battery, in Spanish Fork, Utah, whose task it was to guard the chemical weapons depot in Tooele, Utah. While there Sinner lost a dear friend in a five-ton truck rollover. He had the unenviable task of taking his friend's body to the morgue and removing his wedding ring and a bracelet that had his children's names on it. "This remains one of the most dreadful things I've ever had to do in my entire life," he says.

During his tour of duty for Operation Enduring Freedom in Afghanistan, a fellow Sergeant he'd known for twelve years received word that his wife wanted a divorce. "Because we were the same rank, we shared living quarters together and were quite close both on and off duty." Having been through a similar experience, Sinner's heart went out to his comrade. "I came back to our hooch one afternoon after work and found he'd stuck his M16 under his chin and blown his brains out. I've had a hell of a time trying to get that image out of my head."

∞

Veterans like Inbody and Sinner return home to a population that is largely unaffected by the wars in Iraq and Afghanistan and unaware of the toll that military service takes on one's personal and family life. Most Americans haven't performed dangerous, demoralizing jobs that take them far away from loved ones for long periods of time. They haven't tried to come back from staggering, life-changing injury and emotional trauma. It's often a long and lonely road, and sadly, some don't make it.

∞

We'd arrived in Alaska not knowing one end of the forty-two-foot *HRB* from the other; a week later, we could practically have run the boat by ourselves. Sinner and Inbody were both dab hands at running the dinghy, and I did my best to keep up with the gear, work the traps, and, of course, clean the crabs, shrimp, and fish. Captain Morfit did most of the cooking, set the schedule of events, and acted as navigator. Eventually he'd trained us so well that he'd occasionally take a catnap while Inbody and I went fishing in the dinghy. Sinner would handle the *HRB* all by himself, with the good captain always available for quick advice about our bearings or a needed course correction.

Dinner every evening in the ship's small galley was the highlight of the trip for me. I myself had more than a few funny stories to share over dinner from thirty years in the fire service, and perhaps a few stories that weren't quite so funny. In return, my crewmates shared their stories of a lifetime of service, both at home and abroad, and what it's like trying to adjust to a new normal. We fished alongside each other during the day and opened up about our inner demons each night. And in a week's time, we'd become a tightly knit crew able to anticipate one another's actions almost without speaking. The only thing we hadn't accomplished during our week in Alaska, in fact, was to land a halibut.

∽

By our last day I was fished out, but Sinner and Inbody were still determined to land one of the elusive flounder-like beasts. I was drinking in the scenery when Inbody shouted, "That's gotta be him, boys!" His rod tip dove over the side of the boat, his reel buzzing from the pressure. Inbody's call had summoned us all to his side, and we collectively held our breath as he single-handedly duked it out with his prey.

The halibut would take line, and Inbody would reel him back in toward the boat, back and forth, with no clear winner. Eventually Captain Morfit ushered our small group toward the back of the boat as the epic tug-of-war raged on and on. Inbody seemed to tire before rallying with a burst of energy that finally pulled the halibut to the surface. Captain Morfit ably handled the gaff, and Sinner and I did our best to help pull the beast to the boat. In the final analysis, Inbody's halibut would tip the scale at more than one hundred pounds.

We were collectively elated and exhausted. We took a few photos, told and retold our perspectives on the story, and generally patted ourselves on the back. We spent hours and hours cleaning and filleting the fishy beast, then packed it appropriately for the trip home. Some of the fish would stay aboard the *HRB* as food for the next set of anglers, just in case they weren't as lucky as we had been. We cleaned off the decks, checked the gear, and prepared to reset the traps for the following day. We ate a late dinner that night and cleaned all the remaining gear.

We knew that the following day a new crew would come aboard the *HRB*. They would be awkward and perhaps even a bit nervous. They wouldn't know each other's stories, or difficulties, but that would all change. Eventually the ship's generator would hum to life, announcing to the new and untested crew below that Captain Morfit and the *HRB* were ready to take on another day.

Joel Sinner and Dave Inbody aboard the *Hot Ruddered Bum* hoisting a fine halibut.

HEALING TOWERS

Captain Garry Morfit, who winters in South Carolina, had hoped to take even more veterans fishing by extending his Alaskan season on the boat. And then it occurred to him: some vets might feel more comfortable staying home with their families, who can aid tremendously in the healing process. Morfit knew what he had to do: purchase property in Alaska.

The *Hot Ruddered Bum* moored quietly below Healing Towers. Photo courtesy Garry Morfit.

"When I leased the property," Morfit says, "it seemed more like leasing part of a sheer cliff instead of a place where a home should be. I have to admit, though: the view is amazing, and the twin towers on the house really give it an exceptional look." As Morfit's plan took shape, moving materials and building supplies—and constructing an additional cabin—seemed overwhelming. That is until local Alaskans and veterans who'd spent time aboard the *Hot Ruddered Bum* with Morfit got wind of the plan. Once word leaked out, service members from every branch of the armed forces began to show up to volunteer for work in shifts, some of which stretched on for weeks. Local Ketchikan residents and business leaders provided discounts on products and services, and in one case donated helicopter time to fly in building supplies.

In the end, a small private cabin went up next to Morfit's house overlooking an inlet connected by a wheelchair-accessible walkway. The bathroom and kitchen are likewise situated to serve the needs of veterans who may require extra help maneuvering while staying in the Healing Towers guesthouse.

Morfit operates Healing Towers as its own independent nonprofit and continues to work closely with Project Healing Waters to provide once-in-a-lifetime experiences in Alaska.

NAME: ELIZABETH SPRINGER
RANK: CRYPTOLOGIC TECHNICIAN
TECHNICAL 2 E-5
BRANCH OF SERVICE: US NAVY
YEARS OF SERVICE: 7
HOME BASE: LEAD, SOUTH DAKOTA

"I remember the MRI technician saying, 'Wait right here, the doctor will be in to see you in just a few minutes.' I mean, normally you go in and get an MRI, and they tell you to come back in a few days to get it read. So I knew then and there it must be bad."

Elizabeth Springer, now thirty-four, had joined the Navy to see the world. And indeed, over two deployments spanning nearly a year and a half aboard the aircraft carrier USS

Liz Springer began suffering from debilitating headaches while serving aboard the aircraft carrier USS *Enterprise*. She would later discover the cause to be a brain tumor. Photo courtesy Liz Springer.

Enterprise—no, really—Springer had experienced such exotic ports of call as Portugal, Spain, Bahrain, and Dubai. She had begun as a machinist mate, but a minor back injury and some other issues led her down a different career path: she became a cryptologic technician (a "crypto-tech") responsible for jamming the programming of incoming rockets before they struck the ship.

Springer loved her job and crew and was disappointed when the Navy decided to decommission the *Enterprise* at Naval Station Norfolk in Virginia. She wanted to be with her ship and shipmates until the very end—and was part of the crew taking her apart—when she was waylaid by severe, increasingly frequent headaches.

"At first it wasn't all that bad," recounts Springer. "I would get a few headaches at sea, and they would come and go. But then they started coming more often and stayed longer. I tried to ignore it, but it got so bad it started affecting my vision. Eventually I started seeing double, and I would have to drive from my apartment on shore to the ship using one hand to cover my eye so I could see clearly enough to drive. Finally I said to myself, 'This is crazy. You gotta find out what is causing these headaches and blurred vision.'"

Eventually Springer was referred to Portsmouth Naval Hospital, where a doctor sat down beside her to explain her MRI results. "Your headaches are being caused by pressure on your optic nerve," she remembers the doctor telling her. "Regrettably, this pressure is due to a cancerous mass growing in your brain. We need to operate as soon as possible."

"I was just stunned," Springer remembers. "Still, I was pretty calm about it." The doctor told her that she "had stage four cancer, and the tumor in my brain had grown to the size of a tennis ball. He told me I needed to get my parents here as soon as possible because I was going in for surgery very soon." In fact, less than a week elapsed between MRI and surgery.

Liz Springer seen here early in her Navy career. Photo courtesy Liz Springer.

Liz Springer is all smiles with a brown trout she brought to hand on a Project Healing Waters outing. Photo courtesy Liz Springer.

Springer's parents, themselves both Air Force veterans, flew in immediately. The surgery would involve the left frontal lobe of the brain, which controls memory and motor skills. Springer says that although the surgery went well, a seven-week follow-up of radiation and chemotherapy followed by an additional year of chemotherapy left her unbearably ill. Eventually her mother moved into her apartment near the naval base to help her through the ordeal.

"I was as bald as a cue ball, and I was quite a sight wearing my uniform," Springer remembers. Although she had time off immediately after surgery, Springer volunteered to work in the cancer ward at Portsmouth Naval Hospital while completing her treatment. "They knew I was one of them," she says. "They knew I was not only in the Navy but was familiar with their struggles and could relate." Patients and staff occasionally asked if she was afraid of her treatment or prognosis, and although she was frightened and anxious, she tried not to show it. "I told them all—the patients and the staff—the same thing. I'm a devout

Christian, and as strange as it might seem, I realized I was in a no-lose situation. It dawned on me I was going to be okay either way: I was either going to get better, or I would be spending eternity with Jesus."

Worse than the difficult and debilitating post-op cancer treatment was the knowledge that even if she survived, Springer's naval career was over. "I wanted to do at least twenty years," she says with a catch in her voice, "and in the end I did less than seven years. My dreams of making a career in the Navy were over." Worse still was the loss of control. "When I lost the ability to drive, I was devastated and felt I had no control over my life anymore. I knew I was going to lose my career, I was being waited on by my mom like I was a little kid, and now I couldn't drive." It was humiliating.

"During my recovery period I was in the Safe Harbor program, the Navy's version of a wounded warrior transition unit. During that time I was counseled by retired Master Chief Georgia Monsam and Chief Petty Officer Trini O'Con of the US Coast Guard. I would speak to them often, and they helped me deal with my transition out of the Navy and my recovery. One day Chief O'Con asked if I'd like to go fly fishing. I didn't really know anything about fly fishing, but I liked to fish as a kid, so I said yes."

Both Monsam and O'Con knew of Project Healing Waters Fly Fishing and liked the concept. They put Springer in touch with Bill Campbell of the PHWFF program in Portsmouth. He took her fishing at an area owned by Dominion Power and called the "hot ditch" because of the warmwater effluent that runs out of the power station year-round. "On my very first fishing trip I landed a speckled trout. It was funny because I was pulling in the line, and I thought I was caught on something because it wouldn't come in. Then it started moving away from me. I was like, 'Hey, is someone going to help me here? I got no idea what to do!' Eventually I landed a nice speckled trout and went on to land two red drum all on the same day—and all on a fly rod."

Leaving the Navy was a terrible blow, but "Bill Campbell and Matt Bender and the other guys at PHWFF have helped me begin a new life. They even taught me how to tie flies, which is something I never thought I'd do.

Liz Springer left the Navy and has gone on to culinary school. Photo courtesy Liz Springer.

They've helped me to enjoy something I knew nothing about before my illness. I go to meetings as often as I can and I tell people all the time just how much this program means to me."

Elizabeth Springer was medically retired from the Navy in July 2014. She lives in Lead, South Dakota, and graduated from the Art Institute of Virginia Beach with a bachelor's degree in culinary management.

CASTING IN
THE RAIN

My shift at the fire station had been brutal: though the calls now blur together in my memory, I recall with perfect clarity that I hadn't seen much of my bunk that Saturday night. My wife was still asleep when I made my way quietly into our bedroom on Sunday morning and stretched out beside her, still in uniform, for a quick nap before the kids woke and we began getting them ready for church.

I had only just closed my eyes when the phone rang. "Is this Beau Beasley?" a female voice asked. "This is Beau," I affirmed curtly, annoyed that my Sunday morning had been interrupted by a sales call. "How can I help you?"

"Beau, I am so glad I was able to find you," responded the voice. "I've been thinking about you off and on for the past few days, and I just haven't been able to get you off my mind."

I was certainly wide awake now.

"I'm not sure if you remember me," the voice continued, "but my

Retired Marine Corps Gunnery Sergeant Alex Colonna teaches a young girl to cast at the Virginia Fly Fishing & Wine Festival.

husband and I attended the Virginia Fly Fishing & Wine Festival about six months ago. We met you briefly. My husband was the Army vet in the wheelchair who wanted to learn to fly fish."

At last, memory woke. Nearly a year earlier, I'd been contacted by a reader of an article I wrote for *Virginia Wildlife Magazine*. As a young adult, Jerry had served in the Army for nearly four years; now in his early sixties, he had been ravaged and left unable to walk by complications from diabetes, even losing a foot to the disease. Jerry had always hoped to fly fish, he told me, and after reading my article he'd made up his mind to give me a call.

We had discussed how he might get involved in fly fishing despite his limitations, including attending the upcoming Virginia Fly Fishing & Wine Festival, held at that time on the banks of the South River in Waynesboro. Vets from Project Healing Waters Fly Fishing would be on hand, I reassured him; he wouldn't be alone.

A couple of months after that phone call, an anxious Jerry had called me back. He'd been surprised to discover that the festival was held in a series of tents, that the weekend's weather forecast looked bleak, and that the river lacked access points for the disabled.

"I just don't know what to do," he said. "I really want to come, but I'm so afraid I won't be able to do anything at all."

"Jerry, don't sweat this," I replied. "I've got you covered. I have a handful of Marines at my disposal who regularly volunteer at the festival. I can assure you that if you want to get to the water to cast, those Marines will make sure it happens."

"Really?" Jerry asked hopefully.

"Yes. Jerry, you just get yourself there; the Marines will do the rest."

I hung up and immediately dropped a pair of admission tickets in the mail along with a note that Jerry and his wife were my personal guests to the event.

The festival weekend had arrived, bringing with it weather even worse than predicted. Unfortunately, regardless of the fact that one can spend upwards of a year carefully planning an outdoor festival, the weather remains beyond the show promoter's control. The word of the day became "mud." Some of our dauntless volunteers worked together to create a makeshift boardwalk out of wooden pallets so that attendees could traverse the area *inside* the main tent, which had turned into a shallow lake. Outside the tent, the South River looked like chocolate milk.

I was clutching my head in dismay at the prospect of a year's worth of hard work going down the (storm) drain when a volunteer caught up to me and said breathlessly, "Hey, Beau, I think you might want to see this."

I followed him through the main vendor tent and stepped outside into the downpour. In the middle of the fairgrounds was retired Marine and PHW volunteer Alex Colonna, apparently impervious to the storm, kneeling beside a gentleman in a wheelchair. That's Jerry, I realized—seated in the torrential rain, listening to and carefully observing Colonna, wearing a top-of-the-line Orvis rain slicker hurriedly stripped from a mannequin by a vendor just for this moment—and having the time of his life. Wheelchair-using veteran and senior citizen Jerry was preparing to cast a fly rod—in a near hurricane, mind you—for the very first time.

I held my breath. All I could hear was the pounding of the rain on the tent roof and the pounding of my heart in my chest. All I could watch was Jerry's fledgling cast. PHW volunteers began to amass around Colonna and his pupil. The volunteers appeared to be holding their breath too.

This wasn't a movie, this was reality—so naturally his first few attempts were feeble and resulted in little more than a puddle of fly line at his feet. Teacher and student were undaunted, however, and before long, Jerry's casts improved.

The Virginia Fly Fishing & Wine Festival has become an annual gathering point for many PHWFF participants in the mid-Atlantic. Here an angler stalks a trout on the South River, where the festival originated.

And then beauty happened. That moment came—the moment that every fly angler lives for, when all things shift slightly and inexplicably, and angler, rod, and line move together in harmony in a moment. Jerry's fly line shot straight as an arrow and landed perfectly, about thirty-five feet away. Arms upraised, Jerry shouted with delight. Colonna shouted and slapped Jerry on the back in camaraderie. Heck, we all shouted. Who wouldn't?

Later that summer Jerry called me back with an update. "Guess what I did yesterday? I went out with the guys from PHW and caught a really nice bass! I caught him on a fly rod all by myself!" he gushed. "I'm sure glad I met those guys from Project Healing Waters." He told me about his ongoing care and rehabilitation at the VA hospital in

Richmond and added, "Beau, I'm going to save up and buy your Virginia guidebook and then get you to sign it for me." Immediately upon hanging up, I grabbed a copy of my book from a shelf, signed it for Jerry, and dropped it in the mail.

I'd not heard from Jerry since, so I was pleasantly surprised to hear from his wife that Sunday morning. "I'm so glad I reached you, Beau," she said.

"Me, too," I responded. "How's Jerry doing?" I waited to hear about his progress and his latest catch.

"Beau," she began softly, "Jerry died a few days ago."

I was struck dumb with shock and grief. No well-oiled words of comfort came to me in that moment.

"We're having a service for him later today," she continued, "but before I left the house, I wanted to call you personally and thank you for introducing my husband to fly fishing, and to Project Healing Waters. I can't begin to describe what fly fishing did for Jerry." She cleared her throat and pressed on. "We had such a special time together at the festival—just the two of us. No kids, no hospital visits, no rehab; we just shared a great time together as a couple.

"Jerry was so very happy to be a fly angler. The guys he met were really good to him. I just wanted to say . . . thanks. You don't know what that experience did for us both."

I have no idea what I said to Jerry's wife, though we spoke for several minutes. After she hung up, I turned to my curious wife, relayed the story and the call, held her in my arms, and cried.

The Virginia Fly Fishing & Wine Festival has grown tremendously since those early days. It's moved indoors, to the Farm Bureau building on the state fairgrounds outside of Richmond. The event is well enough protected from the vagaries of the weather that we can thumb our noses at even a torrential downpour while we roam the festival at our warm, dry leisure. Hundreds of enthusiasts have cast their first fly line at the event. And still, every first cast is Jerry's. Occasionally I cross the South River into Waynesboro, and I always see Alex Colonna kneeling beside Jerry's wheelchair. Jerry was a husband and a father and a veteran and a lot of other things, but for me, he will always be a guy making his first-ever cast from a wheelchair—a desperate bid for freedom from a place of isolation. He will always be casting and then raising his arms and his voice in victory over his circumstances—over gravity itself. In my memory, Jerry is forever casting in the rain.

PFC Ali Sarsak and 2LT Eivind Forseth in Baghdad, Iraq, December 2004. Photo courtesy Eivind Forseth.

People join the military for a variety of reasons. Some sign up hoping to do a few years with Uncle Sam, obtain some good training and a bit of experience, then get a job in the civilian world in a similar field. Some enlist as a way to get to the next step in their lives—a transition, if you will. Not so with Eivind Forseth. He wanted to be a lifer. He enlisted as a Private in 1993 and left after being promoted to the rank of Sergeant, whereupon he went to college. After graduation, he returned to the Army, deciding it would be his life's career.

From 1995 to 1996, Forseth served a peacekeeping tour in Bosnia-Herzegovina in support of Operation Joint Endeavor, assigned to A Battery, 1/4 ADA, 1st Armored Division. By 2004, however, Forseth was serving with Task Force Falcon in support of Operation Iraqi Freedom. He was an Airborne Infantry Platoon Leader with D company in the famed 82nd Airborne. In January 2005 his patrol was ambushed by an IED strike in the Yarmouk Circle in Mosul, Iraq. An investigation of the attack revealed that the IED consisted of a 155mm (6.1 inch) artillery round that was placed in a taxicab parked on the side of the road and command-detonated when his vehicle passed. The blast discharged directly beside his vehicle at point-blank range. Both Forseth and his gunner, Sergeant Jose Lopez, were severely wounded. Fortunately, there were no fatalities.

When the smoke had cleared from the blast, Forseth knew he'd been injured; he just didn't know how badly. "I could tell my arm was broken, but I couldn't see through my right eye and didn't know until later most of the flesh under my right elbow and forearm had been blown off. I do remember being unable to move my right hand." Forseth would later find out that both his median and ulnar nerves had been severed, leaving his right hand permanently paralyzed. "Right after the blast, my right arm was pouring blood, and had it not been for my Platoon Sergeant, Sergeant First Class Dasch, applying a tourniquet, I would have probably bled to death right there." Forseth later discovered after the blast that SFC Dasch assumed command of the platoon and had Forseth and his wounded comrade evacuated to the combat support hospital at FOB Marez.

After narrowly escaping death, Forseth woke up in Landstuhl Regional Medical Center in Germany. "When I woke up," says Forseth, "I found I'd been kept in a drug-induced coma for six days. Once I finally came around, I knew it was bad. I'd been around long enough to know if you'd been flown to Germany from the battlefield, you probably weren't going back to your platoon." Within twenty-four hours of regaining consciousness, Forseth was flown to Andrews AFB, then transported to Walter Reed Army Medical Center. What would follow was a grueling three-year process of recovery.

As a Ranger-qualified, prior-enlisted Army infantry officer, Forseth was no stranger to discomfort, pain, or the misery that sometimes comes with being a Soldier serving on the front lines. The pain he

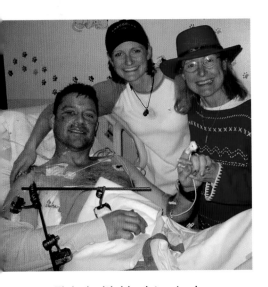

Eivind with his sister, Larissa, and mother, Judith, in the ICU at Walter Reed. This photo was taken a week after his evacuation from Mosul, Iraq, in January 2005. Note the paw prints and Dalmatians on the wall. Due to the volume of injured and wounded warriors returning from Iraq and Afghanistan, the entire pediatric ward was transferred to Bethesda National Naval Medical Center to make room for a larger intensive care unit. Photo courtesy Eivind Forseth.

felt from his battlefield injuries, however, was excruciating, and nothing like he'd ever experienced before. Still, he held out hope that he could go back, lead his platoon, and once again take the fight to the enemy. He was, after all, a warrior, and he wanted to do what he'd been trained to do and go back and serve with his men. "The pain I was experiencing from my wounds was excruciating," says Forseth. "It was hands down the most pain I'd ever endured my entire life. But I could handle the physical pain while harboring the hope that I would recover, regain function, and return to the battlefield. About a month later, the doctors came to my room and leveled with me. 'Listen up, Lieutenant; you've lost the nerves that control dexterity and grip to your right hand. The orthopedic damage to your elbow is also very extensive. We'll continue to do our best to heal you, but you're never going to regain full function of your arm. Realistically, you won't be back in the fight anytime soon.'"

Upon hearing this prognosis, Forseth's morale took a nose dive. "At that moment, my soul was taken hostage by three unforgiving emotions—anger, anxiety, and depression. The emotional pain was overwhelming. The physical pain that was once manageable was now

Eivind Forseth is one of the original participants in Project Healing Waters. Photo courtesy Eivind Forseth.

unbearable. At times, I expressed that it was all too much to bear." Forseth was beyond anger, and beyond any sense of depression that he'd ever experienced before.

"I felt like I was in hell," says Forseth. "I was crushed that my soldiering days were over. In the blink of an eye, I had lost my dream job. I had dedicated my life to serve as an Army officer. That's what I was born to do; I'm a Viking by blood. What now? Then came the outpouring of concerns as to whether I would live a normal life. Will I be able to fish with my dad? Will I be able play baseball with my son? Will a woman ever love a 'half-man'? Will I always need someone to help me cut my food? I couldn't even tie my bootlaces anymore!"

Forseth's seething anger often led to emotional outbursts during his long recovery. It began to turn inward and manifested in terrible depression. In the quietness of his hospital room, Forseth wished for the unthinkable. "I actually began to regret that I was alive. Why couldn't I have just bled out on the battlefield?"

Thankfully, during his recovery Forseth had the support of his family, but it was still tough going and at times he didn't think he'd make it. "My misery consumed me," says Forseth. "And I could only focus on the negative aspects of my wounds. I'd left the war in Iraq only to return home to a war with myself. To make it worse, my loved ones were collateral damage. I watched my devoted mother cry every day. My sister kept a stiff upper lip for my sake, but she was deeply affected by my situation. My stoic Norwegian father was pissed out of his skull, but we didn't even discuss it."

Eventually, however, Forseth began to recover ever so slowly. His skin grafts healed, the torturous occupational and physical therapy with his fingers began to pay dividends, but he still felt empty inside. "One day I was approached by Colonel Bill Howard, chief of occupational therapy at Walter Reed. He knew I was a fly-fisherman from Montana, and it just so happened he was a fly-fisherman himself. The Colonel introduced me to Captain Ed Nicholson, US Navy Retired. 'I told him you're a fly-fisherman, and he would like to take you fishing.' I of course gave Captain Nicholson the standard reply. 'It's nice to meet you, sir.' However, I had no intention of going fishing with Captain Nicholson or anyone else. I just didn't have it in me. I was in the deepest, darkest place I'd ever been. I finally realized for the first time in my life that I lacked courage. I was afraid. I was scared to attempt to fly fish again for the fear of failure. What if I can't do it? What if I embarrass myself? If I try and fail, that will be it. Even my mother pleaded with me to go. 'Please go fishing with Captain Nicholson. Please just try it.' I adamantly refused. Not long after this, Colonel Howard pulled me aside and looked me square in the eye and said, 'Lieutenant, you *will* go fish with Captain Nicholson.' I cursed under my breath, but since I wasn't in the habit of blowing off Colonels, I replied with the appropriate, 'Roger that, sir.'"

Eivind was reluctant to try fly fishing at first, but now fly fishes as often as he can. Photo courtesy Eivind Forseth.

In May of 2005, five months after he'd been wounded, Forseth met with Captain Nicholson and a group of volunteers. The group consisted of members from the Mid-Atlantic Council of the Federation of Fly Fishers and the National Capital Chapter of Trout Unlimited. Because of the age of the volunteers, Forseth was originally unimpressed. "I thought 'Jesus. What a bunch of fossils!'" But Forseth admits that looks can be deceiving. "As it turns out," he says, "these gentlemen were the salt of the earth—guys like George Gaines, who is one of PHWFF's unsung heroes. And John Colburn and I became close friends." Colburn, who was a retired Army Chief Warrant Officer and an expert fly tier, spent a great deal of time with Forseth and really took the young Army officer under his wing, smoldering anger and all.

"That first morning I met John Colburn," says Forseth, "I asked him the name of the fishing organization. I figured it must have some catchy name like all the other groups operating out of the hospital. Colburn replied, 'We really don't have a name yet. I've heard some folks throwing around "Healing Waters." Hmph. It sounds like bottled water, if you ask me.' It still makes me laugh!"

Eventually, Forseth and the other members of the group ended up fishing Beaver Creek, a splendid fishery not far from Hagerstown, Maryland. Mark Eustis, one of the volunteers, helped Forseth string up his fly rod. "We stopped at the water's edge," says Forseth, "and I was mesmerized and felt as though I was back in Montana. I didn't even realize until later that day that I was ignoring my anxiety and focusing on the task at hand. Out there on the water, there was no time for anger or depression. I was wading in a beautiful stretch of water, and I was there to catch a fish. I finally got a good drift, and that's when it happened . . . All I remember is the flash of the trout's nose as it took the fly—like something out of *Shark Week*! The tension on my fly rod surged through my arm and into my chest like a bolt of lightning! That shock reached into my very being and gripped my soul! Nothing had ever rocked my existence with such force—not even the IED blast on 4 January 2005. I kept tension on the line and used my brace to reel. Mark helped me land a ten-inch rainbow trout. We released the trout back into the creek to live another day. And that was it. I was back. I remember thinking for the first time, 'Hey I'm gonna be okay.' That was the beginning of my recovery—my return to the Eivind Forseth that my family and friends knew and loved. That experience saved my life and put me on the road to recovery."

Eivind Forseth has continued to serve in several different military and defense roles. He lives in Camarillo, California, and remains active in PHWFF and cherishes the friendships he has forged there. He's especially thankful to Ed Nicholson, George Gaines, John Colburn, and Mark Eustis, who helped him through some dark days. Forseth mentors fellow veterans and speaks at fundraising events about his journey of recovery.

Like many veterans in the late 1960s, Jesse Garza was drafted into the Army 4th Infantry Division, 1st Battalion, 22nd Infantry. His duty required him to serve in a combat role in the dense jungles of Vietnam. Though his time in service was brief, it nevertheless left indelible physical and emotional marks that he carries with him to this day. He still vividly remembers how he was wounded and when he thought his time had come.

Jesse Garza is a longtime member of the Long Beach, California, program and helps teach its rod-building program. Photo courtesy Jesse Garza.

"Originally there was nothing but the sounds of our boots as we walked. You could have heard a pin drop, and then all hell broke loose. Adrenaline started pumping through my body, and there is no way I can explain the feelings I experienced at that moment. There are no thoughts of home, no thoughts of your family, you just think of yourself and your buddies next to you and you fight as hard as you can to stay alive. Your mind goes blank apart from hearing the bullets and grenades and your brothers yelling for medics.

I received my first injury from an AK-47 bullet which struck my right calf. A short time later I received another bullet wound to my upper leg–buttocks area. I had a difficult time reaching my second injury because I couldn't get the pack off my back to patch it up. I knew I was bleeding pretty badly, and I could feel my leg was going numb. I eventually passed out, and when I came around I soon discovered I couldn't reach my M16. By now I could easily feel the blood running down my leg. In my desperation I reached for my .45-caliber pistol and put it to my head because no one was taking me as a prisoner. Thankfully, twenty minutes later the battle was over."

Jesse was seeking medical treatment at the Long Beach, California, VA when he was first introduced to PHWFF in January 2009. Three of the veterans in the group at that time worked in the VA's lapidary workshop, where Jesse also spent time. He joined as a result of hearing what they had to say about the program, feeling that if it had helped them, perhaps he could get help as well.

"PHWFF has given me many things, among them a passion to fly fish. Along with this came patience, endurance, freedom, and a desire to participate. I now have the patience to learn something new, the endurance to finish what I start, and I'm free from pain when I'm building a rod or tying a fly I made. PHWFF has given me the opportunity to use my mind, hands, and body rather than being cooped up at home doing nothing. I now enjoy being around people, and I want to give back to PHWFF and share with other veterans what's been given to me. I am now the liaison for the Long Beach, California, PHWFF program. I really can't describe it any better than saying being involved with PHWFF is like being in therapy all the time. PHWFF takes you outside and introduces you to Mother Nature, and you get the benefit of making new friends and meeting other vets along the way."

While Jesse has come a long way in his recovery, he points out that the support he's received from PHWFF is unique and not likely to be the same experience that other service members might find when engaging the public. There still seems to be a large disconnect between the average American and the veterans who've served them so well.

"With some folks you can talk until you're blue in the face and get no response. For instance, when we do a Buddy Poppy drive as a fundraiser for our VFW post to raise money to help veterans, eighty percent of the people pass you by, not caring at all. This response disappoints me very much. They just don't seem to understand what the American Soldier has done for this country."

Jesse Garza is currently an active participant with PHWFF in Long Beach, California, and says the same thing to each fish he releases: "I hope I can catch you again sometime when you're one inch longer and one pound heavier."

Lally Laksbergs is a longtime volunteer with PHWFF. She is seen here on deployment in Morocco. Photo courtesy Lally Laksbergs.

"You'll be all right," the Army doctor assured Private Lally Laksbergs. "Rest it, ice it, and take some Advil. You'll be just fine." At thirty-nine, Lalita "Lally" Laksbergs was hardly the typical fresh-faced, insecure recruit; rather, she was mature enough to offer the only appropriate response to this advice: "Yes, sir." Her internal dialogue ran more along these lines: *Doc, that's horseshit, and you know it. I'm in basic training. My drill instructor isn't going to go easy on me because I say, "Oh, pretty please, my hip hurts."*

Laksbergs's daughter Alyssa had enlisted in the Army National Guard during her senior year of high school, reasoning that the move was her way of paying for college to help her single mom. While Alyssa was away at basic combat training and Laksbergs's son Jacob focused on starting his senior year of high school, single mother Laksbergs had begun to consider her own future: When Jacob left, she'd be alone in a small town in Illinois with no family and few friends. An inner voice prompted, "Why not enlist?"

Laksbergs hails from a service family. "My dad served in World War II," she says. "He fled his native Latvia and served with the US Army fighting in Germany. He was wounded in the ankle and eventually landed in a medical facility where he took a fancy to a pretty nurse," herself a Latvian emigre, whom he married not long after. "They put him in a cast all the way up to his hip for an ankle injury. Unfortunately they left it on too long, and when they took the cast off, his leg was fused straight." As a result of the poor medical care he received, one of her father's legs would always be shorter than the other; the family patriarch limped for the rest of his life but never considered himself disabled.

Like so many warriors of his generation, Laksbergs's father "never spoke to us kids about his military service—and I mean *never.*" Her older brother Marty enlisted in the Marine Corps just before graduating from high school, and it was during his background check that his brother learned more about their father's service record than they had ever known before. Marty shared that information with his sister after she graduated from her advanced individual training.

Laksbergs pushed through BCT, gritting her teeth at the excruciating hip pain that no amount of Advil could touch. She eventually discovered that she had twisted her hip bone, causing a small stress fracture. Recruits do a great deal of running in BCT, and Laksbergs, determined to prove herself to the Drill Sergeants and other Soldiers as something other than "Grandma," had put her long legs to work making large strides that she was confident would keep her closer to the front of the pack. They did—but the stretched muscles and ligaments twisted her pelvis until it cracked through.

Army Colonel Gregory Gadson, Fort Belvoir Garrison Commander (now retired), accepts a custom-built fly rod from PHWFF Fort Belvoir volunteer Lally Laksbergs. Photo courtesy Lally Laksbergs.

"During the last week of basic, we were simulating clearing enemy units, doing house-to-house searches," Laksbergs remembers. "During a sprint across an open field, my pelvis finally broke all the way through. The pain was like nothing I'd ever experienced before. I dropped to the ground. It was agony." Fortunately her commander had already seen everything he'd needed to see in her: "He told me I'd already passed all my physical training testing and other requirements with flying colors, and he wasn't about to recycle me—which would have meant I'd have had to go through basic all over again!"

After graduating from BCT, and actually marching through the pain during the ceremony, Laksbergs headed to the Defense Information School at Fort Meade, Maryland, to complete her military occupational specialty training as a public affairs specialist. After graduating, she returned to Illinois to serve in the Illinois National Guard.

After several years serving in Illinois, Laksbergs was asked to do an active duty tour at the National Guard Bureau outside of Washington, DC, as a public affairs specialist. She established herself as a photojournalist documenting service events such as military training operations, various civilian and military support missions, and leadership engagements. The assignment became an extension of Laksbergs herself, a sincere, self-deprecating, and naturally curious person who isn't satisfied until she can understand and express the *why* of a story. In fact, it was her ability to tell a great story about service members through her photojournalism that prompted her older brother Marty to turn to her with a request for help.

"I was at work one day when Marty called and asked if I'd be willing to promote this thing called Project Healing Waters." A volunteer with the PHWFF program at Virginia's Fort Belvoir, Marty knew that his sister's photojournalism, digital media, and public relations expertise could communicate the stories of their program's vets in a unique and compelling way, potentially touching the community beyond the walls of Fort Belvoir. For her part, Laksbergs was so taken with the PHWFF ethos that she also began volunteering. She has since helped other programs improve their outreach efforts.

Lally Laksbergs and fellow volunteer Greg Johnson from the Fort Belvoir program take a break from fishing near Colorado Springs, Colorado. Photo courtesy Lally Laksbergs.

Though Laksbergs hasn't seen combat, both of her children have. Working closely with vets, she's witnessed the disparate impact of our military engagements on service families. She's seen her fellow National Guardsmen leave the battlefield and return home to small towns filled with lifelong friends to whom they can no longer relate. "People seem to think that being in the National Guard is easy. Or that all we do is help out during floods or wildfires. We drill one weekend a month. Yeah, one weekend a month, my ass!" Laksbergs laughs. "Your service can take over your whole life. And when you come home with minimal support, few who can relate to you, and perhaps no military medical facility that can deal with your injuries. . . . Who do you turn to then?"

When Marty first asked for her help, Laksbergs assumed she would snap some photos and write up a brief press release for the program. In truth, she had no idea what she was getting herself into, and that's probably a good thing. "What I didn't understand then but do now is that PHWFF provides a lifeline. It's so much more than fly fishing; it's about being there in good times and in bad. This isn't a volunteer project for me anymore. It's not academic. These are real people with real challenges, and some of them have become my closest friends in the whole world. PHWFF is another family outside of my National Guard family, one that accepts everyone as they are, and I am honored to be part of it."

Lally Laksbergs is still an active duty National Guardsman for the State of New Mexico. She is an active volunteer who doesn't hesitate to give her big brother, former program lead Marty Laksbergs, a hard time any chance she gets. She is most comfortable working behind the scenes and is known for her photography skills.

Semper looked longingly at her master, unsure of what to do. Something was wrong. She'd been carefully trained to watch over him and respond to his every command. He was on the floor and clearly in a lot of pain, choking back tears and breathing heavily. And yet he was sending her away. Why?

"Semper, get on the bed. Semper, get my phone."

The gentle English Labrador retriever, tipping her head to the side as if trying to make sense of nonsense, wagged her tail and drew nearer to lick her master's face. "Semper," came the stern command, "get on the bed and get my phone." Semper slowly backed

Andrew and his faithful companion Semper are rarely more than an arm's-length apart.

away from her master on the floor and turned to jump onto the bed. "That's a girl," the beloved voice said with encouragement. "Semper, bring me the cell phone, girl. Find it. Bring me the phone." Semper nosed through blankets and bedding until she located her quarry. Picking the phone up gently in her mouth, she bounded off the bed and dropped the phone beside her master. "Good girl, Semper," he exclaimed.

"This is 911," said the curt, professional voice at the other end of the line. "What is your emergency?"

"My name is Andrew Laffey," said Semper's master into the phone while she sat beside him. "I'm a disabled veteran, and I've had to call before. I was using my walker to steady myself as I backed up to sit down, but I misjudged how far I was from the bed and missed it entirely. I'm recovering from surgery and I—I'm in my bedroom on the second floor lying on the floor." Laffey's voice shook. "I'm in a whole lotta pain, ma'am. I can barely move, and I can't put any weight on my right leg."

Laffey could hear the dispatcher typing and the quiet, continuous beep on the recorded 911 line. "Please let the medics know I have a service dog here. She's going to be very protective of me, but she won't bite them. I can't let them in to help me, but I can tell you where the spare key is outside my door."

"Sir, you just stay right where you are and try not to move. We're rolling units as I speak. Can you confirm the address?"

With emergency help on its way, Laffey turned to Semper, now lying quietly beside him on the floor. "What would I do without you, girl? What would I do?" Semper only wagged in response. With nothing to do now but wait, Laffey exhaled through the pain, patted Semper, and remembered.

The USS *San Jacinto* (CG-56)—the *San Jac*, as she is called by those familiar with her—is a Ticonderoga-class guided-missile cruiser named for the battle in which Texas won her independence from Mexico. Though nearly six hundred feet long with a crew of thirty officers, three hundred enlisted personnel, and a full complement of missiles, the

San Jac is considered a "small boy"—a smaller fighting ship. Famed for launching the Tomahawk cruise missiles that were the opening shots of Operation Desert Storm, the *San Jac* stopped numerous ships from getting contraband into Iraq and even rescued civilians from pirates operating in the waters around Yemen.

Andrew Laffey, assigned to the *San Jac*, was proud of his ship's storied history. His father and both uncles had served in the Navy; Laffey had grown up hearing their stories of life at sea. He'd gotten a later start than they had, beginning his naval career at twenty-seven. Nevertheless, he hoped to serve for at least twenty years—with any luck, perhaps for thirty.

On October 13, 2012, the *San Jac* participated in a predeployment exercise off the Florida coast in support of the aircraft carrier USS *Harry Truman*, soon heading to the Mediterranean Sea. This exercise, one of the final training and readiness phases in meeting the Navy's requirements for gaining clearance to deploy, happened to fall on the birthday of the Navy. Laffey and his fellow Sailors knew, however, that it would be a workday just like any other.

As a Second Class Petty Officer and a Weapons Supervisor, Laffey's highest-profile responsibility was pushing the button that fired the ship's missiles. Rarely did he push those buttons. Instead he spent the bulk of his time doing maintenance and standing watch. Today, for example, he was scheduled to work on the ship's harpoon missile system. Whereas tomahawk missiles are designed primarily for land warfare, harpoon missiles take out enemy ships that might attempt to shoot down tomahawks. In this way the weapons systems work in tandem.

By lunchtime Laffey had transitioned quickly from his watch station and gathered the appropriate maintenance requirement cards, which laid out all the steps needed to complete the required work. This maintenance included inspecting and securing each of the swing bolts along multiple tubular canisters on the missile launcher. Securing some of the bolts on this particular weapon would require him to be nearly twelve feet above the deck; although the maintenance card listed a safety harness as optional rather than required, Laffey made his case to two senior chiefs and obtained a harness. Next, because he would be operating well above the deck and toward the rear left of the ship, Laffey secured a safety spotter to keep an eye on him and radio the bridge in case something went wrong.

"The only real problem I had," Laffey recalls, "was convincing the guy working with me to stay a safe distance away from me and keep an eye on things. He kept trying to come over and hand me tools, but I insisted that he observe from a safe distance toward the center of the ship—that he follow safety protocols." says Laffey. "I had my harness tethered in place, climbed up the launch structure, and had just tightened the first swing bolt when I felt an unbelievable jerk. The whole ship just shuddered violently and for a second actually seemed to stop. I remember thinking, 'Holy shit—we've either been hit by a missile, or we've somehow run aground!' But, I mean, how could we run aground? We were patrolling in the middle of the Atlantic Ocean."

The *San Jac* had of course not run aground; rather, the ship had made a dramatic and unexpected turn. "I felt almost like a cartoon character," remembers Laffey, "because the line on the safety harness was pulled completely taut. Thank goodness, because that kept me from being thrown overboard. For an instant it was as though I was being held in midair, and then gravity took over. I landed on the middle of my back and hips, and struck the ship's side railings, which are about four and a half feet from the deck. As soon as I made contact with the railing, I bounced up, and the harness again kept me from being thrown overboard. I then fell the rest of the way onto the ship's steel deck, landing mostly on my left hip and back."

Andrew Laffey fly fishes both fresh- and saltwater. Here's a nice flounder he caught at Virginia Beach.

Perhaps he lost consciousness; Laffey isn't sure. "I just remember coming around slowly. I remember hearing alarms sounding; we train constantly to respond to all kinds of incidents. So I can't really say that I *thought*—I simply *reacted* according to my training." Laffey's well-trained reaction saved his own life and probably the life of his safety spotter. Using the same tether on his harness to pull himself up, Laffey looked for his crewmate. "I found the guy with this deer-in-the-headlights look on his face. If he'd been standing beside me, he'd have been thrown overboard. Instead he was wedged tightly between a pair of the missile launcher structure beams. I had to help pull him out."

With the help of his spotter, Laffey wound his way through the ship, somehow climbing ladders between decks, to make it back to his assigned general quarters position in the *San Jac*'s radar room, where Laffey collapsed onto the floor, still wearing the safety harness that had saved his life. "The pain was so intense that I could no longer stand. I just laid there on the floor."

The crew of the *San Jac* had no idea what had happened to the ship until their captain made a ship-wide announcement that stunned them. "First, he congratulated us," recalls Laffey, "on making the ship water-tight in less than seven and a half minutes despite the shock of what had just occurred." Their lookout had spotted a periscope about eighty yards directly ahead of the ship, the captain explained, which is why he had immediately ordered evasive maneuvers. "Even so, we couldn't turn the ship fast enough. We clipped the rudder of one of our own subs—the USS *Montpelier*, which wasn't even part of our group sail. The commander had tried to sneak in during our maneuvers and take a photo of the USS *Truman.* To be able to take such a photo would have demonstrated that he could have torpedoed her had he wanted to." The submarine commander's foolhardy decision was disastrous: both vessels were significantly damaged. Only Laffey's dedication to duty and safety kept the event from costing two lives as well.

As his ship limped back to port, Laffey was still in excruciating pain several days after the collision. Multiple visits to medical staff confirmed that he had sustained significant injuries. The "small boy" *San Jac* had no physician on board; all the ship's corpsman could do was give Laffey anti-inflammatory medication and ice for the pain. It would be *two weeks* before Laffey saw a doctor.

"He told me it was a miracle I could walk," Laffey reports, "and that I had little to no intact cartilage—that it was basically bone-on-bone between my femur and my left hip. He said I would need to be seen by an orthopedic specialist where I could try resurfacing or have my left hip replaced. I opted for the latter."

During his long postoperative recovery period, Laffey began to experience vivid nightmares, waking in the middle of the night in a cold sweat, screaming, and convinced that he was being thrown overboard. "Sometimes the nightmare was so real," he says, "that I'd actually try to jump out of the bed to save myself."

One surgery led to another. "During my second hip surgery my blood pressure began to skyrocket. Someone noticed there was no urine output, and eventually they determined that during the operation a catheter had been misplaced: Instead of going into my bladder, it lanced through to my urethra. They had to stop the operation and call in a urology specialist to deal with the mistake. I pissed blood for nearly a week after that surgery," recalls Laffey with disgust. "It should've been easier than my first surgery. Instead it was far worse. I had to wear a Foley catheter and a catheter bag around my leg."

Laffey's nightmares intensified as complications from both his injury and his surgeries mounted.

"At the time of my second surgery we lived in a small apartment on the third floor. Obviously the steps were very difficult for me to manage. But the complex steadfastly refused to let us out of our lease; the best they could do, they said, was move us to a ground floor apartment. Well, there was mold in that apartment. As a result of being exposed to mold for approximately ninety days, I developed a severe respiratory infection that landed me right back in the hospital."

Over the course of the next five years Laffey would see a series of doctors, physical therapists, counselors, and surgeons. His lifelong dream of serving at sea ended when he was forced to take medical retirement from the Navy. Worse yet, his marriage was also a casualty of his medical situation. "Some days were so dark," says Laffey, "I really didn't know how I would make it."

A fellow veteran Laffey met in a stress management class introduced him to Project Healing Waters and Bill Campbell, the project lead for the Tidewater (Virginia) program. While Laffey continued receiving care at Naval Medical Center Portsmouth, he attended outings with Campbell's program. "Before Project Healing Waters," says Laffey, "my life was 'go to this or that appointment, live with constant pain, and try not to think too much about everything I've lost.' Bill Campbell's positive attitude and the kindness of everyone in the program had a huge influence on me. I began to look forward to our outings. Bill even helped me fish from a kayak."

His extensive injuries meant that Laffey floated from one facility to another—which had a surprising upside: "I was lucky to connect with programs in Virginia Beach, Walter Reed, and Fort Belvoir, and meet folks like Al Warner, the program lead at Walter Reed, and Victor Kernus, who volunteered at Fort Belvoir. No words can express how much these three guys helped me."

Perhaps the brightest light in Laffey's life was a gift made possible by a generous Project Healing Waters supporter: his service dog, Semper, whose name recalls the Navy's strong ties to the Marine Corps. "Had it not been for Semper, I don't know what I would have done. She's so much more than a service dog. Honestly, she's an extension of me. Sometimes she knows me better than I know myself. She even reminds me to take my medicine. She finds my phone and brings it to me on command. I can't imagine my life without her. No one has ever loved me as much as Semper has, unconditionally."

Andrew Laffey has had three left hip replacements and three additional right hip replacements—all before his thirty-eighth birthday. He frequently experiences either numbness or searing pain in one or both legs; at times he loses control over his ability to bear weight on his hips. Sometimes the pain is terrible, like pins and needles being stabbed into him. Other times he suffers near total paralysis that occurs within seconds and with no warning. Damage to his spine that wasn't initially detected has continued to plague him. "Sometimes I've taken eight or nine different medications a day," he says, "and worn out multiple TENS units in a desperate effort to just find some relief from what seems like never-ending pain." Between his injury, his long and painful road to recovery, the loss of his career, and the collapse of his marriage, one might assume that Laffey would be bitter.

One would be wrong.

"Through Project Healing Waters I've built relationships with people who have changed my life. I attended an event at Rose River Farm a few years ago where I heard Keith Gilbert's moving, motivating, inspiring story—what he went through and what his road to recovery was like. I could really relate to him. He opened my eyes to accept the things that I couldn't change and make the changes I *could* make. I thought then and there, 'I want to be like Keith Gilbert. I want to give back too.'" Laffey says he has a long way to go. "But now I know I don't have to go it alone. Guys like Al Warner, Bill Campbell, and Victor Kernus have really been there for me. They've helped me get my life back. I want to do the same for others on *their* road to recovery. I want them to know that you *can* have a real life after your injury. You don't have to go it alone."

Andrew Laffey is currently completing his college education to become an electrical and computer engineer and formerly served as the project lead for the Raritan Valley program and Lyons VA programs in New Jersey. Semper continues to keep watch over her master and is seldom more than arm's-reach away.

NAME: DAVID CURTIS FOLKERTS

RANK: CAPTAIN

BRANCH OF SERVICE: NEBRASKA ARMY NATIONAL GUARD / US ARMY

YEARS OF SERVICE, NEBRASKA ARMY NATIONAL GUARD: 5

YEARS OF SERVICE, US ARMY: 3

HOME BASE: FREDERICK, MARYLAND

David Folkerts, at right, on his first mission outside of his Forward Operating Base (FOB) in Taji, Iraq, March 2005. Photo courtesy David Folkerts.

The small divided highway ahead seemed to stretch on endlessly; I thought I could see some mountains on the horizon, but I had no idea which range they were. Both sides of the roadway were flanked by green-tinted fields. Intermittent patches of sagebrush clumped together like mischievous youngsters. Apart from the sagebrush the area was mostly flat. Honestly, we'd been driving for hours, and I wasn't certain where we were.

We had spent the past few days in Shawnee, Colorado, at the Battle at Boxwood. This Project Healing Waters Fly Fishing fundraiser, the brainchild of retired National Hockey League player Steve Payne, ran from 2010 to 2018 in Shawnee at the Boxwood Gulch owned by Dan and Karen Mauritz. As if the fly fishing weren't enough, teams of veterans dined in style courtesy of the All American Beef Battalion.

The Battle at Boxwood behind us, our van full of five men and enough gear to stock a small fly shop was pretty snug. David Folkerts, a medically retired Army Captain, was at the wheel when we spotted a woman walking along the road ahead. She ginger-ly hopped onto the shoulder as we approached and back onto the

David interacting with local Iraqi children near Taji, Iraq, March 2005. Photo courtesy David Folkerts.

road after we passed. One of the guys commented that it was probably unwise for someone to be walking alone in the middle of nowhere, espe-cially where there's no cell phone reception. A mile later a car slowly came into view, and by the looks of it the driver had barely made it to the shoulder before the car gave up the ghost. We deduced that this was the origin of the walking woman: she'd experienced car trouble and decided to hoof it back to the small town we'd passed not long before. Glancing at the stalled car, we noticed a youngish man sitting in the rear passenger seat; he nodded to us as we breezed past.

"What kind of man lets a woman walk miles for help while he sits in the car? What a jerk!" said one of the guys. We all grunted and murmured our agreement. Still, we had a plane to catch—and this really wasn't any of our business.

"We're going back," declared Folkerts as he slowed the van. "We have to go back. I know it sounds crazy, but I think God is telling me that we need to go back and help those folks. I know it's out of our way— heck, we'll be going in the opposite direction. I just have a sense that we need to go back and lend a hand."

Now, David Folkerts is as steady as they come. Not one of us said a word as he turned the van around and headed back up the highway.

We approached the stranded vehicle, and it struck me again how odd it was that the young man was sitting in the back seat of the car all by himself. Then the rear passenger-side door opened, and a prosthetic leg extended to the gravel as the young man pushed himself out and made his way toward the van. Mystery solved.

Greeting us with a cheerful smile, the young man told us that when their car died a half hour before, his wife had convinced him that she should go for help while he stayed with their infant. "Your *what*?" Yes, the young father confirmed, "We have our baby girl in the car seat there." He pointed to the seat beside his own in the back. "I wanted to walk into town, but my wife was afraid that I might not make it, given the distance. I'm sure glad you guys stopped to help!"

"Your wife was right," replied Folkerts solemnly. "That would've been a painful hike."

David Folkerts knows a thing or two about pain.

∞

In 1999 David Folkerts joined the Nebraska Army National Guard, out of which grew the desire to pursue an active-duty full-time career in the US Army. In the fall of 2002 he joined the US Army ROTC program at the University of South Dakota and enjoyed participating in both the Nebraska Army National Guard and US Army ROTC throughout his final two years of college. Graduating from college in May 2004, Folkerts was commissioned as a Second Lieutenant in the Army Corps of Engineers; he spent the rest of 2004 completing the Engineer Officer Basic Course at Fort Leonard Wood, Missouri, and US Army Ranger School at Fort Benning, Georgia.

In January 2005, Folkerts was assigned to the 70th Engineer Battalion of the 3rd Brigade Combat Team, 1st Armored Division at Fort Riley, Kansas; by March he had been deployed to Iraq in support of

Operation Iraqi Freedom.

While on a dismounted patrol near Taji, Iraq, on April 22, 2005, Folkerts and three other Soldiers were hit by an IED. Miraculously, none of the four were killed. Folkerts received shrapnel wounds mostly to his left arm and leg and the left side of his face, including a wound right below his left armpit that lacerated his artery and ulnar and medial nerves. These injuries left him with permanent artery and nerve damage and a partially paralyzed left hand.

Improvised explosive device (IED) was a bomb attack that ripped through the pavement and threw David nearly twenty feet in the air. Photo courtesy David Folkerts.

"When I was hit by the IED," recounts Folkerts, "my platoon members' eyewitness accounts report that myself and the Soldier standing next to me were thrown about twenty feet up in the air and off the road. The blast knocked me unconscious, and I do not know how long I was out, but I remember waking up and feeling like I had just done a belly flop onto the ground from a two-story building. My head was pretty rattled and I was very disoriented. I remember first looking down at my legs to make sure they were still there. I remember having trouble standing up because my head was spinning; I had trouble controlling my balance. When I was finally able to stand up I noticed that my left arm was severely wounded. I was bleeding out pretty badly with blood squirting out from my severed artery with every heartbeat. I saw the other guys involved in the blast and went to them to make sure they were okay. One of them had a severe leg wound. I realized there wasn't much I could do to help because of the severity of my own wounds.

"I ran back to our Platoon Sergeant's Humvee, about a hundred meters from where we were. I think I tried to call for a medevac, but my Platoon Sergeant had already done so. Between the blast rattling my head and the shock and blood loss my body was going through, I had difficulty thinking straight. Our medic treated me: she put on a tourniquet and other bandages to help control the bleeding and set up an IV. I remember being cold and thirsty, having a dry mouth, and feeling very sleepy—all symptoms of massive blood loss. I kept repeating that I wanted to go to sleep—and my Platoon Sergeant kept shaking me and looking into my eyes and telling me to hang in there and that the medevac was coming soon."

The medical helicopter arrived about thirty minutes after the blast, ferrying Folkerts and his fellow injured Soldiers to the Army field hospital in Baghdad's Green Zone. At the hospital, "A young Soldier from the medical unit callously told me I was going to lose my entire left arm. His comments made me really angry," Folkerts says. "Later, when the military doctors came to see me, I told them that I wanted them to do everything that they could to save my arm, and they agreed to do an emergency surgery that involved taking a vein from my left leg and grafting it into the artery in my left arm. This kept the blood flowing to my arm." The surgery was successful. "Believe it or not, they put leeches on my fingers to suck out the 'bad blood' that hadn't recirculated after having the field tourniquet on for some time."

Eventually Folkerts was flown to Germany, where doctors stabilized him, and then on to Walter Reed Army Medical Center in Washington, DC. At Walter Reed he faced numerous surgeries, including a nerve graft in which doctors took a nerve from the back of his left leg and grafted it into his left arm. "At the time," remembers Folkerts, "my left hand and wrist were completely paralyzed. No movement. I was told that the surgery was unlikely to be successful and that amputating my left hand and using a prosthetic might be the better option. I was devastated—severely depressed for months. I was dealing with a lot of anger as well as graphic memories from the explosion.

"And it was about this time that I was introduced to Project Healing Waters."

At Walter Reed, Folkerts met fellow officer Eivind Forseth, an infantry officer who also had completed Army Ranger School.

David receiving his Purple Heart medal from Secretary of Defense Donald Rumsfeld at Walter Reed Army Medical Center in April 2005. Photo courtesy David Folkerts.

Forseth had combat injuries similar to Folkerts's own. "Eivind kept pestering me to try flying fishing and to join Project Healing Waters," Folkerts says. "Fly fishing looked complicated to me—and my left hand was still mostly paralyzed. I was reluctant. I was afraid to try something new and then fail to be able to do it because of my injuries. It would have made me even more depressed and angry."

Forseth continued to prod. Ed Nicholson, the retired Navy Captain who'd founded PHWFF at Walter Reed, and Army veteran John Colburn, who taught fly tying there, also urged Folkerts to give the organization a shot. And eventually Folkerts overcame his fears.

He could cast a fly rod, he soon realized. In fact, he adapted quite well to fly fishing. "I eventually went on my first fishing trip and caught my first trout, and the rest is history," Folkerts says. "I fell in love with Project Healing Waters and with fly fishing in general. It sort of flipped the switch in my head—it got me thinking positively and changed my outlook on life and on what I was still able to do. Soon I was giving back, getting as many other wounded vets at Walter Reed involved in

David Folkerts was one of the very first participants in PHWFF. Photo courtesy David Folkerts.

the program as I possibly could."

Many mistakenly believe that they must travel the road to recovery alone. "The truth," says Folkerts, "is that you need to be brave enough to let someone know you need help." Reaching out is difficult, but Folkerts believes that bottling up one's pain is "the worst thing you can do" because eventually that pain will "eat at your soul and mind and take you to some really dark places. It'll leave you isolated. Sharing my struggles with others and being around people who are positive lights in my life—this is the best help I can get. In return, I try to help others on their own road to recovery."

∞

When the young husband and father, stranded alongside the road with his infant, told us that he and his wife had prayed for help, David Folkerts just smiled and offered to turn around and pick up the young man's wife, take her to town, and bring her back to the car. I pointed out that, notwithstanding our good intentions, the young mother was unlikely to get in a van full of men she didn't know. Instead we ought to get *out* of the van and wait with the husband, baby, and broken-down car while Folkerts, armed with the names of both husband and baby, went on ahead to assist the mom.

Within half an hour or so, Folkerts returned with the young mother in tow; they had been to town and found a local mechanic who could work on the car, but apparently the needed parts wouldn't be available for a few days. We looked on mutely as the grateful couple quietly debated how to manage a hotel stay with a baby.

Mentally calculating a midpoint between the airport and the couple's hometown, Folkerts offered, "Why don't we just take you with us? I think we can swing it. Perhaps one of your neighbors could meet us." Mouths agape in disbelief, the young couple argued that they couldn't possibly inconvenience us further. The rest of our group quickly rallied behind Folkerts's suggestion, assuring the couple that we had plenty of room and couldn't imagine leaving them stranded. Without another word they opened the back doors of the van and began to eject and then rearrange our mountain of gear.

The baby's car seat went in first, right in the middle of the back seat. Baby cried initially, of course, but settled after Mom joined her. Dad sat up front next to Folkerts so that he could stretch out his leg and still be able to turn and see his daughter. The rest of us piled in as best we could. It was a tight squeeze, to be sure, but absolutely worth it to all of us.

We learned a bit about our new friends during the drive. Dad was a youth pastor who had lost his leg to infection following a tragic motorcycle accident. He shared his own arduous road to recovery and the many obstacles he and his wife now faced, including the mounting medical bills, his ongoing health problems, and the family's uncertain economic future. The couple had carefully planned a much-needed respite,

David and Lindsay Folkerts have been a part of PHWFF from the very beginning. Photo courtesy David Folkerts.

only to have their car break down in the middle of nowhere. When we told them why we were in Colorado in the first place, the pastor responded, "God must have sent you to us." Folkerts just smiled and kept driving.

When we reached the Walmart where we planned to rendezvous with the couple's ride home, the young mother told us, "We're going to be able to spend the night in our own home tonight because of you. My husband and I could have managed, I guess, but the baby is going to be much more comfortable sleeping in her own room." Her husband agreed and offered Folkerts some cash, saying, "We can't thank you enough for stopping to help us. Your kindness in going out of your way not just to help us but to make sure we got home was more than anything we could have hoped for." Voice cracking, he continued, "It means a lot to me and my wife."

"No," said Folkerts quietly, refusing the money. "We were just at the right place at the right time, and glad to help." The young man tried again to give us something, but Folkerts took a small step back and shook his head. "No," he said again. "We're with Project Healing Waters. This is just who we are. This is what we do."

Eventually the happy couple and baby were picked up by family members. We said our goodbyes and the mom teared up and gave us all a big hug. After our goodbyes I admit we were all a bit choked up and we still managed to make it to the Denver airport in plenty of time.

David Folkerts was one of the very first veterans to enter Project Healing Waters and eventually worked for the organization for fourteen and a half years in many leadership roles. It is nearly impossible to determine how many of his fellow veterans Folkerts helped and had a positive impact on, but it easily numbers in the hundreds.

It's 5:30 on a Monday morning and nearly everyone boarding the plane is bleary-eyed and trying to remember why in the name of all that's holy they booked a flight so early. About ten rows back from the front of the plane sits a man wearing the familiar uniform of a commercial pilot. He is eager to get airborne and begin his workday. He avoids making eye contact with the boarding passengers—not because he's too proud to mingle with the riffraff but in an effort to delay the inevitable.

Regional coordinator Curtis Boatman, at left, with his friend Graham Walker, who served in the United States Marine Corps. Photo courtesy Curtis Boatman.

Nevertheless, the wisecracks eventually begin: "Hey, fella, you know you're sitting in the wrong seat, right?" "If you're back here, who in the world is flying this thing?"

Curtis Boatman has been an American Airlines pilot for more than twenty-four years, which means "I deadhead a lot." Airline industry professionals "deadhead" when they're off duty but in uniform, ferried from one duty location to another on a passenger plane, with little to do between assignments but read or complete crossword puzzles. In any given week Boatman might fly to and from Alaska, Mexico, Aruba,

Nearly every year Curtis Boatman spends a week out West trout fishing with his close friend Bob Gartner. Photo by Bob Gartner.

Maine, and anywhere in between. So he's been on the receiving end of passengers' friendly one-liners hundreds, perhaps thousands of times. Boatman takes the ribbing in stride, though he sheepishly admits that he fantasizes about replying, "Well, I was supposed to fly today, but my arms are tired. I'm just gonna sit here until I rest up, and then I'm back in business!" Of course Boatman thinks too much of his employer to ever joke; instead, he nods and smiles as successive waves of passengers delight in teasing him.

Boatman was on Colorado's Frying Pan River when he saw a sign that read "Project Healing Waters Outing." "I'd never heard of this group before," he says, "but I was curious." A subsequent internet search turned up Project Healing Waters Fly Fishing, and as soon as Boatman returned to his home outside Washington, DC, a call to PHWFF national headquarters in La Plata, Maryland, directed him to the Fort Belvoir program in nearby Alexandria, Virginia.

"I spoke with Dr. Mike Cherwek, who was at that time the Fort Belvoir program lead," Boatman remembers. "I made it clear that I wanted to help out, and I didn't care what I had to do. They could have told me I had to mop floors and wash dishes, and I'd have done it, I just wanted to lend a hand." Looking back over his life, Boatman continues, "As a younger man I had the choice of serving in the military. I didn't go. In some ways I've really regretted that. But now I've found a way that I can give back to folks who have done so much for me and my family."

After beginning to volunteer, Boatman met Bob Gartner, to whom Cherwek passed the torch of the Fort Belvoir program. According to Boatman, Cherwek and Gartner shared the same philosophy: "It's all about the guys. I can't tell you how much gear I saw provided to veterans while I was there—everything from rods and waders to flies and nets. And it didn't cost the participants a dime."

After nearly six years of faithful service to the Fort Belvoir program, American Airlines transferred Boatman from DC to Atlanta, where he discovered PHWFF at the Shepherd Center through their SHARE program, which is an initiative to treat and rehabilitate wounded veterans. While injured warriors progress through the Shepherd Center's unique, intensive recovery program, PHWFF advances their rehabilitation with skills-based recreational therapy like fly tying and fly rod

When not flying commercial airlines for a living, Curtis Boatman is fly fishing somewhere. Photo by Bob Gartner.

building. From developing their eye-hand coordination to helping them relearn how to follow a sequence of repetitive steps, PHWFF activities are a natural fit for SHARE.

Early in his volunteering with PHWFF at the Shepherd Center, Boatman recalls a Marine who knew that he traveled frequently asking, "Hey, Curt, can you fly fish in the Smoky Mountains?" Boatman responded that you could indeed, and that he had done so. "About fifteen minutes later," says Boatman, "he repeated the question. I figured he hadn't heard me, so I responded a bit louder." In fact, the injured vet asked Boatman the same question several times. He slurred his words and was "hunched over" and seemingly "confused a great deal of the time," remembers Boatman. "I thought maybe his many medications had something to do with it."

Not long after meeting that Marine, Boatman became increasingly busy at work. After about two weeks away from the PHWFF program at the Shepherd Center, Boatman returned, and bumped into the curious Marine again. "His voice was crystal clear, he was fully attentive, and he looked me directly in the eye!" recalls Boatman, who was shocked when the Marine proudly showed off a fly rod he'd built for his father. "When I get out of here," he assured Boatman, "he and I are going to go fishing. And I want him to use this rod."

Boatman would go on to become a PHWFF regional coordinator, overseeing the needs of programs and program leads in Georgia, South Carolina, and a few other states, as well as liaising between program leads and the national office. Boatman loves the area and the volunteers and veterans he works with: "That Georgia and South Carolina charm thing is for real: those guys are the salt of the earth."

In 2015 Boatman pitched an idea to staff in the military and veterans' initiative at American Airlines: a collaboration with PHWFF using AAdvantage Miles for travel on designated PHWFF trips. American

Airlines liked the idea so much that they asked Boatman to get straight to the numbers and bypass the sales pitch. "The whole thing took about forty-five minutes, maybe less. They were as excited about the idea as I was." In 2018 alone American Airlines helped thirty-five veterans reach their destination; to date, American Airlines has donated six million AAdvantage Miles to assist veterans during travel to sanctioned PHWFF events.

Following a promotion, Curtis Boatman was transferred back to the DC area. He currently serves as regional coordinator for the National Capital Region and frequently visits the Fort Belvoir program in between flights in and out of Reagan National Airport or Dulles International.

CAKE AT THE POPE RANCH

Chris Matthews wielded the chainsaw like he'd been born to the task, deftly thwacking limbs of cedar and mesquite off a threatening brush pile as if he were a sword-swinging knight battling a dragon. Apparently he'd worked as a lumberjack at some point in his life—experience that clearly paid off now. Mesmerized as I was by Matthews's nearly effortless parry and thrust with the twisted tree limbs, I barely made out the voice shouting to me over the chainsaw's deafening buzz: "Hey, dumbass. You gonna stand there and stare at Matthews's ass, or you gonna do something productive? The firewood isn't going to load itself. Anytime you're ready, sweetheart—start loading."

Paul Norman, Alex Colonna, and Chris Matthews all served as Marines. Sitting around a campfire with close friends is a great way to end any day.

"Ease up, cupcake," I replied to retired Marine Corps Gunnery Sergeant Paul Norman, who had invited me along on this wood-gathering foray. "I'm going as fast as I can without getting clocked in the head by a piece of flying wood." Norman, a mountain of a man with a thick black beard, penetrating brown eyes, and numerous intriguing tattoos, could be the motorcycle-gang extra straight out of central casting. He looked like he might be fully capable of chewing up a handful of nails and spitting out thumbtacks.

Best get to loading, I decided, and began stacking wood in the back of the Gator. Having slain his wooden dragon, Matthews climbed into the front of the Gator; Norman, rifle slung across his lap, folded himself into the passenger seat. I hopped into the Gator's bed alongside the firewood, wondering all the way back to the ranch if my coccyx would ever be the same again.

∞

Every November, Temple Fork Outfitters founder Rick Pope invites friends to his Texas ranch to celebrate the birthday of the Marine Corps. "I never served," explains Pope. "When some of the friends I'd met through Project Healing Waters said they'd like to hunt . . . well. I was all in."

Ranch rules are simple: Licensed hunters may take aim at deer, coyotes, and turkeys, and are encouraged to shoot any wild pigs on sight. All game must be tagged immediately and treated with care even after being harvested. The ranch's numerous does and immature bucks are the principal targets; those with defective antlers or oddly shaped racks are culled so as not to pass on bad genes. Hunters may also take a trophy buck, which must be mounted by a local taxidermist; few actually take such bucks, however, seemingly more inclined to admire them through binoculars. Strictly off limits are aoudad—Barbary sheep, which can weigh in at well over two hundred pounds—and yearling deer. Every guest winds up taking home as much harvested game meat as he or she desires.

Guests are likely to see game all over the ranch, but certain sweet spots—with names like Flat Rock, Big Oak, the Pens, High Point, and Onion Pond—feature small wooden blinds with benches. Flip's Bowl,

The Pope Ranch is a beautiful place of solitude where friends gather every year to celebrate the Marine Corps birthday.

named for renowned angler Flip Pallot, is simply a great place to sit and wait for game to amble by.

Safety is paramount at the ranch: hunters mark where they're headed on a map and check in regularly, either face-to-face or via group text, with fellow hunters.

Texas's state plant, the prickly pear cactus, is well represented across the nearly two thousand acres of the Pope Ranch. "Feel free to

take a few back home with you," jokes Pope, "because we have plenty." Still, beyond the hard, dry ground, large boulders, and scrub brush are some beautifully green low-lying pastures, lush and healthy, that support a few head of cattle. Often among the cattle are deer enjoying the feed left for them by "Miss Bettie," Pope's mother, who lives next to the upper pasture in a tidy cottage. Pass those deer in a truck, and they'll hardly notice: they seem to know that they're on hallowed ground at Miss Bettie's, where nothing and no one will harm them.

The local rattlesnakes, by contrast, had better watch themselves. Miss Bettie quickly dispatches *those* with a .38-caliber Colt revolver.

Paul Norman heading out for a hunt.

Not far from Miss Bettie's, down a winding and bumpy dirt road adjacent to the lower pastures, stands the hunting cabin. Originally a one-room schoolhouse in Texas's frontier days, the cabin was disassembled and relocated to the property before the Pope family purchased the ranch. Pope has since made his own improvements to the small structure, outfitting it with plumbing, electricity, and a concrete porch.

The cabin's two rooms and two doors open up to the lower pastures. One room contains a small kitchen area, with a sink and large freezer against one of the walls for storing harvested game. On the other side of this room is a small, comfortable couch that has seen better days. In the center of the room are a single table and an assortment of mismatched chairs, and the walls are covered in hunting calendars and hunting and fishing photos. Near the kitchen sink sits an old coffeemaker with a scorched glass carafe that's rarely empty. An eclectic collection of weathered coffee cups lines the kitchen shelf as if on picket duty just above the pot; surprisingly clean, these cups are sporting enough to hold bourbon, Scotch, or rum come evening.

The second room contains two sets of wooden bunk beds—old but quite sturdy. A space heater warms Texas's cold (and sometimes rainy) November mornings. A rack in the corner of the room holds a variety of hunting clothing: light jackets, flannel button-down hunting shirts, and corduroy "bush pants" to protect hunters from the ubiquitous cactus, mesquite thorns, and tasajillo. The relentless tasajillo, called by the deceptively charming name of desert Christmas cactus, is a misery when it embeds itself into your skin. Ask me how I know.

The cabin's single bathroom is small, but what it lacks in size it more than makes up for in character. A tottering stack of hunting and fishing magazines rivals the commode in height. The tiny sink perpetually bears a slight brown stain from the dripping faucet. The shower "curtain"—a plastic sheet—is held up by metal rings that produce an unholy shriek when pushed aside. Inside the shower one typically finds a can of shaving cream and a wide variety of soap chips on offer. My wife wouldn't come within fifteen feet of the place; the hunters don't seem to mind it at all.

Mismatched chairs and numerous gun racks dot the dusty concrete front porch. On one side of the porch is the large map of the ranch on which hunters mark their locations. Countless mementos decorate the exterior porch wall: an array of antlers is on display along with various signs, one of which, no doubt "borrowed" by a Marine, reads "Danger! Stay back one hundred meters!" in Arabic with the English translation beneath. Opposite the map, across the porch, stand a pair of commercial refrigerators, their doors whimsically wallpapered with stickers: TFO, Patagonia, Shiner Bock, and more. Inside, hunters might find Texas craft beers, a half bottle of vodka, or perhaps a large glass jar of pickled eggs or pigs' feet. A closer inspection reveals several dozen pounds of deer and wild boar meat wrapped in plastic bags and carefully labeled with a Sharpie, ready for transport home.

A large shed flanks the hunting cabin, where a pulley with ropes is secured to a nearby hook; occasionally the carcass of a harvested deer or boar hangs here, waiting to be cleaned. All day long a campfire smolders out front, revived as evening approaches. Hunters often gather round the fire after dinner, coffee cups in hand, to discuss the day's hunt and make plans for the morrow.

Admittedly, some of the parts of the ranch's hunting cabin don't amount to much, but the cabin is more than the sum of its parts. Despite its ramshackle look, this humble shelter is a second home and a sanctuary to its many visitors—priceless, beloved, and yes, some might even say holy.

On the highest plateau of the ranch sits the main house. Its generous open kitchen features a grand island that is both a practical food-prep area and a great place to sit and chat. The island competes for the title of Favorite Gathering Spot with an antique Jacobean dining room set. Rick Pope's wife, Ginny, received the finely carved table and chairs from her parents, who brought it with them when they emigrated from England. Running nearly the entire length of the back of the house is a large deck with commanding views of the ranch below as well as of Lake Buchanan.

Rick and Ginny Pope share the main house with their loveable English Golden Retrievers Ducky and Teddy, impossibly large lapdogs who live for a good scratch behind the ears. "They shed like a son of a bitch," says Pope, "but I like to think of them as live dubbing dispensers." Expertly managing this human and canine menagerie is the unflappable Otis, an orange tabby cat of noble mien who lets visitors know in no uncertain terms when he is and is not amenable to being rubbed.

The week culminates in an evening celebration of the birthday of the Marine Corps, for which Ginny Pope generally outdoes herself: hors d'oeuvres, fajitas, chili made from deer harvested from the ranch, cornbread, fruit salad, and green beans feed eighteen or so guests. Bobby Creech and his wife, Kathy, longtime friends of the Popes, usually attend and bring along some of Bobby's delicious homemade popovers. So many desserts put in an appearance that one might assume the ranch features an onsite bakery. The mood is festive—unsurprising when Marines have had a few adult beverages—and Ginny Pope manages it all with effortless hospitality and grace.

When the meal ends, the room's mood changes.

In the corner of the dining room next to the fireplace, a white table-cloth covers a small table set for one. The single glass is turned upside down, the solitary plate empty. A lone candle flickers, casting shadows across the cool white cloth. The table is set for every warrior who won't come home. Some lie buried with comrades in foreign fields; others have never been found.

∞

After dinner Chris Matthews stood at the edge of the antique table. All eyes were fixed on him as he solemnly sliced into a birthday cake decorated with an anchor and globe insignia. "In 2004," began Matthews, "Sergeant Patrick J. Salmon served in the combat logistics battalion during one of the many battles over Fallujah in Iraq. Salmon participated in the cake-cutting ceremony at headquarters, but he knew that other Marines fighting on the front lines hadn't received any cake. Crazy as it sounds to those who aren't Marines, Salmon set out to find every Marine on the front lines and take them a piece of cake—firefight or no firefight. Each Marine took a turn eating a piece of cake, one at a time, while comrades fired on enemy positions. Many Marines have taken cake to the front lines; Salmon is just the latest in a long line of Marines who have upheld our traditions."

Chris Matthews's dedication to Sergeant Salmon left few eyes dry in the house. Following Marine Corps tradition, the youngest Marine present—none other than Chris Matthews—received a piece of cake from former Gunnery Sergeant Alex Colonna, the oldest Marine in the room, in a gesture signifying a passing of the torch. Colonna then read aloud a

Table set to remember those who lost their lives while serving in the Marine Corps.

statement prepared on November 1, 1921, by General John A. Lejeune, the thirteenth commandant of the Marine Corps, to commemorate annually the birthday of the Corps: "On November 10, 1775, a Corps of Marines was created by a resolution of the Continental Congress. . . ."

As General Lejeune's words washed over the silent room, I glanced at Matthews, standing at attention like a sentinel carved from granite. Yes, he wore a beard now. And sure, he'd undoubtedly put on a few pounds since leaving the service. But those eyes remained fierce and alert. They were focused on something real, something only he could see—perhaps on a firefight in a distant land, perhaps on fallen comrades who never came home.

I looked at Paul Norman; he too was standing ramrod straight. He too was as alert as Matthews—just as present and just as distant. Indeed, every Marine was at attention, simultaneously in the room and on the battlefield. "I served, and I'm no one's hero," their faces seemed to say. "I did my duty. I did what Marines do. I did what all my comrades-in-arms did. And I'd do it again."

Standing together in solemn reflection with Matthews, Norman, and everyone else at the ranch that evening, I realized that there were really only two types of people in the room: Marines—and those protected by Marines.

Chris Matthews operates Semper Fli Guide Service in Springfield, Oregon, and is a frequent visitor to the Pope Ranch.

Every parking space is taken at the Anchorage Marina in Atlantic Beach, North Carolina. Along the weathered boardwalk, vessels that might fairly be described as yachts are moored alongside low-profile skiffs and modest fishing boats. I make my way to the large white tent teeming with more than a hundred fellow fly anglers and fly-fishing guides, all buzzing with excitement for the Cape Lookout

Chris Thompson is an avid fly tier and enjoys teaching fly tying. Photo courtesy Chris Thompson.

Albacore and Redfish Festival. These devoted anglers have gathered to land a few hard-fighting albies, knock back some local microbrews, and raise money for Project Healing Waters Fly Fishing.

"You look like hell, Beau," quips Curt Boatman, regional coordinator for PHWFF in Northern Virginia, as he navigates through the crowd toward me. "I thought firefighters are supposed to be tough. You look like you need to go back to bed, dude! What's wrong? Forget your Metamucil this morning?" A chorus of laughter erupts behind Boatman, who continues, "I really wanted a good fly angler to partner with for this tournament. I mean, saltwater fly fishing is demanding and often requires significant skill. You have to be a good caster because of the wind," he says, while the anglers and guides around him nod solemnly in agreement. "You have to make solid hook sets—and then the *real* challenge begins as you try to land these speed demons. Unfortunately for me," sighs Boatman, bringing his speech in for a landing, "all of those really skilled guys were busy this weekend—so I got stuck with you!"

Chris Thompson's familiar bellow interrupts the general hilarity. "Okay, people, listen up: We have a schedule to keep, and I aim to keep it." The retired Marine Gunnery Sergeant is heavily bearded, topped by his customary orange Temple Fork Outfitters ballcap and swathed in a long-sleeved T-shirt that features Bigfoot clutching a fly rod—appropriate for the six foot four Thompson, who is himself affectionately known as Sasquatch to the fly anglers who love him.

"We have gifts, provided by our generous sponsors, for all competitors," continues Thompson. "I want all the teams to register and pick up a copy of the rules." Thompson then turns the event over to his fellow board of directors member Tommy Bennett, who quickly assures all attendees with his disarming Carolina drawl that this event will be run by the book. Peering over wire-rimmed glasses, Bennett intones, "If you don't register correctly, and abide by all the rules—well, you're more than welcome to fish, but you won't be part of the tournament. Nor will you be eligible for any of the trophies or prizes. *No exceptions*," concludes Bennett flatly, holding up a list of rules for all to see.

"No lines in the water before 8 a.m.," begins Bennett with the soberness of a county judge. "All boats must return to the marina with their scorecard by 3:30 p.m. . . . ." Boatman, our guide, Captain Tom Roller, and I listen closely. Bennett concludes his solemn reading: "In the event of a tie, unforeseen conflicts, or other such circumstances, the decisions of the board of directors for the tournament is final." Bennett takes off his glasses and sits down, at which point Thompson immediately responds, "And may the best Marine win!"

The tournament was born in 2002 when Charlie Utz set up the Cape Lookout Albacore Festival to raise money for Duke Children's Hospital and Health Center, which successfully treated his two-year-old daughter, diagnosed with a brain tumor. The event was a success and enabled Utz to contribute funding to children's cancer treatment at Duke Children's Hospital. The event raised over $300,000 before becoming inactive for several years.

In 2014 a group of self-confessed albie addicts, Thompson, Bennett, John Snipes, and John Mauser, decided to revive the event with Utz's blessing. Acknowledging the region's strong ties to the military, planners concluded that the new tournament would raise money for Project Healing Waters Fly Fishing. The group secured sponsors, established rules and guidelines, organized logistics, and recruited volunteers to take disabled veterans fishing near shore for albies. Thompson's then-girlfriend Kellie Sutton joined the cause, working behind the scenes to secure morning coffee, breakfast, and afternoon lunches for the dozens of guides and partici-pating veterans, and to coordinate the captains' party and awards banquet. The group took turns fielding hundreds of calls and emails, finding raffle items, setting up tents, and generally putting out fires.

At this year's event, as always, Sutton is busy anticipating needs and responding to requests, but she's also got one eye on

Lefty Kreh and Chris Thompson enjoying a moment together.

Thompson. She knows how devoted he is to the festival. Routinely the life of the party, Sasquatch may be overheard quipping, "Drinking rum before 10 a.m. doesn't make you an alcoholic—it makes you a pirate!" While Thompson smiles, laughs, talks, and mingles, Sutton watches for signs of pain—and when she sees them, she insists he sit down. Few know how long a road Chris Thompson has traveled to get here.

∞

As a teen Thompson loved airplanes, participated in Civil Air Patrol (CAP), and dreamed of becoming an Air Force pararescueman. During a three-week CAP summer encampment at Marine Corps Air Station Cherry Point, however, the young Thompson met a Marine Corps Master Sergeant who left an indelible impression. "He had such a sense of purpose," Thompson remembers, "such a commitment to doing a good job that then and there I knew I wanted to be a part of the Marine Corps." On April 14, 1991, Thompson found himself standing on a pair of Parris Island's famed yellow footprints; he graduated meritoriously from boot camp as a Lance Corporal and never looked back.

Thompson spent the next ten years at Camp Lejeune, where he served in three different infantry battalions and as an instructor at the School of Infantry. "I don't care what you think you're going to be in the Marine Corps: baker, tailor, candlestick maker. First and fore-most," Thompson insists, "you're going to be a rifleman. You're going to learn every aspect of rifleman skills. We're the smallest of the armed services. We're trained so that no matter where we are or what we're doing, within a moment's notice we can pick up a weapon and become part of a platoon."

Assigned to Marine Corps Security Force Company Europe in Rota, Spain, Thompson served for eleven months until injuring his back during close combat training. At first he believed he could "shake off" the ever-worsening pain; then he learned that he had broken some of the facets in his lower back—the small bones that look like little fins that come off the spine. Therapy helped until swim qualification training: "I got out of the pool easily enough, but once out I slipped and fell on the concrete pool deck. Lucky me." Thompson's fall reinjured his back, and he began the healing process all over again. In time he made a complete recovery.

During his service, Thompson deployed aboard the USS *Iwo Jima*, USS *Wasp*, and USS *Bataan* in the Mediterranean with Marine expeditionary units. He was deployed to various locations within the European theater, including Yugoslavia, Kosovo, and Albania, as well as to Okinawa and mainland Japan. In 1994, he was part of a Special Purpose Marine Air Ground Task Force that was sent to Haiti to restore Jean-Bertrand Aristide, the country's first democratically elected president, to office after a military coup sent President Aristide into exile. Thompson also served with Naval Submarine Base Kings Bay in Georgia.

By the time Thompson arrived at Marine Corps Base Quantico, the famed "Crossroads of the Marine Corps," he had served twelve years and risen to the rank of Staff Sergeant. He was soon promoted to Gunnery Sergeant and shortly afterwards became the Operations Chief of The Basic School. All commissioned USMC officers are required to attend the Basic Officer Course of The Basic School, which focuses on learning to lead a rifle platoon. Sure, he would have preferred a combat role, but Thompson was sent to Quantico on a humanitarian transfer. He accepted his role and knew training was integral to the Marine Corps—and he had to admit to himself that his life at Quantico was pretty good. "I was living in a nice townhouse," Thompson remembers. "One day I was taking some laundry downstairs when my 125-pound Rottweiler stood on a sheet I was carrying. The sheet got wrapped around my legs, and I fell ass-over-teakettle down the stairs and landed on my back. The pain—the pain was immediate and intense. It took two medics and four firefighters to get me out of the house on a backboard. I was in agony."

He spent the next sixteen months in a cycle of physical therapy and doctor appointments. The pain was such that even standing up from his desk became almost unbearably difficult. "I nearly passed out at times from the excruciating pain," Thompson says, and he popped pain pills like candy. When Thompson's doctor suggested a spinal cord stimulator, he was intrigued. "They did a minor procedure and slipped some electrodes into me. The results were amazing. When the pain got bad, I could just dial a little gizmo and block it." The stimulator did not repair his injury, but the pain block was a revelation, and Thompson thought he might just see a light appear through the clouds. That's when the doctor delivered the bad news: They would need to permanently implant the device inside him. This would provide significant relief, but it also meant the end of his career in the Marine Corps.

"I went from joy at the thought of getting serious long-term pain relief to despair when I realized that my life as a Marine was over. I simply couldn't imagine what that looked like." Meanwhile, Thompson's marriage was falling apart and ended in divorce. "It was the darkest time in my life," he recalls. "I was angry and disappointed and—it's really hard to put into words, but I felt like life as I knew it was over."

While at Quantico, Thompson met the late fly-fishing legend Lefty Kreh, then the most famous angler in the world, who impressed Thompson as "a regular guy who treated me like an equal." Through Lefty, he met Rick Pope of Temple Fork Outfitters, who "has become one of my closest friends," says Thompson. "Lord only knows how much gear TFO has donated to help guys like me." It was through Pope that Thompson heard about a new fly-fishing program called Project Healing Waters. He was invited with his brother Marines Alex Colonna and Paul Norman to attend the PHWFF 2-Fly Tournament at Rose River Farm in

Syria, Virginia. There he was introduced to PHWFF founder Ed Nicholson and chairman of the board Douglas Dear. Before his discharge, he connected with PHWFF program lead Marty Laksbergs, also a retired Marine, who "went out of his way" to bring Thompson into the fold. Laksbergs, Thompson, and Jim Bensinger, all Marines, helped start the Quantico program. They are the last three original members still associated with PHWFF. About Bensinger, who taught weekly fly-tying classes at Quantico, Thompson jokes, "Though I would never admit it publicly, Bensinger is one hell of a fly tyer. He's an excellent instructor. Fly tying soon became an outlet when things were really bad." Fly fishing and fly tying helped his recovery, but Thompson insists that "it was the people I met that really made the difference."

✍

The following morning, Boatman and I meet Captain Roller at the marina. Dozens of veterans with their guides, along with other paying festival participants, are setting their gear in boats and wishing each other good luck as we head out to the fishing grounds. Before we leave, Kellie Sutton ensures that each of us has a boxed lunch as well as all the donuts and coffee we can reasonably hold. Before we even leave the marina, Boatman starts in on me: "If you need any pointers today, Beau, you just let me know!"

Albacore fishing is a rush: These bruisers routinely push nine to twelve pounds, with twenty-pound-class fish common in the Cape Lookout area, and cruise at about thirty-five miles an hour. Once hooked, they can peel off a hundred feet of fly line and then an additional hundred yards of backing in mere seconds. Anglers must cast weighted fly lines into the wind from a bobbing boat deck. Schools of albies pop up out of nowhere as they chase smaller fish along the surface, while opportunistic seagulls dive into the froth to pick off the wounded and stunned baitfish.

Chaos ensues when baitfish leap for their lives—and the pursuing albies chase them straight to the boat. One moment a school is a hundred yards away headed in the wrong direction; the next moment the same school is a few yards away and headed straight toward the boat.

When anglers tire of chasing schools of surface-feeding albies, they can cast flies behind commercial trawlers such as shrimp boats. Commercial anglers are required to return undersized fish or shrimp (called bycatch) from their nets. Once they've taken the desired species on board, commercial anglers pitch their bycatch back into the ocean. Albies swim in schools behind the trawlers like a pack of ravening wolves, waiting for an easy meal. Hopeful anglers cast their flies behind the trawlers along with the bycatch and wait for a strike—at which point they really don't so much set the hook as hold on tight. Albie takes are so strong and sudden that the inexperienced fly angler is lucky when the rod isn't snatched right out of their hand.

Boatman lands his first albie while fishing behind a trawler. Naturally I miss mine. He hooks up again. I miss again. "Let me know if I need to cast for you, Beau," he says. Captain Roller rolls his eyes. I realize it's going to be a long day.

Anglers often target shrimp trawlers when fishing for false albacore or blacktip sharks.

Roller eases the boat in line behind the trawler, and we cast again—no small feat on his part or ours, as dozens of other boats are also lining up to take a turn in a carefully orchestrated maritime dance. A boat zips in, an angler hooks up, and then the next boat in line takes its turn. Mixing it up with the albies are some large and threatening party crashers:

blacktip sharks, their distinctive dorsal fins standing out ominously against the froth when they break the surface of the water. Oh, they'll eat the bycatch in a pinch, but their real targets are the albies themselves.

Boatman continues to land albies, and somehow even I finally manage to bring one to hand. "I'd love to catch one of those blacktips one day," I say offhandedly.

"Uh, no, Beau—you really don't," replies Boatman.

Well, in for a penny . . . "Yeah, I really do," I reply.

Minutes later Roller has tied on a wire leader complete with a white streamer. "Cast it out there," he says, pointing about thirty feet behind the trawler. "Don't strip it—just let your fly drift." I follow his instructions, and less than a minute later a massive dark gray head surfaces and just as quickly submerges, taking my fly along for the ride. I set the hook. Hard. Nothing happens. I tug to get a good hook set. Still nothing. "It's so large it doesn't know it's hooked yet," comments Roller.

Yet? This can't be good.

Slowly my line grows taut. Boatman is watching me, a Cheshire cat grin spreading across his face. I swallow hard.

The blacktip makes a run for deeper water, and for fifty agonizing minutes it shows no sign of letting up. I gain a few feet of line, and my quarry peels off twice as much. Throughout the struggle Boatman laughs and taunts. "I told you not to do it, but oh no. 'Sure would love to catch one of those blacktips,'" he chirps in a charming falsetto—an imitation of me, apparently. "Well, have at it brother—it's all yours!"

The fight goes on, my forearms begin to burn, my hands grow numb, and finally I cave: "Curt, I can't see. Can you wipe the sweat out of my eyes?" Boatman dashes over, on the way deftly scooping up the towel Roller has used to hold the albies when removing our flies. The thing smells absolutely awful, but beggars can't be choosers. He begins dabbing my head with the smelly towel as though we're a surgical team,

Saltwater fly anglers have a number of species to target, including this colorful dorado caught off the North Carolina coast. Photo by John Snipes.

although the dabbing does precious little to remove the sweat. Roller laughs, I continue to struggle, and Boatman dabs on. "Come on, dude," I beg, "I'm dying here!" Boatman relents. Moments—and a lifetime—later the blacktip is alongside the boat. "She'll go about six feet," says Roller with confidence, "and about one hundred twenty-five pounds." Roller expertly releases the shark unharmed, handing me the fly as a keepsake. Boatman flashes his Cheshire cat grin once more, and I collapse onto the gunnel, panting.

I go on to land several more albies—even more than Boatman, who dutifully records our catch.

∞

The Cape Lookout Albacore and Redfish Festival may have begun as a small regional event, but by 2016 its notoriety had spread far beyond North Carolina. All of the hard work that Thompson and his colleagues had put into the event, PHWFF's first saltwater fundraiser, paid off.

The event, which features youth, women's, and conventional fishing divisions, spotlights the region's fishing opportunities to a whole new category of tourist, proving a boon to local hotels and restaurants. Each year dozens of veterans flock from across the country to participate in "Albiefest," some passing up opportunities to fish in storied locales such as Colorado, Montana, and Alaska. The festival has even been featured on an episode of *The Seahunter*, a national fishing show on the Outdoor Channel, and in periodicals such as *American Angler*.

∞

Back at the marina the white tent is pulsing with excitement as anglers line up to turn in their scorecards and swap stories about the one that got away. Others carefully check their bids at the silent auction. Thompson and Bennett welcome us all back, John Mauser offers up a quick prayer, and we sit down to a veritable feast of fried chicken, Carolina-style barbeque, coleslaw, all the sides, and biscuits—with vets at the front of the food line. I'm sitting alone at a table when Thompson sidles up and clears his throat. "Ahem. We need to talk," he mutters.

"Well, that doesn't sound good," I reply.

"I wanted you to hear it from me first. You've won first place in the fly-angling category."

I am stunned but quickly recover. "Uh, no. No. No, that's not going to happen. A veteran is going to win that trophy and prize. Not me. I just came down to have a good time! Heck, Boatman even paid all the fees! I'm not going to accept it."

"Yeah, I knew that would be your response," replies Thompson, "and I told the board of directors you wouldn't take it before I even approached you. But here's the deal, Beau: You won it fair and square. Curt abided by all early registration rules. There's no way around it. You can argue with Tommy Bennett all you like, but I wouldn't advise

Chris and Kellie Thompson often fish from kayaks near their home.
Photo courtesy Chris Thompson.

it. I know the guy. He ain't going to back down, and neither is the rest of the board. Rules are rules."

And that is that. But when I accept the trophy later that afternoon, I quietly give the first-place gear to a participating veteran.

The following day I'm honored to bear witness to an even more important and memorable event. As the sun begins to set, a gentle sea breeze brings with it the unmistakable, savory tang of a Lowcountry boil: the delicious smell of shrimp, sausage, potatoes, and Old Bay hangs in the air. A long table is set with flowers. Soft music plays in the background. And we are all mesmerized by the lovely Kellie Sutton.

Beside her, ramrod straight, stands Chris Thompson. Before them both is Rick Pope. The burly Texan beams as he speaks to this gathering of friends about love and commitment and being there for each other when it matters most.

Finally, and most importantly, he says, "I now pronounce you man and wife." Thompson kisses his blushing bride before turning to his friends.

"Hey—I can tell folks I was married by a Pope! Who wants to cast some fly rods before dinner?"

Chris Thompson now serves as the North Carolina regional coordinator for Project Healing Waters Fly Fishing. He currently works at Marine Corps Base Camp Lejeune, just down the road from Marine Corps Air Station Cherry Point, where he first dreamed of becoming a Marine. Both he and Kellie continue to volunteer for Project Healing Waters Fly Fishing and assist with the Cape Lookout Albacore and Redfish Festival, held each October.

Jim Bensinger is an excellent fly-tying instructor. He is seen here tying with Travis and Thea Vanderberg, who are regular supporters of the Quantico program. Photo courtesy Jim Bensinger.

The traffic on Interstate 95 resembles nothing so much as one of Dante's infamous circles of hell, but then, that's nothing new for Northern Virginia. I creep along with the rest of the damned until I spot a sign indicating my salvation has come: Marine Corps Base Quantico is just ahead on the right. Thank God.

Though giddy with the desire to floor the gas pedal—because I can—I watch my speed when I hit the base. I'm on my way to the Project Healing Waters meeting at Quantico's Weapons Training Battalion. From the parking lot I notice a circle of Marines sitting cross-legged on the grass, apparently completely enthralled by a lecture. Weapons and packs are stacked neatly around them. About fifty yards away from the class is a nondescript single-story white building that could easily pass for a derelict garage. The sign in front of the building reads "Scout Sniper School," and a small pile of skulls at the base of the sign suggests that numerous woodland creatures met a merciful end.

Inside, the "government issue" color scheme of gunmetal

gray–meets–olive drab is deceptive; for a moment, a visitor might be misled into believing that this could be any ordinary government office. A quick look around dispels that notion: This humble structure houses some of the best firearms instructors in the world. The walls inside are lined with countless photos of young Marines receiving instruction while standing, kneeling, or prone. Beside the photos are hung numerous awards, commendations, ribbons, and medals. The paper image of a shadowy, menacing figure with closely trimmed beard, sunglasses, skullcap, and automatic weapon is taped to the wall for target practice. This generic bad guy is none other than retired Marine Chris Thompson, who used to work at Quantico and whose image glares out from firing ranges here and at other Marine training sites.

As I enter the building for the first time, I spot Jim Bensinger, who will teach the evening's fly-tying class. I also can't miss the enormous black rifle mounted on the wall in one of the back classrooms. "What kind of weapon is that?" I ask Bensinger. "Who in the world could fire something that large? Looks like the recoil could tear your shoulder off."

Stifling a laugh, Bensinger replies, "That's a model of an M16 service rifle—a model that for instructional purposes is about five times larger than the real thing."

It comes as no surprise that Marines are trained to know their weaponry inside and out, but Marine Corps marksmanship is in Bensinger's blood: His father was a Korean War–era Marine and his grandfather fought at Belleau Wood. His son James was medically retired from the Marine Corps after serving two combat tours in Afghanistan. Bensinger's last duty assignment was as the Company First Sergeant for the Marksmanship Training Company at Quantico; after serving twenty years, he is now a civilian who serves as the deputy director of the Corps' Marksmanship Program Management Section.

Over the course of his career Bensinger estimates that he has taught marksmanship skills to about ninety thousand Marines. "Teaching someone to shoot is pretty easy," he says. "It's all about building rapport and getting into their heads that you have confidence in them. They'll normally rise to your expectations." Just how good is he at what he does? "Hell, man," quips Bensinger, "I could teach Ray Charles to shoot. If it's got a trigger and a .50-caliber round or smaller coming out of it, I can teach you to shoot it." Then he adds, "Grenade launchers, too."

When he puts down the firearms, Bensinger picks up fly-tying materials. This diehard tyer—whose motto, if one is to judge from his extensive materials stash, appears to be "have at least one of everything"—has spent nearly every Wednesday evening for several years teaching fly tying at Quantico. During class Bensinger normally sits at the head of a long wooden table flanked by four to six students on each side, most of whom are active duty or former Marines—though the occasional civilian or member of another service branch shows up. In his element when teaching, Bensinger resembles nothing so much as one of those many-armed Hindu deities. Apparently on autopilot, Bensinger guides, instructs, jokes, and counsels, rarely even glancing down at his own creation. Somehow he simultaneously stays ahead of the fastest student while managing not to leave behind the slowest. Bensinger's passion for tying has resulted in him starting his own business, Fiber Flies Dubbing; he's also on the national pro staff of Norvise.

"At this point," instructs Bensinger from his vise, "you want to keep your thread tight and snug against the eye of the hook but not too tight. Keep it away from the hook point or—" A high-pitched pinging sound interrupts him, his severed thread curls upwards, and his pattern begins to unravel. Bensinger's face flushes, and the room erupts into laughter as he expresses himself colorfully. "Or you'll break your thread from too much pressure," he continues.

"Or you'll have to start all over again because you're too much of a dumbass not to overpressure the freaking wrap or nick it on the hook point," says Travis Vanderberg, a fellow Marine and one of Bensinger's closest friends. Bensinger responds with a finger gesture.

For years Bensinger has served as assistant program lead at Quantico, working closely and effectively with program lead and fellow retired Marine Marty Laksbergs. Both men have seen active combat, and neither is eager to speak about it. "My combat service wasn't shit compared to lots of other Marines," says Bensinger. "I only fought maybe four or five days in Desert Storm; hell, I know guys who fought for months on end. I mean hard and dangerous house-to-house fighting. I have nothing but respect for those guys." He adds quietly, "Some of them didn't make it back home."

In the late '80s Bensinger was assigned to weapons company TOW platoon 1st Light Armored Infantry Battalion at Camp Pendleton. He served as the gunner on the four-man crew of the Light Armored Vehicle-Anti-Tank variant (LAV). Later he was transferred to 1st Marine Division G3 to serve as the driver for the Assistant Chief of Staff G3, or as he puts it, to be the "Colonel's gopher." Eventually he deployed to the Persian Gulf War with the division forward command. Once while tracking unit movements, Bensinger thought he heard radio traffic indicating that his old LAV unit had taken some casualties. His command post was close to the front lines, occasionally making it difficult to hear transmissions clearly over the sounds of battle. Later, when he was able to track down the written communication of the transmission he thought he'd heard, he discovered to his horror that it was true. "They took a direct hit to their rear hatch," he says solemnly. "They all died—every last one of them. Corporal Ismael Cotto, Lance Corporal Dave Snyder, Lance Corporal Dan Walker, and Private First Class Scott Schroder." Like so many combat veterans, Bensinger expresses

Jim shows off some of his fly patterns tied with alpaca dubbing.

survivor guilt: "I feel guilty as hell that I wasn't there with them. I know it sounds crazy, but I feel like I should have been with my crew. Don't get me wrong—I love my life and especially my wife, Gail. But sometimes I feel like I cheated death."

Bensinger has some scars of his own, but they're less visible to the rest of us. "When you're in a firefight or clearing houses, going room to room, you're pretty hyped up," he recalls. "I mean, you have your weapon at the ready, and the target area is going to be empty or there's going to be some sort of firefight. If the bad guys don't want to give up quietly, the shit's going to hit the fan pretty fast. It's very intense. In the end it's just you and your guys, and you can't be certain what you're going to find. One thing is certain: It can get real ugly real fast."

At the Kuwait International Airport, Bensinger saw "ugly" up close. The building's height and location made it ideal for enemy snipers, so it had to be cleared. "We entered one room," Bensinger says quietly, "and I could see right away it was bad. I mean really bad." In the corner of the room lay the body of a Kuwaiti teenager. "It was obvious the Iraqi soldiers had raped her. They always traveled in packs and acted more like wild animals than soldiers," he says in disgust. "The pieces of shit that hurt that little girl . . ." His voice breaking, Bensinger continues,

"Those sadistic animals had tortured her first. Those bastards cut off her nose, they cut off her nipples, they . . ." He stops, and his eyes fill with tears.

In a final act of barbarism, the enemy soldiers had dressed their defenseless victim in an American service uniform and shot her in the back of the head. "I had nightmares about that poor little girl," Bensinger says. "I have daughters of my own now. I still have nightmares about her sometimes."

Bensinger finds healing at his

Jim caught this trout at Harman's Cabins on a pattern he tied. Photo courtesy Jim Bensinger.

fly-tying vise, just as his students do. In addition to teaching fly tying at Quantico, Bensinger has participated in the PHWFF Fly Tying Marathon that occurs each March. Now in its eighth year at the National Museum of the Marine Corps, the event is quite popular. Members from both the Quantico and the Fort Belvoir Programs attend the event, founded by retired Marine (and favorite paper target bad guy) Chris Thompson. To date the marathon has donated more than ten thousand flies to veterans.

The museum itself is an unforgettable experience. Incredibly, the 120,000-square-foot structure is shaped to resemble the Marines' iconic Mount Suribachi flag-raising on Iwo Jima. It houses more than sixty thousand artifacts, from medals to letters to jeeps to jets, and features chilling re-creations of Corps battles fought all over the world. Etched into the stone wall near the entrance of the museum are these stirring words, attributed to two-time Medal of Honor recipient Sergeant Major

Dan Daly to his men at Belleau Wood in 1918: "Come on, you sons of bitches, do you want to live forever?"

My young son Jeremiah and his friends were struck dumb by the exhibits when I took them a few years ago. On our way out to the car, they asked to come back. "That was amazing. It was just so cool," said my son on our way out to the car after a full day. "We have to come back. I can't believe it's free to get in. I mean, it's *free!*"

I stopped the boys there in the parking lot and put my arm around my son. "Jeremiah," I said, "the admission fee isn't free. It's very, very expensive. It's just that the price has been paid in full by Marines."

Jim Bensinger continues to teach fly tying and serves as the program lead for PHWFF at Quantico.

NAME: HARRY YATES
RANK: COLONEL
BRANCH OF SERVICE: US ARMY
YEARS OF SERVICE: 28
HOME BASE: AUBURN, ALABAMA

"Itold you: I'm fine, Doc," Colonel Harry Yates told the young Army captain examining him. "Really. I feel fine," he said sternly, mustering all the intimidating power of his rank. "I don't have any complaints."

Some have nicknamed Army Colonels "birds of prey," in reference to the silver eagle emblem pinned to their uniforms and to the aggressive, no-nonsense demeanor for which they're famous. Just now, Harry Yates acted the part. "I'm ready to go back to work," he insisted, repeat-

Having hidden his injuries for a long time, Harry Yates eventually realized he needed help. Fly fishing has proven to be just the outlet he needed. Photo courtesy Harry Yates.

ing a lie he'd told so many times that he himself had begun to believe it. In the end the doctor relented, and Yates left the hospital and headed straight for his office.

Yates, who had spent nearly three decades serving his country, was the Chief of Staff of the 335th Signal Command (Theater) in Kuwait. His office, which oversaw 4,500 Soldiers, essentially determined who could talk to whom and when. This covered everything from service members who were Skyping with family members back home to Soldiers using radios involved in combat operations. One evening after work, Yates was pedaling to his quarters on his bicycle when he turned a corner and saw a jeep about the size of a Suburban barreling toward him. He slammed on his brakes, but they couldn't prevent him from slamming into the vehicle, which bore a General's insignia. He looked up from the ground where he'd landed and into the eyes of the young Soldier who had jumped out from behind the wheel of the vehicle. "Holy shit!" exclaimed the driver in dismay. "I ran over a Colonel!" Dazed, Yates replied, "Holy shit! I've just been run over by a General!"

After a thorough examination at the ER, Yates was happy to learn that he hadn't broken any bones. In fact, he figured he was pretty darn lucky. Yes, he'd had the wind knocked out of him. Sure, he had severe road rash. And he had a monster of a headache, which wasn't surprising given that his helmet had been split nearly in two. Discharged on the understanding that he would indulge in at least a few days of bed rest, Yates returned to duty stiff, sore, and happy to be alive.

He was less happy to be alive when, over the course of the next several weeks, the headaches set in. He began to experience a persistent ringing in his ears. He became irritable, found it difficult to concentrate, and soon struggled to read because of blurred vision. Even when he could see well enough to read, he struggled to process what he'd read or apply it in any meaningful way. He began to feel dizzy.

Slowly, almost imperceptibly, Yates compensated for his increasing inability to do his job. To avoid reading, he called his subordinates to his office for briefings on various subjects. "My staff was excellent," says Yates. "In fact, I couldn't have asked for better folks. They worked hard, required little supervision, anticipated what needed to be done, and did it like the true professionals they were."

Meanwhile, Yates's headaches had become nearly unbearable and he began to forget things. He couldn't read more than a few sentences without losing the thread of the document. Then his gross motor skills began to suffer: he struggled even to kick a ball while engaged in team sports meant to lift morale for those serving overseas. "I was so bad that at times folks laughed out loud at me—and that's pretty rare when you're Colonel," he says. Yates continued to go in to work every day, but he began closing his office door, avoiding meetings and talking about anything complex. In hindsight he believes that, toward the end of his tour, he was taking advantage of his staff, passing on to them the work that he was no longer able to do. Yates eventually rotated stateside, where he continued to cover up his failing health.

In the end, Yates was felled by a high-blood-pressure event that occurred during a routine dental visit—so high, in fact, that it sent him in an ambulance to the ER, where he finally broke down and came clean to a doctor. He couldn't sleep, couldn't concentrate, had intermittent dizzy spells and terrible headaches, and could barely understand anything he read.

"Were you near any explosions while you were deployed?" the doctor asked him. "Are you sure? Did you fall down while you were overseas?" "Well," Yates eventually responded, "I did get hit by a vehicle. Does that count?" The doctor immediately suspected Yates had a traumatic brain injury and subjected him to a series of questions. "I had a perfect score," says Yates, "meaning that I had every single symptom consistent with a brain injury."

His life was in a tailspin. His career—which he loved and had dedicated most of his life to—was effectively over. Colonel Yates, who'd held sway over thousands of Soldiers and made split-second, complicated, life-and-death decisions had become Harry Yates, who couldn't figure how to leave a tip for lunch. Even worse, he and Margie, the love of his life, divorced before his last deployment.

Living alone in a one-room apartment above a garage, Yates tacked up blankets over the windows to block out the sun and mitigate his headaches. It didn't matter that he could no longer tell day from night; he couldn't sleep anyway. "I didn't pay my bills, I didn't communicate with anyone. I just isolated myself and thought about all that I'd lost."

Medically discharged from active duty, Yates entered an intensive rehabilitation program at Atlanta, Georgia–based Shepherd Center, renowned for its treatment and rehabilitation of spinal cord and brain injuries. He endured grueling days of cognitive motor-skills training, counseling, and numerous other therapies. One day recreational therapist Sherry Kelly suggested he consider a new type of therapy that revolved around fly fishing. "Sherry was really gung ho about this program and recommended it strongly. Since I like fishing, I thought, heck, why not? This was my introduction to Project Healing Waters."

While an avid trout angler, Yates doesn't mind fishing the flats either. Photo courtesy Harry Yates.

At a PHW meeting Yates met and befriended Atlanta program lead Ken Griffin, former Special Forces and a decorated Vietnam vet. On his first PHW "field trip," Yates did some fly fishing in the mountains of Blue Ridge, Georgia. The trip had been organized by Carl Riggs, the longtime program lead for that part of the Peach State: "I'll never forget that first day," he says. "I probably didn't cast my fly more than three times before I caught my first fish, and it was nothing short of amazing. I can't describe it. I can't put words to it, but there is something special about having the water rush past you and the feeling of peace that comes over you. I also appreciated all the support I received from Ralph Artigliere, who guided me to my very first trout. It's a day I'll never forget as long as I live."

Eventually Yates traveled to Alaska to spend a week aboard the *Hot Ruddered Bum,* the fishing vessel owned by longtime PHWFF supporter Garry Morfit. Yates and his son Quint spent their time fishing for salmon and trout in the mornings and putting down crab traps at night. They would often eat for dinner what they'd caught that day themselves. More than anything, Yates relished the time with his son.

Upon his return from Alaska, Yates's life began to fall into some semblance of order. He still had headaches. He still had a raft of other challenges to face. But he also had something he thought he'd lost for good a long time ago: hope.

"I kept going to PHWFF meetings," says Yates, "and I soon learned that tying flies was really therapeutic for me. I actually built my own fly rod and found that if I really applied myself I could follow a sequence of directions, which was something I struggled with regularly. After going on a few more trips, which were completely free, I discovered something: it wasn't the fishing after all! It was the people involved in the group. They really cared about me, and that made a difference. The doctors with all their degrees and their specialized training surely helped me. But it was the *people* of Project Healing Waters who reached out to me and pulled me from a very dark place. Guys like Ken Griffin, Bill Beach, Gene Barrington, Carl Riggs, Curtis Boatman, Ed Nicholson, and many others have meant a lot to me, and I really appreciated their support. They encouraged me to come out of my shell and be a part of something special."

Harry and Margie Yates were remarried by Captain Garry Morfit aboard the *Hot Ruddered Bum* in Alaska. Photo courtesy Harry Yates.

His new friends turned out to be more than fishing buddies. "They didn't want to just give me free stuff; they wanted me to connect with them. They'd say, 'Hey, Harry, we're getting together or going on a trip on such and such a day. Why don't you come along and bring your girlfriend?' I explained that I didn't have a girlfriend; I had an ex-wife. They said, 'Who cares? Bring her along!'"

From the very beginning, Margie Yates had taken all of the twists and turns of Yates's challenging career in stride. Nor had she been a fair-weather friend when their marriage ended and his fortunes turned: she had repeatedly called to check up on Yates while he lived alone in his tiny, dark room over the garage. Now Yates began to see more of Margie, and a new relationship began to blossom between them.

In 2014 Harry Yates once again found himself on the back deck of the *Hot Ruddered Bum*, quietly gazing out over the majestic Alaskan wilderness and marveling at the turn his life had taken. Beside him stood

Margie, the love of his life. Their son Quint and a magnificent waterfall stood as witnesses behind them. And before them stood Captain Garry Morfit, who by then had grown to be one of Yates's dearest friends. By the bright light of a northern sun and with the power vested in him by the state of Alaska, Morfit pronounced Harry and Margie Yates husband and wife once more.

Harry and Margie Yates are active PHWFF members in Auburn, Alabama, where Yates serves as the assistant program lead.

NAME: JULIE KEENE
RANK: SPECIALIST E-4
BRANCH OF SERVICE: US ARMY
YEARS OF SERVICE: 2
HOME BASE: FREDERICKSBURG, VIRGINIA

Julie Keene can often be found fishing for shad and smallies on her home waters, the Rappahannock River near Fredericksburg, Virginia.

From the front porch of her home, Julie Keene watches Virginia's Rappahannock River roll away to the Chesapeake Bay. The river is usually placid; resident osprey and eagles, diving for their fish dinner, provide most of the excitement for river watchers like Keene. Locals know, however, that this peaceful water has a wild side: inattentive anglers who wade too far out into the heavy current can easily be swept downstream. The Algonquian Indians knew what they were about when they named this river Rappahannock, which means "rapidly rising and falling waters." Indeed, tidal changes greatly affect the lower part of the river.

Wading the Rappahannock is a gamble primarily because the river bottom seems to be in a continual state of flux. Small islands appear and disappear almost overnight, a testament to the Old Dominion's powerful and unpredictable thunderstorms: high-water events will sweep enormous tree limbs—and sometimes whole trees—downstream until they eventually lodge in shallower parts of the river, collecting sand and other sediment and quickly coalescing into islands and deep side channels. The ebb and flow of the Rappahannock, its regal grandeur and its unpredictability, its tame side and its wild side—both facets appeal to Keene.

Nearly three decades as a police officer has taught Keene that, like the droplets that quickly become the thunderstorm that changes a placid waterway into a raging torrent in the blink of an eye, any individual call for help can turn violent with very little notice.

"All I ever wanted to be," Keene says, "is a police officer. I made up my mind by the time I was thirteen: it was the job for me. My mom and dad divorced my final year of high school; that was really tough for me. My father had been a military police officer in the Army. When I told him what I wanted to do, he told me in no uncertain terms that I wasn't going into the Army." Keene grins. "So of course that's exactly what I did."

Keene followed in her father's footsteps and served as a military police officer for two years at West Point. "We'd spend one week on patrol," Keene recalls, "and then the following week doing pomp and circumstance. I also served in the honor guard, and we did things like work the parade grounds, raise and lower the flag, and fire the ceremonial cannon. It was pretty cool. Most people have no idea how many thousands of people come in and out of West Point in the course of their operations. I very much enjoyed serving there." Once out of the Army, Keene wasted no time in applying for what she knew was the job she'd wanted all her life—and was over the moon to be accepted as a police cadet in historic Fredericksburg, Virginia.

Now a veteran cop, Keene has seen a great deal of the raging-river side of life: domestic disturbances, bar fights, DUIs, rape victims, abused children, shootings, stabbings. She's seen things she desperately wishes she could forget. "One of the worst things I ever witnessed was someone on fire from the waist down. It was simply horrific. You see a lot of bad stuff, and you just try to do your best and not let it eat at you." Keene rarely speaks of what she's seen to anyone who isn't a cop or a Soldier perhaps because it's difficult for civilians to wrap their minds around the stress and anxiety inherent in her job.

On one memorable occasion, Keene—along with cops from multiple jurisdictions—was involved in a protracted high-speed chase on I-95. The suspect got off the interstate near Fredericksburg, but when he cut off his headlights in an attempt to elude authorities, he lost control of his car on the highway off-ramp. Quickly exiting the vehicle, the suspect ran up an embankment, where Keene overtook him and placed him in custody. She may have been the last police officer engaged in pursuit, but it was Keene who was credited with the arrest of a man she later learned was wanted for a double murder.

Keene loved her job—and yet she knew that something was wrong. For months she struggled with persistent headaches. Inexplicably, her joints ached. What she describes as "brain fog" meant that she couldn't recall otherwise memorable events. No matter how much she slept, she didn't feel rested. Indeed, at times she woke feeling more tired than when she had gone to bed. When she finally consulted a doctor, Keene was diagnosed with Lyme disease.

Initially Keene ignored the diagnosis. She was edgy, pretending to feel fine when she really just wanted to lie in bed all day. After months of attempting to hide her symptoms, a friend pulled Keene aside and insisted that she pursue an outlet to escape the pressures of her illness and the stress of her job. At a meeting of the Falmouth Flats Fly Fishers at her local Gander Mountain store, Keene learned that the group hosted an annual fishing trip on the Rappahannock with Project Healing Waters. The fishing trip coincided with the river's famed shad run.

"I first met Marty Laksbergs and Jim Bensinger from the Project Healing Waters program at Quantico in the spring of 2012. Those guys really made me feel at ease. I can't really describe it—I just felt immediately comfortable with them. Jim really took me under his wing and taught me how to tie flies. Jim's an excellent instructor, and when it comes to fly tying, he really knows his stuff. He would invite me over to his house, and we'd spend hours and hours tying flies. His wife Gail would fix dinner for us, but to be honest," Keene says, laughing, "I'd be so engrossed in what he was teaching me that I didn't want to stop and eat. Gail and Jim always made me feel welcome, and it really made me want to learn all I could about fly tying. God only knows how much fly-tying material I bought that year."

Julie Keene served in the Army and loved it. She is seen here with a catfish, a species not typically landed by a fly angler.

Keene eventually became a regular at Bensinger's fly-tying sessions. Tying flies brought her a sense of peace and well-being she simply couldn't find anywhere else. She received the ultimate compliment on her fly-tying skills the day she landed a Rappahannock striped bass on a fly she'd tied herself. Fly tying had become so important to Keene that she went to Laksbergs to volunteer: "I offered to do anything they needed help with, from logistics to helping put together fly-fishing outings for the group."

Keene has nothing but praise for her program leaders. "Marty Laksbergs and Jim Bensinger are some of the finest leaders I've ever seen. I've had my own set of challenges, including days that I didn't think I could make it. But when I see all the other veterans struggling with what they are going through, I count myself lucky," she insists. "I'm not an overly religious person, but sometimes you need to stop and thank the man upstairs for all your blessings. And Project Healing Waters has certainly been a huge blessing in my life. When I started volunteering, I thought I was really helping others. Turns out I needed the help just as much as any of them did—I just didn't want to admit it.

"I know there are lots of men and women who could benefit from this organization. Sometimes I see folks at a single outing, and then I don't see them anymore. And that's unfortunate. It's okay, though; some folks just aren't as ready to take on their demons as others. We all have our own pace, and I just hope they stay with it. As for me," says Keene, "I'm going to stay engaged with Project Healing Waters and help out any way I can as long as they'll let me. Guys like Marty Laksbergs and Jim Bensinger and the other guys who are part of the Quantico program have really helped me. They have more or less become extended family members. I'd follow those guys anywhere."

Julie Keene is a retired law enforcement officer and has served in various roles within Project Healing Waters. When she's not volunteering or tying flies, Julie can be found plumbing the depths of the Rappahannock River in search of anything that will bite a fly.

AN ANGLER IS BORN

Down on one knee, Bob Gartner struggled to fit a pair of waders onto irrepressible thirteen-year-old first-time fly angler Stetson Bardfield. The youth was full of energy and champing at the bit to get into the river, and with good reason: after months of casting fly line at cardboard cutouts of fish, today he was ready to leave the practice casts behind and catch his first fish on a fly rod. What could possibly go wrong?

Normally mild mannered and quiet, Fort Belvoir PHWFF program lead Bob Gartner's cheeks grew more flushed as his frustration increased. Like Stetson, Gartner had waited for this day for months. Unfortunately, the waders he'd banked on using today were proving unmanageable.

Stetson Bardfield's positive attitude is infectious. He was incredibly popular with veterans in the Fort Belvoir program.

Earlier that year on his way to a program for children of veterans, Stetson had seen PHWFF members casting in front of the USO building at Fort Belvoir. He'd never seen anything like fly casting and was immediately intrigued. For weeks he pestered his mother to ask the veterans to teach him how to cast; for weeks she denied his request because, she told him, he was not a veteran. Eventually Stetson's persistence paid off: his mother gave him permission to ask. Gartner quickly agreed that if the young man wanted to learn how to fly fish, then he had come to the right place: "How can I turn down a child—especially the child of a veteran—who wants to learn how to fly fish?"

While Gartner continued to struggle with the waders, Stetson's mother, Chris Laidir, made an unusual executive decision: "I think you'd better just take your legs off. I mean, really—this is pretty silly. Bob's done all any reasonable person could do to get those blasted waders on. Besides, we haven't got all day—and I want to see you catch a fish!" The rest of the group looked on in stunned silence as Stetson moved to obey his mother.

Adversity is nothing new to Stetson. Because he was born with arthrogryposis, a rare birth defect that manifests itself in severe congenital joint contractures, even routine, everyday tasks like eating and dressing pose significant challenges. At birth Stetson's legs, folded and

A custom rod made for Stetson by the members of Fort Belvoir's program. He's seen here on the lawn in front of the USO building where the Fort Belvoir program regularly meets.

crossed at a forty-five-degree angle, could not possibly grow to carry his body weight or allow him to walk unassisted. His arms were locked straight as well, and his elbows were fused. He also was born with "windswept hands"; that is, his hands were turned inward toward his forearms completely when he was born, and his thumbs were fused to his hand. Whereas most people have a flat hand and evenly divided fingers, Stetson's fingers are very close together and unable to bend.

Upon Stetson's birth, his mother retired from her army career, and she and her then-husband, Chief Warrant Officer and Blackhawk helicopter pilot Shai Bardfield, plunged headlong into managing Stetson's care. They faced a dizzying array of medical appointments, surgeries, and castings of their son's arms and legs. The goal of this care, from the medical community's point of view, was to enable Stetson to one day sit in a wheelchair, attend school, and feed himself. Conventional wisdom said that Stetson would never walk, much less play sports.

Maddeningly, Stetson Bardfield and his parents have consistently refused to obey conventional wisdom.

By the time he was three years old, Stetson was crawling around the house on his knees. He'd scoot around the floor just as fast as he could go, just like any other toddler—except that this toddler was dragging his deformed legs behind him. Chris watched her son for a long time before giving voice to a question—a horrible question—that had been nagging her. What if, she eventually asked Shai, doctors could take Stetson's admittedly useless legs off at the knees? Could he be fitted with prosthetics instead? He was already darting around the house like any healthy child; clearly his knees were strong. As disturbing as the idea might initially seem to anyone with healthy limbs, electing to remove the legs that were holding him back would undoubtedly enhance Stetson's quality of life.

"When I posed the idea to my son's doctor," Chris reflects, "he wasn't enthusiastic. He agreed that the idea had merit, but the procedure had never been done for anyone with Stetson's condition. And he wasn't about to be the first doctor on record to attempt such an operation." In search of emotional support, Chris turned to fellow parents of profoundly disabled children—and got a response she hadn't expected: "They acted like I was some sort of monster for suggesting that Stetson have his legs removed. They really made me feel like a horrible mother. I couldn't believe the words they used to describe me simply because I wanted to try something different."

More than a dozen specialists refused them before Chris found pediatric orthopedic surgeon John T. Killian, who agreed to perform the first surgery to voluntarily remove an arthrogryposis patient's legs. (Since then, surgeons have only attempted the procedure three other times worldwide.) Outfitted with prosthetic legs and a grueling physical therapy regimen, the boy who would never walk began to walk on his own. The Bardfield family—now grown to include younger sisters Jamesen and Emmerson—never looked back.

Back on the banks of the river, it was time for a little out-of-the-box thinking: Stetson removed his prosthetic legs, and Bob Gartner deftly inserted them into the waders. Stetson's metal-jointed prosthetics might easily pinch the waders, they realized; another angler offered a gravel guard from his boot to add to the padding, creatively solving yet another problem. Standing, outfitted, and ready to fish, Stetson realized that the mighty Shenandoah River that beckoned to him was still a good hundred yards away over uneven ground.

"Ready to go?" asked Stetson's mother. "Yes, ma'am, I am," he replied with gusto. Chris stood in front of her son, hunched down, and threaded her arms through her son's arms, which are nearly permanently crossed in front of him. Lifting him onto her shoulders as if he were a backpack, she leaned forward and trudged toward the river.

After thirty years in the field as a firefighter and paramedic, I've seen more trauma than most people can even imagine. Still, nothing prepared me for the sight of mother carrying son to the river that day. Over the riverbank, which moments before had been teeming with eager and noisy anglers and veterans from all walks of life, there fell an awed silence as countless eyes followed the pair to the water.

With a shake of my head I came to my senses and realized that I was wearing waders and Chris was not. I hurried to her and immediately offered to take her place. "Sure—if you think you can manage." Swallowing hard, I asked Stetson if he was ready to catch a fish. "Heck, yeah!" he replied. "That's why I'm here!" Just as his mother had done, I threaded my arms through Stetson's, lifted him to my back, and made my way to the water.

Stetson on his way to the Shenandoah River with his mother and program lead Bob Gartner for his first fishing trip. Soon after entering the river, he landed his first fish on a custom rod made for him by members of the PHWFF program at Fort Belvoir.

We had just entered the water when over my shoulder Stetson shouted, "Stop! Stop!" Terrified that I'd injured him or damaged his prosthetics, I jerked to a standstill and craned my neck around to look at Stetson. "The water's making my feet cold," he said. His humor effectively broke the tense silence on the bank, and the crowd of PHWFF anglers and volunteers—and I, I'm willing to admit—howled with laughter.

Some PHWFF programs confine their support to veterans alone. Gartner, however, believes that healing that encompasses the entire family is healing that sticks. He encourages wives and husbands, sweethearts, and children to attend group events when appropriate. And he isn't the only program lead who feels that way. "Family members of our veterans are suffering in countless ways today; few people realize that. With more and longer deployments, things only get harder," argues Quantico program lead Marty Laksbergs. "In many cases, the sacrifices of the military family go unnoticed, but make no mistake—they desperately need our support."

Stetson Bardfield was finally on the water, but he continued to fight for traction for his prosthetic feet on the Shenandoah's uneven riverbed. Bob Gartner moved to one side of the boy to support him while PHWFF volunteer Steve Christopherson moved to the other. Christopherson was no stranger to Stetson: he had handcrafted a specialized fly rod for the boy and worked with him for months on casting the rod over the grass in front of the USO building at Fort Belvoir where PHWFF holds its weekly meetings. Other volunteers had tutored Stetson in fly tying, and the program presented him with a specialized reel, a fly line, and a box of flies. All that remained was the fishing.

Standing in the Shenandoah, Gartner tied on a fly for Stetson while Christopherson gave him a few last-minute pointers. "Cast the same way we did in practice, Stetson," he said. "Just let that line fly go, but keep an eye on your pattern." Gartner stripped off some fly line from the reel, Christopherson and I arranged Stetson in the river, and as the young man finally made his long-awaited first cast into the Shenandoah, a beatific smile broke over his face.

Stetson's medical condition requires a modified casting stroke in which he places one hand on the base of the rod and the other above the reel, not unlike Spey casters do. After someone pulls out a little line for him, Stetson can use the surface tension of the river to catapult his line several yards downstream.

Back and forth Stetson's fly rod moved as he cast, first with only a few feet of line, and eventually with several yards. At one point he lost his balance and nearly fell over, which might have been fatal: He would of course have been entirely unable to right himself in the water. The uneven terrain nearly bested him a second time, but the stalwart Gartner and Christopherson were there to prevent him from going under.

"Okay, Stetson?" queried Gartner, the concern evident in the tone of his voice. "I'm just great—never been better!" Stetson called in reply as Christopherson stepped in to reposition him. Gartner and Christopherson continued to fuss over Stetson like mother geese over a gosling while Stetson continued to cast.

"I've got one!" Stetson cried before long. Sure enough, much to the surprise of the adults whose attention had been focused on his safety, Stetson's eyes hadn't wavered from his pattern. A wild cheer arose from the crowd ranged along the bank as Stetson brought to hand a lovely smallmouth. As far as those present were concerned, that little bass was worth many times its weight in gold. Stetson's months of training and dedication—and the commitment and expertise of all the volunteers who'd assisted him—had finally paid off. In the thrill of that first catch, Bob Gartner's face, shimmering with spent tears, was nearly as incandescent as Stetson's own. What a great day it was to be on the water—and even better, to be a PHWFF volunteer.

In 2019 Stetson Bardfield won a Gold Medal for marksmanship at the Pan American Games in Lima, Peru.

I don't doubt that Stetson will remember that day for the rest of his life. I suspect that the rest of us will too.

After participating with the Fort Belvoir Virginia program, Stetson Bardfield moved to Colorado, where he developed a keen interest in marksmanship.

NAME: JOHN PARAMORE
RANK: MASTER SERGEANT
BRANCH OF SERVICE: US ARMY
YEARS OF SERVICE: 25
HOME BASE: OZARK, ALABAMA

"When I realized that I couldn't feel anything below my waist," remembers John Paramore, "when I realized I couldn't move my legs, toes, feet— I think I experienced every emotion a human being is capable of."

Growing up in a farming community in Alabama, John Paramore—thrill seeker and snappy dresser—knew he wanted to do something different. And Army life seemed about as different from the life of a farmer as could be. Though he began his

John Paramore was told by one physician that he would never walk again. John made an amazing recovery and is seen here preparing to wade fish for trout at Harman's Cabins in West Virginia.

career as an artillery mechanic, then a combat engineer, Paramore served for twenty years as an explosive ordnance disposal technician in such far-flung theaters as Kuwait, Saudi Arabia, Iraq, and Bosnia and Herzegovina. Central to Paramore's job was locating and detonating or disabling lethal ordnances, so it's ironic that when he nearly lost his life on his way to work, his near-death experience took place a few miles from his home in Southern Virginia.

It was Paramore's custom to ride his motorcycle the thirty-four miles to Fort Lee in Petersburg. On a rainy June 15, 2009, Paramore discovered that the rain suit he'd worn over his clothes on his way in to work had a hole in it; his clothes had gotten soaked during the trip. He turned around and headed back home to change, but when he pulled into his neighborhood, "Suddenly a car pulled out from a side street directly in front of me. There was nothing I could do."

The accident is mostly a blur. What Paramore does remember with excruciating clarity is waking up in the hospital in indescribable pain—and being unable to move his legs. "The impact of the wreck was devastating: a burst fracture of my L1 vertebra, significant spinal cord damage, a hemopneumothorax, flail chest, approximately thirteen broken ribs, a broken collarbone . . ." The truth is that Paramore was lucky to have survived the accident at all.

In the blink of an eye, his entire life had turned upside down. "I was a Soldier doing pretty much whatever I wanted to do," says Paramore, "running a couple miles a day, riding my motorcycle, cycling. Until I wasn't. From Soldier to wounded warrior and disabled veteran. I was angry that the other driver had been so inattentive. Scared about how my life was going to change. Anxious about living life as a paraplegic. I felt helpless. I'd always been healthy, and now I faced the possibility of having to rely heavily on others. I hated asking for help. I wallowed in self-pity for a long time. I was depressed at a level that most folks can never understand."

Now the thrill-seeking Paramore was in for the assignment of his life. He spent 23 days in the Medical College of Virginia's Neuroscience Intensive Care Unit and another 107 days in rehabilitation at McGuire VA Medical Center, both in Richmond. Eight more weeks of outpatient therapy followed.

Long, slow, painful, awkward days of recovery turned into weeks and then months. And then a doctor stopped by to drop some devastating news. "He didn't sugarcoat it at all," recalls Paramore, "but looked me straight in the eye and told me that only about two percent of patients in my condition ever walked again."

Paramore continued outpatient rehab after leaving the hospital, "and it was during this time that Paulette Beasley," a recreational therapist at McGuire Hospital, "tried to get me involved in fly fishing and Project Healing Waters." Paramore was clear: he had no interest in either. Several months later, however, Paramore found himself standing in front of a flyer pitching Orvis's Fly Fishing 101 school. "The classes were free, so I thought, What the heck, why not try it out?" Paramore signed up on the spot.

He immediately connected with Duber Winters and Mike Hatfield, his "great and talented" Orvis instructors. "They really know their stuff, and they made me feel confident," says Paramore, who caught Winters and Hatfield's fly-fishing fever and decided to track down Paulette Beasley back at McGuire. Paramore told her of his newfound love for the quiet sport and asked if the fly-fishing program she had pitched to him was still active. Beasley connected Paramore with McGuire program lead Phil Johnson, and Paramore has been active ever since.

"Through PHWFF at McGuire, I found individuals like me. Struggling like me. Some had traumatic brain injuries. Some had other significant medical problems. But all of them were dealing with something." Paramore felt a sense of relief just attending the meetings. "We'd get together and learn how to tie a particular fly, and just talk. I found that time just flew, and I started tying flies at home. Much to my surprise, I found I could spend three or four hours at a time just tying flies. It is such a relief to not think about how much you hurt or what you might be dealing with.

"And then it dawned on me," continues Paramore, "that fly tying was like the render safe procedures I followed in the field with an explosive:

John is known for his quiet leadership and his excellent casting skills.

When you tie a fly you have to do things in a certain way, the same way, every time, to get the desired result. You have to focus on what you're doing at the moment. Your mind can't really wander. You have to maintain focus. And that's something I understood. And when you're done? You have a completed fly. You have a real sense of accomplishment."

Over the past few years, Paramore has worked to hone his fly-tying skills. And ironically, his limited range of motion has forced him to become an excellent flycaster. His roll cast in particular is a thing of beauty. The fly angler employs a roll cast—using the surface tension of the water to cast what looks like an unrolling fly line—when in tight cover, usually surrounded by a canopy of trees. Paramore can roll cast significant distances with great accuracy, as though he directs the line with nothing more than his mind, and his well-tied pattern simply goes along for the ride.

Project Healing Waters has changed Paramore's life—but that doesn't mean he's had an entirely smooth ride. "People sometimes assume that all the members are there as a result of combat injuries. They seem surprised that guys like me are involved.

"Don't assume anything about a veteran's injuries," says Paramore. "You see a guy missing a leg and assume he lost it in an explosion. You don't know. You deduce that the missing limb is his biggest struggle. You don't know. The truth is, lots of veterans suffer from things that have no connection to their combat military service. There are also lots of scars on the inside. There are scars that aren't obvious. Snap decisions about who people are or what they're facing are a mistake. We are all unique. In the end, we all have to come to grips with who we are. We're responsible for our own recovery and our own happiness."

John Paramore is an at-large member of Project Healing Waters while residing in Ozark, Alabama. He fishes often at various locations around the country and remains the best-dressed member at any event.

Ceamus McDermott serves in the Army National Guard and quickly returned to duty after his hand injury. Photo courtesy Ceamus McDermott.

Fly fishing was something Ceamus McDermott enjoyed as a boy but left behind when he moved on to college and eventually the National Guard. McDermott clearly loves being a warrior, and it seems to have filled every fiber of his being. He's the sort of guy who, when he hears that a brutal winter storm is approaching, rather than hunkering down next to a fire and waiting out the tempest, heads straight for the woods to camp out in the elements.

McDermott is comfortable in his own skin. And although he isn't the hulking GI Joe of popular imagination, it's difficult to imagine him as anything other than a Soldier. Wiry and reserved, what he lacks in stature he more than makes up for in steely self-confidence. In conversation his hazel eyes penetrate. In social situations he is neither anxious nor paranoid, but he's always on alert. McDermott knows that someone needs to be ready for any eventuality—and he is that someone.

Like so many Soldiers, McDermott's easy self-confidence makes him seem almost bulletproof. Though he's seen his share of combat, he speaks of it while stateside only when he comments that he'll soon be returning to "play in the sandbox." My sense is that McDermott, whose old call sign in the field was "Irish," has little tolerance for insincerity—and that he can spot bullshit a mile away. I also firmly believe that when McDermott leaves the sandbox, there are fewer schoolyard bullies standing than when he entered it.

Brushing aside what he refers to as his own minor injuries, he insists that servicemen and women return with much more significant and unseen injuries that haunt them for years. "When guys come back from fighting overseas," he says, "the first thing we have to do is make sure their noggin is right." McDermott gained this insight the hard way: his life was changed forever in Afghanistan.

Having just returned from a patrol in an insurgent area, "I was finishing unloading my gun truck," McDermott says. "While I was climbing out of the turret, I held an extracted .50-caliber round in my hand. I slipped getting off the truck, and I put my hand out to break my fall. Unfortunately, this caused the round to explode, which tore off most of my right index finger, broke my right thumb and middle finger, and gave me flash burns to my face. At first the pain was incredible, but as I came around my first thoughts were I couldn't believe I'd been injured in such an absurd way. I'd survived at least a half dozen very hot firefights and countless mortar attacks without a scratch, and then I had to get myself hurt at my own secure firebase falling off my own damn truck!"

McDermott was flown to Walter Reed Medical Center for physical therapy. When he came home to heal, he also came home to fly fishing. Former Soldier John Colburn had been teaching fly-tying classes at

Ceamus McDermott with his son prior to deployment. Photo courtesy Ceamus McDermott.

Walter Reed, and he spent many hours with McDermott, encouraging him to tie as often as possible. Fly tying helped McDermott to regain strength and mobility in his injured hand, although the poor circulation he suffered from his injury meant that his right index finger would eventually need to be amputated.

"My physical injuries were not as severe as many others who were recovering at Walter Reed," McDermott recalls, "and [the facility's] exceptional therapy and access to therapy modalities sped my recovery. In the end, building my fine motor skills and hand strength through something as enjoyable as fly fishing was a great aid in my healing."

Eventually McDermott made a full recovery and even returned to the battlefield. He enjoys fishing as much as he ever did and is also an avid marksman and hunter. He participated in a PHW trip at San Rafael Ranch, a beautiful South Texas homestead owned by the West family, who had heard of PHWFF through a friend and offered to host a hunt on their property for a group of veterans. McDermott was keen on taking one of the local bucks on the ranch and he did.

Despite his injuries, despite losing comrades in arms, despite the many deprivations of combat service, McDermott is humble and sanguine. "My injuries were not as severe as many others who were recovering along with me at Walter Reed. The hospital's great staff provided exceptional care. In the end, building my fine motor skills and hand strength through something as enjoyable as fly fishing was a great

Although Ceamus McDermott is an avid trout angler, he doesn't mind chasing bonefish either. Photo courtesy Ceamus McDermott.

aid in my recovery. There is no way I could have gotten on with my life as fast as I did without PHWFF.

"It might be hard to believe," he continues, "but the simple rhythm of casting a fly rod, whether to rising trout or to a Hula-Hoop on the front lawn of Walter Reed, was (and still is) my greatest stress reliever. For that moment in time, all that matters is that rhythm: the curve and loop of the line, the leader turning over, and the fly alighting onto the surface of the water. The human body will heal itself, especially with modern medical technology. Project Healing Waters helps heal the *spirit*. They help to heal the unseen wounds that linger long after the bandages have come off and the scars have faded."

Ceamus McDermott is an artist who enjoys sketching trout as often as he can. He enjoys sharing his love for the outdoors with his son. Ceamus remains an active duty member of the Army National Guard.

Walt Cary was meticulous in the construction of his beloved popping bugs.

The Popping-Bug King

In a humble rambler on a heavily treed street in a quiet residential neighborhood there lives a king. His house and its surroundings may seem ordinary, but that's only because the unassuming workshop out back is where the magic happens. The monarch in question, Walt Cary, is lord of all he surveys—in his workshop fiefdom, anyway.

Walt Cary is Virginia's undisputed popping-bug king.

Every year on my way to the Cape Lookout Albacore and Redfish Festival—Project Healing Waters Fly Fishing's first-ever saltwater fundraiser, held in October in Atlantic Beach, North Carolina—I swing by Walt Cary's house, off I-95, just north of the state line that runs between Virginia and North Carolina. I saw more of Cary when he lived closer to me, farther north in Front Royal; he moved to the southern part of the Old Dominion to be closer to his daughter, April.

This year, as I pull into Cary's driveway, he emerges beaming from the house before I even make it out of the car. "Hello, old man!" says Cary, nearly forty years my senior, throwing both hands above his head and waving them as if he were in a Pentecostal worship service. He hurries over and envelops me in a hug, still smiling from ear to ear. The king is wearing his standard regalia today: bright eyes, slightly stubbly chin, long-sleeved flannel shirt, and red suspenders. Classic Walt Cary.

In the kitchen we grab quick cups of coffee before angling toward his workshop.

The workshop is an olfactory assault: the smells of lacquer, glue, various solvents, paint, and God only knows what else initially take one's breath away. For Cary these are the smells that say home. Rank on rank of half-finished cork popper bodies line the tables of the workshop like toy soldiers, each one waiting for the master's final touch. Nearby are small bins full of thousands of unpainted cork bodies in various shapes and sizes, neatly arranged in a corresponding binary numbering system that Cary meticulously designed himself. Thousands of hooks—and an assortment of feathers that might put a fly shop to shame—round out the supplies.

Walt's poppers came in a variety of colors and styles and were sold nationwide.

Lining the workshop walls is a fishing life in memorabilia: Snapshots of a young Cary with stringers of smallmouth bass, each of which weighs in at three or four pounds. Pictures of friends who are no longer alive. Nearly a dozen state citations for smallmouth bass and other species. And holding a place of honor on one wall, a plaque acknowledging Walt Cary as the 2007 Virginia Fly Tyer of the Year.

On another wall at the far corner of the workshop is a framed copy of *Fly Tyer* magazine that features one of Walt's famed fire-tiger patterns on its cover. I wrote that article and consider myself fortunate indeed. Few people have secured an interview with Cary, much less gained access to this little workshop-kingdom of his.

Walter Oliver Cary was born in Strasburg, Virginia, to very humble beginnings. His father worked multiple jobs to keep the family fed; one of these consisted of cleaning local churches. Cary has fond memories of working alongside his father, sweeping, replacing hymnals in the backs of the pews, and polishing the brass fixtures. He remembers many, many crosses and stained glass windows that seemed to come alive in the full sun. It wasn't glamorous work, but it was honest—and the family needed the money.

Cary enlisted in the US Army at nineteen. At Fort Sill, Oklahoma, he received an education in artillery operations as well as specialized training—quite advanced at the time—for about six months. That training enabled him to work on the front lines in Korea between 1950 and 1951 as a forward observer, keeping a close eye on enemy positions and calling in artillery strikes to keep the enemy's progress in check. Essentially, Cary's training helped him mathematically reverse engineer the origin point of an enemy round and project how to fire back effectively. (The 2005 book *Fire for Effect! Artillery Forward Observers in Korea* by Anthony Sobieski accurately describes Cary's experience.)

"It's called the Korean War, but we spent most of our time fighting the Chinese," Cary remembers. "It was bitterly cold. We spent an awful lot of time underground; at times I felt like a wild animal living in a hole. We dug holes for everything: We dug slit trenches, we dug in for artillery pieces, we dug holes for damn near everything. If anyone stood still long enough, we were tempted to dig a hole around them, too."

Nearly seventy years later, Cary's combat experiences—seeing death up close in the kill-or-be-killed reality of the front lines—still haunt him. "More than once I should have died," he says, "and I honestly don't know why I didn't. Heck, one time I walked right through a booby trap." His foot had hit a trip wire, and when Cary turned back to learn what his buddies were yelling about, he saw that he was dragging a "potato masher"—a Chinese hand grenade—behind him. "So many close calls like that," Cary says, laughing, "and I lived. Guys thought I was good luck to be around. One guy said he wanted to stay in my back pocket until the war was over, because he was sure a guardian angel was looking over me. He was convinced the safest place on the front lines was directly beside me."

Not a particularly religious man, Cary was deeply moved by the visit of a priest: "He came to the front lines in a jeep and set up a little chapel right there. He prayed and took out a red cloth and put a big brass cross on the hood of the jeep. And all I could think about was being back in church with my daddy." Suddenly Cary was weak in the knees. "I almost started crying. It bothered me so much, I've hardly stepped back into a church to this day."

There are good memories, too. "A full-bird Colonel came to our base at the front lines with a box full of medals to congratulate me and the other guys for hitting a major weapons cache with one of our counter mortar rounds. 'Sir,' I said, 'you can keep your medals. Truth is, it was blind luck: I returned fire and hit the weapons dump. It's that simple.'" Initially taken aback, the Colonel quickly recovered, but not before

Cary pressed his advantage. "I don't want your medal, sir—I want to go home. I've been here way past my time of rotating out because my job is so specialized. I want to go home, sir. I just want to go home!" Learning that the successful strike had been a lucky accident, the Colonel withdrew his medals. Nevertheless, he'd had made an impression: Four days later a jeep showed up for him. Walt Cary was going home.

Being back in bucolic Strasburg was both a blessing and a curse. Cary had left the horror of the front lines, but the war continued to ravage him. He struggled to fit in among people who couldn't imagine the emotional scars he carried. He stayed out late most nights and often slept in until late morning, a schedule unheard of among his country neighbors. He was edgy at the best of times. "I got to drinking pretty bad because of what I'd seen and been forced to do," Cary says. "Eventually I didn't want to be too far from a drink, no matter where I was. Problem was that I couldn't really have liquor bottles at my parents' home. So I would buy liquor and then hide the bottles around town. See, when I was growing up, indoor plumbing consisted of large flush boxes. You'd pull a chain, and the water in the upper cabinet would rush down a pipe and flush the commode. So I'd sneak the liquor bottles in the flush boxes in restaurants all over the county." Cary grins. "This kept my liquor safe—and cold, too."

Cary had desperately hoped being home would make everything right—that he'd reclaim some peace of mind and return to the simple life he'd known before war. Instead he harbored a rage that smoldered inside, flaring into a conflagration at the slightest provocation. He lived with nightmares he couldn't discuss with anyone.

His luck changed rather suddenly. One day Cary was in the parking lot outside of the liquor store when he spotted a cute blonde in the passenger seat of a pickup truck. "I strolled right over to the window and asked her if she wanted to go to the local barn dance that evening," he says. The young woman, Gloria, agreed. "I showed up at her house later that evening, and I could hardly stand upright because I'd had so much to drink. She told me to wait outside while she got her coat. As soon as she got in my car, she asked if I would buy her a cup of coffee. I thought it was odd, of course, but when I got back to the car with the coffee, she said, 'Oh, the coffee is for you, not for me.' We sat there and talked for hours—and never did make it to the dance."

Walt Cary had found the love of his life. Gloria immediately made one thing clear: he could have the liquor, or he could have her—but he couldn't have both. Cary chose wisely, and the two were soon married. Gloria also came from tough country stock, and she quickly adjusted to the rigors of military life.

"I had gotten a letter," remembers Cary, "asking *had I gotten married*—I hadn't yet—and *had I started college* and *did I have any health irregularities*. I didn't like the sound of that at all, so I went back up to DC to find out what was going on." To Cary's dismay, he learned that his specialized skills were in high demand, and the Army intended to send him back to Korea. "My time on the front lines had earned me so many service points that I qualified for placement in the Army Reserve as soon as I returned stateside. Now they were going to send me back. Right there I asked the recruiter if there was any way out. 'Sure, you can get out of going back,' he said. 'You have to join another branch of the service.'"

Hell bent on avoiding Korea, Cary immediately enlisted in the US Navy, where he found his true calling. Cary's aptitude for breaking problems down into manageable pieces led the Navy to send him to the Royal Naval School of Work Study in Portsmouth, England, where he studied industrial engineering and graduated at the top of his class. His stint on the other side of the pond, Cary likes to joke, marked the only time in his life someone called him a Yankee.

Cary served in the US Navy for twenty-eight years and retired as the Command Master Chief of the USS *Forrestal*. Command Master Chief is the highest enlisted rank in the Navy; aboard ship Cary's only supervisor was the vessel's captain. At its construction, the USS *Forrestal* was the largest aircraft carrier ever built, with a crew complement of more than 5,500.

During the Cuban Missile Crisis Cary was ordered to report to the naval air station immediately; fewer than six hours later he had been transferred. "They refused to tell me where I was going," he says. "As a matter of fact, I was told to pack my winter and summer uniforms because they didn't even want me to know what part of the world I was being sent to. They wouldn't even let me contact my wife until I had been gone for three weeks." When pressed for details, Cary replies, "The Navy has not informed me that I am at liberty to discuss what I did for them. Until I hear otherwise, I have nothing else to say."

Walt Cary made the first of his now-famous poppers from the remains of discarded champagne bottle corks he came across while tending bar in a chief's club. Noting the waste of perfectly good material—and short on the funds he needed to support his growing family—Cary set about inventing what would become one of the best-known popping bugs in the country. His original poppers were carved with an X-Acto knife and colored battleship gray with leftover ship's paint. One of Cary's first customers was a young outdoor writer from Frederick, Maryland, named Lefty Kreh.

Some avid fans may treat their Walt's poppers like works of art, purchasing them to grace shadow boxes. Cary has always insisted, however, that his poppers, known as the everyday angler's go-to patterns for their high quality and classic good looks, "are not works of art. They're tools for the working man to catch fish." Today art meets real life at the Fly Fishing Museum of the Southern Appalachians, where one of Walt's poppers, returned to Cary by a grateful customer who claimed he caught over two hundred bluegill on the now-bedraggled fly, is enshrined in a display.

He began crafting his poppers in the winter of 1959; in all that time, Cary has never advertised. And yet, "It's been all I could do just to keep up with the orders." Over the years Cary has had to turn away retailers because "I won't rush; I won't make something just to sell it." It is precisely because of these exacting standards that shop owners and managers have learned to be content with whatever product they receive. Ironically, Cary's prickly disposition has actually contributed to his cult following: He doesn't allow just any store to carry his poppers. If he likes you, he'll send you what he can when he is darn good and ready. If he doesn't like you, you'll be shoveling snow in purgatory before your order shows up. And the size of an order makes no difference to Cary. Big or small, he's in it for people and relationships and perfect poppers—not the money or the numbers.

Back in Cary's workshop, I have apparently grown accustomed to the smell—which can't mean anything good for my brain cells. Instead I'm mesmerized as Cary ties popper after iconic popper. Some of these beauties will receive an amazing seven coats of paint before their debut, rendering them nearly bulletproof. After painting a bug and tying the tail, Cary runs rubber legs through with a needle. All of this magic happens on an unassuming old vise that acts almost as an extension of Cary's hand, and that I have a hard time believing was once upon a time brand-spanking new. This old workhorse has probably turned out fifty thousand poppers. At the height of his tying career, Cary would produce an astounding one thousand dozen poppers or more in a single season. He still makes a few for personal use, but Cary eventually signed a contract with Solitude Fly Company, which now makes them available commercially.

Walt Cary with a framed copy of *Fly Tyer* sporting his popper on the cover. Note the multiple citations for smallmouth bass in the background.

I ask Cary if he thinks tying flies has helped him. "I suppose so," he says eventually, "but I never gave it much thought." I ask what he thinks about organizations that reach out to service veterans—if he believes they might help those vets adjust better to civilian life than he did. "I don't know, Beau," he says, his hands in perpetual motion. "I really don't know. I mean, it sounds good. But you know, some of those guys and gals never even saw combat. I mean, there was nothing when I came back from overseas—absolutely nothing."

I consider this comment. "Well, Walt," I begin carefully, "I think every veteran deserves my respect, whether he or she saw combat or not. I think if you served, we should be grateful. We should try to meet your needs. I don't care how you got injured. I only care that you served when you were needed. Now these vets need *us*. *We* should be there for *them*."

Cary mulls this over at his vise, his deft hands still moving. "I never thought of it like that before, Beau," he says at last. "Perhaps you're right."

For the rest of the afternoon Cary regales me with stories of his adventures at sea: when he thought he might die; when he helped Sailors salvage their careers after they had made terrible mistakes; when he trained superior officers, which all good noncommissioned officers do from time to time; and when he was such a sought-after leadership school instructor that the Admirals would call his duty ship to ask for him. I've heard many of these stories before, but I don't mind. The more I hear the stories, the less likely I am to forget them when Walt is no longer around to tell them anymore.

That night we eat Cary's fresh catch: fried bass, cooked in enough grease and butter that it could swim in the pan. It tastes fantastic. We talk about politics, life, women, children, family responsibilities—and of course poppers and how to fish them.

The following morning we share breakfast and a pot of coffee. Sitting on the kitchen table next to my coffee cup is a small box of #6 poppers. I spot a classic Carolina blue popper, a black popper with yellow stripes that Cary calls the Bee, and my personal favorite: an olive-and-tan-bellied spotted popper that mimics a frog. "I thought you could use these later next year," Cary says as he hands me the box.

I finish my coffee and breakfast before heading back out to my car. I wave a last salute to Walt from the driver's seat, and he waves back. "Take care, old man," he calls out to me. "Come back as soon as you can!"

In recognition of his unique patterns, Walt Cary was inducted into the Fly Fishing Museum of the Southern Appalachians Hall of Fame. He and his beloved daughter, April, were fixtures at fly fishing events across the mid-Atlantic until his death in 2021.

Author's Note: Walt Cary passed not long after this book was in its final editing stage. He was my friend for many years, and I will never be able to look at a popping bug and not think of him and his amazing work.

George Draper suffered a severe back injury from a rappelling accident. Photo courtesy George Draper.

It was the tapping on the van window that finally woke him. Slowly opening his eyes, George Draper struggled to take in his surroundings only to realize he'd done it again. The window tapper was a familiar waitress from the local truck stop where he'd parked his van last night because he'd had too much to drink. "Hey, George, rise and shine," she said with a smile. "You don't want to be late for work now, do you?"

Draper smiled his thanks, rubbing the sleep from his eyes and experiencing the immediate onset of a throbbing headache. They frequently plagued him after a night of drinking. The only thing worse than the headaches was the searing pain in his lower back. "It's gonna be one of those days," Draper said to himself, pulling out of the parking lot and acknowledging that his entire existence had turned into "one of those days."

As the oldest of three boys, Draper had spent nearly his entire youth working alongside his father in the family masonry business, which meant long hours, few days off, and nearly backbreaking labor.

Summer vacations and lazy Sunday afternoons were for other families, not his. "I was taught two things as a youngster," Draper says. "Men are supposed to work hard, and men never complain about their situation. Ever. My father and I always worked with our hands—I mean, really physical stuff," he remembers. "It was hard work, but there really wasn't much of an option." Draper felt a profound sense of responsibility as the oldest son of the family, particularly because one of his younger brothers was deaf and the other suffered from severe educational challenges and seizures. And, both younger brothers were still in school. Like most families they had their ups and downs, but Draper loved them and desired to do all he could to be a help and not a burden.

Given his masonry background, it's no surprise that Draper enlisted as an Army combat engineer—a Soldier specializing in building, landing-zone, and even bridge construction in combat zones. The downside of combat engineering is, of course, that these construction projects don't take place in small-town America; instead, combat engineers build in places where hostilities may erupt at any moment.

Originally from Maine, Draper's Army career began in January 1977 at Fort Leonard Wood, Missouri. He also served at Fort Devens in Massachusetts (39th Engineers) then in Eschborn, Germany (317th Engineers) operating heavy equipment. Draper ran road races representing the Army and accomplished his first marathon in Frankfurt, Germany. Eventually he landed at Fort Campbell, Kentucky (20th Engineers) working in S-3 as Training Operations Sergeant. There he became involved in training other Soldiers. He had successfully completed Air Assault School training, which was just the sort of physically demanding activity that came naturally to him. He enrolled in Rappel Master Course, which would enable him to be a lead instructor of rappelling classes.

A completion requirement for the Rappel Master Course was a final rappel and then a sprint to the finish line in full gear. Well prepared for his final rappel, Draper was the last man out of the chopper. And that's when routine became harrowing.

"About halfway down in my descent," Draper says, "I got tangled up with the other ropes coming out of the chopper. The ropes somehow got wrapped around me as well as my gear. I had my backpack and weapon, and everything else, and I couldn't even look up. I was sort of trapped: I couldn't go down, and I most certainly couldn't go back up. At one point I remember one of the ropes getting around my neck, and I really thought I was going to pass out. I think they tried to lower the chopper some for me because they could see I was having serious trouble. I recall one of the people above me trying to holler down to me, 'You're okay now,' and I thought that meant I was close to the ground. So I let go. What I thought was going to be a short distance ended up being approximately thirty-five feet."

Draper landed flat on his back. His fellow Soldiers ran to him, no doubt fearing he was past saving. Instead of lying still and waiting for aid, Draper asked for their help in crossing the finish line. "I could see the end of the course, and there was no way in hell I was going to quit. Not after all I had done, not after all that training. I could literally see the finish line!" With the immeasurable help of his team members, Draper crossed the line under his own power and successfully completed the course.

After completing the Rappel Master Course, Draper immediately went to the infirmary. Inexplicably, the staff didn't order X-rays and instead handed him Tylenol and some other pain medications and told him to be on light duty for the next few days. In a great deal of pain from the fall, Draper remembered his father's mantra—"a man doesn't complain, no matter what"—and kept his suffering to himself. He feared what might happen to his career if he talked about the pain: "In those days, if you had anything wrong with you medically, they kicked you out of the Army. And I didn't want to leave." General pain led to knee problems and then to severe hip and neck pain. Though he remained stoic, Draper began to realize that he had been seriously injured in the fall.

Draper's career came full circle when he received orders to report to Drill Sergeant School at Fort Leonard Wood. "It was where I had started out in the Army. After graduating and being assigned my second training cycle, I filed for a divorce. I was left with very little money to live on but had to move the ex-wife and kids back to Maine." He visited his family in Maine while on leave for Christmas, hoping to impress his father. "He told me being a drill instructor was a desk job," remembers Draper, "and not really a hard assignment." Crestfallen, Draper tried to express the job's rigors to his father. "I told him how physically demanding the job was, and how I did everything with my recruits—and I mean everything. There wasn't one run, one challenge, or one obstacle course that I didn't run with my men." Unfortunately, his father remained unimpressed, and Draper returned to Fort Leonard Wood feeling dejected. Not long after returning to work, his captain informed him that his father had suffered a fatal heart attack. Deeply shaken, Draper was overwhelmed with regret that he and his father had not parted on the best of terms. All he had to cling to were the clothes that the paramedics had cut off his father's body as they worked to save him. He kept those clothes as a memento of the man he loved and admired so much. Although his father never admitted it to him, Draper later learned from others that his father often praised his accomplishments to his friends and co-workers.

After the sudden loss of his father, Draper resigned from the Army in 1984. He tried to sign with the local Army Reserve unit to stay active, but there were no openings for active duty, so he headed home again to Maine to provide for his mother and younger brothers. There he also served four more years with the Army Reserve Unit in Lewiston, Maine.

Draper had left the Army, but his service injuries hadn't left him: he experienced almost constant back pain. He experimented with chiropractic care and other modalities, but the pain continued unabated. After reading about Boston's Lahey Clinic, which specializes in injuries like his, he booked an appointment that he paid for out of his own pocket. "The doctors there told me I was badly injured and needed surgery. They told me my L2 through L5 vertebrae were a mess." Nevertheless, Draper put off surgery, opting instead to grin and bear it—and supplement his pain medication with alcohol.

By 1985 Draper was working full-time trying to keep the family business afloat. He excelled at some aspects of the job—like building fireplaces and completing other construction work—and struggled with other aspects—like the all-important paperwork. Particularly demoralizing were the employees he took the time to train and, upon receiving the benefit of his expertise, left the business to compete with him. Worst of all, his mother no longer wanted him in her home. "People began telling me they thought I had a drinking problem. Once my sister Terry told me, 'From now on, you can only have one drink a day.' That wasn't a problem: I simply filled up a two-liter bottle with whiskey and told her this was my one drink. She wasn't impressed."

In May 1985, "I woke up one morning and discovered I couldn't walk." Though he eventually made it out of bed, Draper was in constant pain, moving unbearably slowly, hunched over and shuffling like an old man, and clinging to his coffee cup with both hands to keep from dropping it. "I went to the VA and applied for help (seeing how it had only been fifteen months out of active duty) and was denied. They gave me a bottle of pills and sent me home. Thank God for my best friend, Ricky Brewer," says Draper. "He was like a second brother to me and moved in with me to help me with the financial strain. Had it not been for Ricky's support, I don't know what would have happened to me."

By his birthday on December 7, 1986, Draper's life had spun out of control. He was drinking at least a case of beer or an entire bottle of whiskey a day, and on really bad days he'd consume both. He'd begun doing drugs. Despite all this, he was in near-constant back pain. On his birthday, Draper put on his father's old clothes—the same clothes his father had been wearing when he died—and indulged in what he assumed would be his last binge of booze and drugs. And then the phone rang. On the other end of the line was his uncle, from Robinson, Maine, who had been a firefighter as well as a second father to Draper. "He and my aunt told me they loved me and they wanted me to meet them at a hotel in Bangor, Maine. They talked me into going to rehab. They told me they would be there for me if I wanted to get sober. That call made all the difference."

Draper entered rehab the next day—and began the process of turning his life around. Draper has stayed sober, eschewing alcohol and drugs, ever since that fateful December day—and that's no small feat when one considers that he's had numerous injury-related surgeries.

In 2005 Draper was sitting in his vehicle in traffic when it was struck from behind by a car doing nearly fifty miles per hour. As a result, he had to undergo a fifth back surgery, second neck surgery, and surgery on his left shoulder. Now Draper's financial situation became dire. He worked as often as he could, making hand carvings, furniture, and taking on odd jobs to make ends meet. Draper had gone through the VA's thirty-day rehabilitation treatment program and continued AA meetings with the sponsorship of Larry Marcotte. These helped him create a support system outside the VA. Though Draper was as reluctant as ever to ask for help, Maine vocational rehabilitation specialist Judy Danielson was convinced that he would qualify for some sort of disability from the Veterans Administration. Previously, in 2003, Draper had received a disability rating of 40 percent; when he was reevaluated

George caught this salmon on the fly in Alaska. Photo courtesy George Draper.

in 2005, he received a disability rating of 100 percent. "I can't begin to describe," he says, "what a blessing it was to have the Veterans Administration come through for me in the end."

"A Vietnam vet friend Louie, knowing how active I used to be and how depressed I was, encouraged me to take up fly tying. He loaned me a Joan Wulff video because I knew nothing about fly tying or fly fishing."

Recovering from his final surgery, Draper enrolled in a pain clinic class in which one of the self-relaxation techniques was to imagine himself fly fishing. Here he also learned about an adaptive sports class starting up at the Togus VA Medical Center called *Project Healing Waters*. In 2007 Draper was among the very first group of veterans who came to hear about the program from Navy Captain Ed Nicholson, PHW founder, and Eivind Forseth, a combat-injured Army Captain—and he was immediately smitten. "I'm not the kind of guy who can just sit around, and I wanted to learn how to tie flies." Draper's hands, trained on rough masonry, became so adroit with small hooks, delicate thread, and tiny flies that he won first place in a nationwide PHWFF-sponsored fly rod-building class.

In 2009 Draper found himself in the wilds of Alaska aboard the *Hot Ruddered Bum*, operated by PHWFF volunteer Garry Morfit, himself a Vietnam vet, who gives PHWFF members the opportunity to fish for multiple species of salmon, and even halibut, at no charge. Visiting veterans stay aboard Morfit's boat for up to seven days, fishing in various locations and setting traps for shrimp and Dungeness crab, which they then eat. "I spent nearly all my time topside," says Draper. "I almost never went belowdecks as I wanted to take in all the scenery that I could. It was so beautiful!" In fact, Draper left a lasting impression on Morfit: When he went belowdecks to use the head, the interior doorknob came off in his hand. Draper was stuck in the lavatory for more than half an hour while his fellow anglers fished and Morfit skippered the craft. When Draper was finally freed, everyone had a good laugh. He continued to work with Morfit and Healing Towers, serving on their board while helping design and construct their facilities.

"I can't begin to express what Project Healing Waters has done for me," says Draper with conviction. "I'm never satisfied to sit back and do nothing, and this organization has introduced me to people who really care about me and care about veterans as a whole. I feel like in some ways my life began when I was introduced to Project Healing Waters because I was nearly always alone. Now I've made lifelong friends here, and there's a place for me here. I have a real sense of belonging now. I honestly don't know what I'd have done without Project Healing Waters."

As positive and hardworking as ever, George Draper served thirteen years as a volunteer with PHWFF, teaching rod-building classes and serving as a regional coordinator to grow the New England program.

Kyle McAdams with a massive thirty-inch fish he caught on the Conejos River with his guide Ron Sedall from Taos Fly Shop. Photo courtesy Kyle McAdams.

The only thing Kyle McAdams might enjoy more than wading into and fly fishing a mountain trout stream is covering the twenty miles to the stream by mountain bike. Occasionally, however, he indulges in sedentary activities like the rest of us and plants himself in front of a screen for some mindless entertainment. While watching an old movie one evening he reflected on his grandfathers, both of whom were veterans: one served in World War II and one in Korea. Not long after, McAdams happened to catch an episode of *Fly Rod Chronicles* that highlighted veterans and their involvement with Project Healing Waters Fly Fishing. "I made an immediate connection," McAdams explains. "I thought, 'Hey, why can't we do that here in Texas to honor our veterans? There must be plenty of folks who'd be willing to get involved with a project like this.'"

McAdams contacted PHWFF and immediately faced an obstacle. He was told that he would need to align himself with a local fly-fishing club—but no such club existed locally. Undeterred, McAdams emailed several fly-fishing friends with his vision, and within days the Amarillo Fly Guys was born. As far as McAdams knows, AFG is the only fly-fishing club in the country that was founded for the sole purpose of collaborating with PHWFF. He became AFG's first club president as well as the program lead for PHWFF. The club grew quickly. Happily, the Local Veterans of Foreign Wars Post 1475 donated meeting space to AFG to accommodate fly-tying and rod-building classes.

"Once we got set up, we were fortunate to have the support of Mike Meinen and David Crabtree, who both worked at the Thomas E. Creek Veterans Hospital in Amarillo," says McAdams. "If these guys hadn't stuck their necks out for us, I'm not sure we could have gotten into the local VA system. Because of their help we currently have around fifteen active members and volunteers. But several more pay dues in order

Kyle McAdams holding a permit caught by his son Hayden while fishing in the Florida Keys. Photo courtesy Kyle McAdams.

to support our mission. Our dues are $50 annually, and one hundred percent goes to fund supplies for our tying classes and outings. By doing this we don't use much, if any, of our national budget from PHWFF, so that those funds can be used on other chapters who are trying to get established. Because of strong local support we've been able to take veterans on several local outings and onto private property where the fishing is excellent. We've also taken our veterans to out-of-state locations like the Enchanted Circle in Taos and Cow Creek Ranch in the Pecos Wilderness.

"On one particular trip to New Mexico," McAdams remembers, "we fished the Cimarron River. At the end of the day we managed to arrange a private evening tour of the David Westphall Veterans Foundation, the first national Vietnam veterans memorial in the country. Though all of our veterans were younger guys from Iraq and Afghanistan, they could really relate. After a while I could see they were hugging each other and some were crying. That's when I had my aha moment. That's when it hit me that veterans, regardless of their age or their time in service, are a real *brotherhood*. They share each other's pain because they've been there themselves, and they know the struggles that few if any of us who haven't served can ever understand."

As luck would have it, McAdams eventually met Curtis Fleming of *Fly Rod Chronicles* through his connection to PHWFF. The two fished together, filming an episode about PHWFF as a guest of Brazos River Ranch in northern New Mexico.

Kyle McAdams still works with members of AFG and believes that one should "never miss an opportunity to express your gratitude and use your God-given talents to help those around you."

Josh Williams is one of those people who can light up a room with a smile alone. His optimism is as infectious as his fly patterns are addictive. He's built a solid reputation as one of the most talented fly tyers in the mid-Atlantic—indeed, his Josh's White Lightning, Josh's Wiggle Hellgrammite, and Josh's Tactical Reaper Midge patterns work well for bass and trout anglers alike.

Josh Williams served as an automatic rifleman with the 1st Cavalry Division. This photo was taken in Sadr City, Iraq, on his twenty-first birthday. Photo courtesy Joshua Williams.

Coming home without any visible injuries after thirteen months in Iraq as an infantry machine gunner, Williams admits that he was already suffering from PTSD as well as significant hearing loss in his left ear. One day while riding his motorcycle to Fort Hood to take up his position on guard duty, a young driver ran a stop sign right in front of him, and Williams struck the car.

"I went straight through the driver's side window and then out the front windshield," recounts Williams. "I immediately lost my right arm above the elbow. I also shattered my right femur as well as my right ankle and broke three bones in my back." When he was eventually able to take stock of his injuries, he was devastated: "I remember thinking, What kind of career can I have now? What girl would ever want me? I could never hunt or fish again. I became severely depressed and began to wish that I hadn't survived the wreck."

Williams eventually met Ed Nicholson and John Bass while recovering from his injuries at Walter Reed Medical Center. Initially he wanted nothing to do with PHWFF—but he hit it off with both men and became especially fond of Bass. Through PHWFF, Williams received a Vivarelli reel, a specialty fly reel that one-handed anglers can easily use because it retracts line with the action of a single finger. "That reel gave me the courage to try fishing, and then eventually hunting again." Bitten by the fly-fishing bug, Williams took the next step: "I tried to tie my first fly on the line," no small matter with only one hand. "When I finally managed to tie my first fly on a tippet, it took forty minutes. Before that, I had to pack up and leave whenever I broke off or got flies tangled in the trees.

Josh Williams is quite passionate about fly tying and has several original patterns to his name. Photo courtesy Joshua Williams.

Tying on that first fly was huge for my morale. Tying that fly on the line eventually led to me tying my own shoes, and eventually tying my own flies."

Josh Williams with a hefty smallmouth bass he caught on Virginia's Maury River on a pattern he tied. Photo courtesy Joshua Williams.

Today Williams is happily married to his wife, Lisa, who he claims is his personal hero. They both enjoy watching their eleven-year-old daughter, Emma Jo, and nine-year-old son, Wyatt, scurry around his fly-tying bench. Fly tying has become such a part of Williams's life that both children often sit alongside him, tying flies in the evenings and at shows when he volunteers to teach youth. "I do more now than I did when I had two arms. All the things I did before, I just had to learn how to do differently. That's the biggest thing PHWFF taught me: how to think outside the box. The program took a broken, depressed guy and gave him a reason to live again when all hope was lost."

Williams helps fellow veterans through various channels whenever possible and fishes as much as his busy family life will allow. It's the peace that attracts him as much as the fishing. "There's nothing in the world like it. Going out there in God's backyard and tricking a living creature you have so much respect for into thinking you actually have real food on the end of your line. I love the reminder of what fly fishing did and still does for me. That's what it's all about."

Josh Williams fishes widely and graduated with a mechanical engineering degree from Old Dominion University in 2014. He and his family are usually in the woods fishing, hunting, hiking, or camping.

ROSE RIVER FARM

On a beautifully clear morning in late April, a motley crew of unlikely anglers and their grateful guides plied the waters of Virginia's Madison County. Serious angling was happening here at Rose River Farm. It was quiet now.

It certainly hadn't started out that way.

In fact, the morning's most apt descriptor might have been "loud." Earth-quakingly, bone-shakingly loud. The cheers of a hundred smiling bystanders—some with their index fingers stuck in their ears—had been drowned out by the roar of the motorcade. More than two dozen motorcyclists from the Virginia Patriot Guard, wearing jackets that proudly displayed patches of old military units, had queued up at the Best Western in nearby Culpeper to escort visiting dignitaries through the rural Virginia countryside on their way to Rose River Farm. They'd

Flags waving in the breeze greet veterans and guests attending the 2-Fly Tournament fundraiser. Photo by Douglas Dear.

delighted the crowd by periodically revving their engines as state troopers and deputy sheriffs stopped traffic to enable the unusual motorcade to get on and off State Route 29.

Bisecting farms and fields, the VIPs and their exuberant escorts had eventually passed through a flag-festooned fence to Rose River Farm, crossing a small bridge and turning down a gravel road that runs parallel to the river itself, passing a makeshift field-turned-parking-lot packed with cars bearing an inordinately large proportion of Purple Heart license plates. Coasting to a stop, the doors of the escorted white van opened and poured out about a dozen extraordinarily ordinary Americans with one thing in common—military service.

These veterans, in vests, waders, and battered ballcaps, had come together for their comrades in arms at Project Healing Waters Fly Fishing's original fundraising event, the annual 2-Fly Tournament. The brainchild of Rose River Farm proprietor Douglas Dear and Project Healing Waters founder Ed Nicholson, the 2-Fly paired angling veterans with veteran anglers—that is, armed services vets with professional fly-fishing guides and longtime fly anglers.

Douglas Dear, a strong supporter of Project Healing Waters from the very beginning, served as the nonprofit's first chairman of the board for a decade, dedicating untold hours to the as-yet little-known organization with an as-yet uncertain future. Dear and Ed Nicholson, both passionate fly anglers and upland bird hunters, developed a firm friendship and an equal determination to see the organization thrive in its mission. To meet the needs of the country's vets, they reasoned, Project Healing Waters required a unique fundraiser—-something beyond the expensive per-plate banquet that had the flair of the famed One Fly tournament in Wyoming, something that didn't tell—something that showed.

Enter the 2-Fly Tournament. What better way to raise money for a nonprofit that heals through fly fishing than an event that gets vets

Douglas Dear and Ed Nicholson have a passion for fly fishing and upland bird hunting. Photo courtesy Douglas Dear.

on the water? The inaugural 2-Fly paired vets from Walter Reed National Military Medical Center in Washington, DC, with professional guides. Each pair would fish as a team, ostensibly in friendly competition with every other angling team. Whereas the angling vets could use as many flies as they liked, the guides were limited to just two flies—and with that stipulation, an event moniker was born. As word of the 2-Fly spread, fly-fishing guides from as far away as Montana vied for a coveted spot on a team.

As the 2-Fly took off, corporate sponsors—venerable names such as Orvis and Hook & Hackle—came on board. Rick Pope, founder of Dallas-based rod manufacturer Temple Fork Outfitters and 2-Fly sponsor, often attended the event in person. During the 2-Fly, the banks of the Rose River became a veritable Who's Who of fly fishing. In any given year, spectators might spot leading anglers such as Lefty Kreh, Ed Jaworowski, Flip Pallot, Blane Chocklett, Walt Cary, Bob Clouser, or Joe Humphreys. *NBC News* anchor Tom Brokaw, *ABC News* special correspondent Bob Woodruff, and *Fox News's* Shannon Bream participated in the 2-Fly as guests of honor or masters of ceremony. Medal of Honor recipients spoke and even fished in the tournament.

Although the 2-Fly became a very popular venue with the support of many luminaries, it is well to remember that the real luminaries were the disabled veterans who participated and shared their stories with heartfelt testimonies and interaction with the assembled attendees.

And yet, says Dear, the success of the event could be chalked up not to the extraordinary but to the radically ordinary: "Yes, well-known participants helped with sponsorships and casting lessons and more. And we're so grateful. But make no mistake: It was the strong support of local volunteers and headquarters staff that made the event happen year after year. Without them there was no way to pull off something this special. Without them, there was no 2-Fly."

The fledgling daylong fundraiser eventually spread its wings. First, organizers added a pre-event day of casual fishing so that veterans could get to know and bond with their pro partners. Then a post-tournament dinner was added so that angling teams and interested stakeholders could nosh and mingle under a large tent that evening.

The 2-Fly became synonymous with Rose River Farm. Dear opened his home—which overlooks the river—to tournament guests, and he also put them up in the yurts he normally rents out to his fee-for-fishing clients. In addition to the Rose River's wily trout, numerous warmwater species inhabit the farm's large pond, the site of veterans' kayaking forays and impromptu panfish tournaments. Local children and other community groups also fish there. Two platforms alongside the Rose and three on the farm pond, field-tested by countless veterans, enable the wheelchair

Lefty Kreh, who was a regular guest at the 2-Fly, seen here with his good friend Tom Brokaw. Photo by Douglas Dear.

users to fish safely. Its warm welcome, its wily brown and rainbow trout, and its accessibility earned Rose River Farm its Project Healing Water Fly Fishing "home waters" status many years ago. Fewer people know, however, that Dear's idyllic farm has also served as a place for fundraising and fishing opportunities for other nonprofits, such as Casting for Recovery, Reel Recovery, the Mayfly Project, and the National Capital Chapter Trout Unlimited Tri-State Youth Camp.

On the banks of the Rose are two monuments, which those unfamiliar with Project Healing Waters Fly Fishing and the 2-Fly Tournament could easily overlook. One monument remembers board member and early supporter John Bass; the other memorializes early tournament participant Staff Sergeant Brian Mancini. The modest monuments, deliberately placed where Bass and Mancini loved to fish, are fitting tributes to two men who gave so much of themselves to Project Healing Waters, to the nation's veterans, and to their country.

"It's amazing," reflects Douglas Dear, "when I consider how many people have come through here and fished at this farm and had a chance to connect with the outdoors and other veterans. I think every fly angler knows how good fly fishing is for the soul. I can't ever walk along this river and not think of the lives we've helped to change."

Douglas Dear continues to be a strong supporter of Project Healing Waters Fly Fishing and continues to open his doors to local events. When not angling, he's likely to be found working one of his bird dogs with his close friend Ed Nicholson.

NAME: CHARLES TRAWICK
RANK: SERGEANT E-5
BRANCH OF SERVICE: US ARMY /
TENNESSEE NATIONAL GUARD
YEARS OF SERVICE: 13
HOME BASE: FAYETTEVILLE, TENNESSEE

Charlie Trawick comes from a large family with a strong tradition of military service. As one of twelve children, he thought it only proper to follow in his brothers' footsteps: Five of them went into the military; four served in Vietnam, and the oldest earned a Purple Heart. With his mother's approval, he joined the Army on a delayed entry program and, after initial training at Fort Benning, Georgia, was assigned to the 25th Infantry Division in Hawaii. He was only seventeen years old.

Charlie Trawick was just seventeen years old when he entered the Army and served with the 25th Infantry Division in Hawaii. Photo courtesy Charles Trawick.

Primarily Trawick worked as a forward observer with various Special Operations units, searching for and seizing intelligence from the front lines and reporting back with the least amount of contact with the enemy as possible. His training assignments varied from cold-weather operations with the New Zealand Special Forces to training with the Navy SEALS in Coronado Beach, California. He also trained alongside the Air Assault School teams in the rain forest of Wahiawa on the island of Oahu. In 1981, he found himself in the Philippines.

Charlie worked as a forward observer in the Army and participated in the invasion of Panama. Photo courtesy Charles Trawick.

"During jungle warfare training," says Trawick, "I was the point man for my team in the Philippines. I climbed up a tree to observe a forward position, and the branch I was standing on suddenly broke. I fell directly from the tree onto my feet and then went straight down, striking my tailbone and spine. The fall was so hard that I actually bounced when I made contact with the ground. I crushed parts of my spine, my shoulder, and my hips. When I received my initial medical assessment, they told me that I'd sprained my back and gave me handfuls of anti-inflammatories—better known as 'grunt candy.' I really didn't understand the consequences or repercussions of my injuries or how they would affect me for the rest of my life."

During Trawick's physical therapy in 1981, a doctor told him that he had a serious injury that would only worsen over time. "Son," Trawick recalls the doctor saying, "you'll have a monkey on your back for the rest of your life. You just don't realize that now." Says Trawick, "I really should've listened to him, but I was gung ho and had a 'bring it on' attitude."

Trawick left active duty in 1983, serving in the 251st Tennessee National Guard for the next five years. "I married my wonderful wife, Maggie, in July 1984 and then decided to go back into full-time service in 1988. I eventually went on to participate in the invasion of Panama in 1989 with the 5th Infantry Division."

In 1991, however, "I felt my back pop," Trawick recalls, reactivating his back injury when he tried to pick up some track pads for a Bradley Fighting Vehicle. "I was eventually released from the military with a minor medical evaluation and no psychiatric evaluation of any kind."

Trawick left the Army, went back to school, and became a mechanical design engineer—but he knew something was wrong. After the invasion of Panama, even his mother told him that he had changed. And yet it wasn't until 2012 that he was diagnosed with post-traumatic stress disorder and some of his symptoms began to make sense to him.

"In hindsight," says Trawick, "I realized I'd had issues even while I was on active duty—but I'd had more after I was released. I started looking back at some of the conflicts I'd had, and in particular my anger. At times I directed that hostility toward my family, my friends—God help me, even my own dear mother, God rest her soul. I became aware of just how severe this was, and I thought they'd all be better off without me. I stay at a regular base pain level of about eight, and when it reaches the level of ten ... it triggers my PTSD, anxiety, panic, anger, and sometimes rage."

Trawick was introduced to Project Healing Waters through the Veteran's Recovery Center (VRC) in 2010, and he credits them with beginning the long process of recovery. In fact, PHWFF became so important to Trawick that he

Charlie's family has a long history of military service. Photo courtesy Charles Trawick.

Captain Rob Fordyce, host of *The Seahunter*, holds a baby tarpon that Trawick landed while recording an episode about veterans and PHWFF. Photo courtesy Charles Trawick.

wrote a song about his experiences—titled "Healing Waters"—which was adopted by the organization as its official song. Trawick went on to represent PHWFF on a nationally televised fishing program called *The Seahunter* with Captain Rob Fordyce.

"I've gotten the professional help I needed to regulate my mood swings by working through these issues at the VRC. They've given me methods and a toolbox of options to help me deal with my illness. The support from VRC has been just overwhelming. The VRC and PHWFF have been literally like a second family to me—very supportive. The PHWFF events and camaraderie have made a world of difference to me. May God bless the United States of America, Project Healing Waters Fly Fishing, and everyone involved in ensuring that veterans have a better quality of life."

Charlie Trawick is still active with the VRC in Murfreesboro, Tennessee, and helped found the Southwest Florida program located in Cape Coral, Florida. He insists that if anyone deserves a medal, it's Maggie, his wife of thirty-five years.

NAME: BUBBA HOLT
PHWFF ROLE: DIRECTOR OF TRAINING AND STANDARDIZATION
YEARS OF SERVICE: 10
HOME BASE: PARKERSBURG, WEST VIRGINIA

Bubba Holt is a native West Virginian and has fished nearly every trout stream in the state.

Spend just one day in the presence of Bubba Holt, and you're sure to hear him say either "I'm the luckiest man in the world" or "My name is Bubba, and I'm from Odd, West Virginia"—and quite possibly both. In marked contrast to his bald head is his full beard, and he often wears his hat backward when fishing. Add his heavy country accent, and one may be forgiven for assuming that one has come face-to-face with a stereotypical good ol' boy. But if you've judged this book by its cover, it's time to read a little deeper: Bubba Holt's humble demeanor and self-deprecating humor hide the fact that he is less a hillbilly and more a Hill William—perhaps a more sophisticated redneck than he might appear to the casual observer.

Native West Virginian Brandon Calloway Holt—first called "Bubba" by a younger brother who couldn't pronounce Brandon—reads people nearly as well as he reads the water he fishes. He became the youngest certified ham radio operator in West Virginia at the tender age of twelve.

An avid reader, Holt won his state's highest academic award for state history. After attending Governor's Honors Academy, he rose to the top of his class at Pikeview High School.

"I really enjoyed school," says Holt, "and my parents always pushed me to excel scholastically. At Presidential Classroom, you learn all about how government works, and we even held our own elections. I ran for president on the platform 'Once you go Bubba, there is no other!' I broke my ankle right before Presidential Classroom, so I spent the entire time there hobbling around on crutches. To be honest," admits Holt with a laugh, "I think I won on a sympathy vote."

Holt went on to college, working toward an education degree with a minor in chemistry and physics. Because he has a photographic memory, Holt didn't bother to purchase a single textbook; instead he read the books at the college's library.

In 2010, program leads Marty Laksbergs and Bob Gartner asked Holt to guide participating veterans at their annual Harman's event; he was "honored to be asked and very moved by the experience." At Harman's, Holt met a veteran who wore a collared brace because he'd severely injured his neck. Despite his injury, however, the veteran was determined to catch a wild rainbow on a fly. "I remember the guy being highly motivated," says Holt, "and while it took some doing because of his mobility challenges, I was able to put him on a wild trout. I was pleased beyond all description when I saw the expression on the guy's face when he landed that fish."

By 2011 Holt had completed an applied sciences degree from West Virginia University at Parkersburg and landed his dream job as a chemical analyst at Constellium Rolled Products. He had met Sarah, the love of his life, and the couple had two small children, Brett and Emma. Life was perfect.

Late on the night of June 25, 2013, Holt drove his jeep on Interstate

77 near Parkersburg. "I was driving in the left lane a few vehicle lengths behind a state safety truck, which was traveling in the right lane. I'd planned on passing the truck when a deer ran from the median strip into the highway. I merged into the right lane, but when I did, the truck slammed on its brakes, and I had a fraction of a second to make a decision: I could hit the truck from behind or try to swerve around it and try passing." As Holt swerved to miss the truck, he approached a curve on the highway and T-boned the guardrail going nearly seventy-five miles per hour. "The jeep hit the guardrail so hard it went straight up what seemed like eight feet, and then back down. The jeep's roll bar kept me from being completely crushed, but it did land on its roof. Within seconds, I found myself hanging upside down from my seat belt and had difficulty breathing."

Consummate outdoorsman that he is, Holt had a pocketknife on him. He fished the knife from his pants and cut himself loose from the seat belt, kicking out the broken back windshield and exiting the vehicle. Miraculously, an ambulance was nearby and happened across Holt's wreck. "They were on the scene so fast, I could actually hear the call being dispatched over their radio while they were putting me on the stretcher. I wrecked around 11:30 p.m., but according to my hospital records I was there by 12:05 a.m. That's really something when you consider the hospital was nearly twenty-five miles from the site of the wreck. I'm thankful those folks didn't waste any time getting me where I needed to be."

At the hospital, things looked grim. Holt hadn't so much as a scratch on him—but his internal injuries were severe. X-rays indicated that Holt had broken his C4 and C6 vertebrae, and that his C5 vertebra was totally shattered. The doctors wanted to operate immediately but hoped to wait for the swelling in his neck to decrease. As Holt began to lose feeling and motor control from the neck down, however, the surgeons resolved to act. "When I woke from surgery, my right arm and hand seemed completely normal. I could also move my legs, but they felt like Jell-O." Unfortunately, says Holt, "my left arm and hand were dead."

Though he'd survived what should have been a lethal wreck, Holt descended from gratitude to depression. "I went from being a strong man who could provide for his family to a complete burden to everyone around me. You suddenly realize you can't do anything for yourself. You think your life is over and everything you have ever known is gone, including your independence. I can't begin to describe what it does to your sense of self-worth when you're a thirty-year-old man and your mom has to wipe your butt. It was very hard on Sarah and the rest of my family."

In the midst of this descent into depression, says Holt, "Marty and Bob and others from PHWFF called me every single day I was in critical care. They checked on me—and not just me but Sarah and the kids, too. They were really there for me, and I was blown away by the outpouring of support. I should have been peripheral to them; I wasn't in their programs, and I only saw them a few times. And yet they went all out to support me and Sarah. I will never forget that."

Though he did recover the use of his left arm, it doesn't function correctly. "I have no feeling in my pinky finger or my ring finger on that hand, and I have almost no feeling on the underside of that arm." Pointing to a circular scar on his left arm, Holt recalls, "I was at my cousin's place in Colorado, and she had one of those glass flat-top electric stoves. The burner had recently been turned off, but I didn't know it. I came into the room and nonchalantly leaned on the stove while I was having a discussion. Someone said, 'What's cooking?' Much to my surprise, it was me! I'd scorched myself badly, and I never felt a thing."

Holt takes nearly a dozen medications because he also suffers from chronic pain as a result of nerve damage. Throughout each day he'll feel a tingling sensation across his entire body and experience what he likens to the shock he received licking a battery as a child, "except it's like licking a car battery," he adds dryly. He has headaches, dizziness, occasional lack of bladder and bowel control, and difficulty breathing as a result of nerve damage to his diaphragm. On bad days he has to lie down frequently, which is a challenge for someone as active as he is. He also endures vivid nightmares stemming from the horrific accident. "I was in a pretty bad place," says Holt, "but then I thought about that Soldier and his determination. I thought, if he can do it, maybe I can do it too."

Spurred by gratitude for the support he'd received from Laksbergs and Gartner, Holt helped start the PHWFF program in Parkersburg; he and his good friend Nathan Leasure, the assistant program lead, have created a vibrant and active program. "I never served in the military myself, so I want to do all I can to give back to these men and women who have given so much." Holt has been wildly successful in his outreach efforts, hosting dozens of angler trips and volunteering hundreds of hours each year.

In addition to this vocation, he routinely hosts groups of veterans at both the Holt family cabin (near the Greenbrier River) and the mountain camp (near the Greenbrier's headwaters). He also hosts or helps plan a few fishing tournaments throughout the year that raise money for PHWFF.

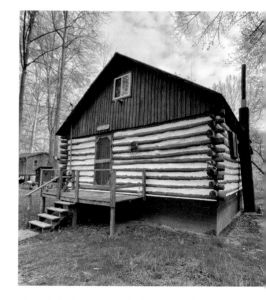

The Holt family cabin is located on the banks of the Greenbrier River and is visited by dozens of visiting anglers each year.

Bubba has taken hundreds of veterans fishing; it's his favorite pastime. Photo courtesy Bubba Holt.

Holt heads the annual Thornwood event in Pocahontas County; drawing as many as seventy participants and nearly as many volunteers, it's wildly popular with veterans and support staff alike.

Whether fishing, guiding, or organizing a veterans' program, Bubba Holt takes every opportunity to express gratitude for the simple things. "I can hug my wife, see my kids grow up, and share my passion for the outdoors with people I admire." In spite of his harrowing accident and chronic pain, he firmly believes that "I'm the luckiest man in the world."

Bubba Holt previously served as the regional coordinator for Project Healing Waters Fly Fishing in West Virginia before being promoted to director of Training and Standardization. His wife, Sarah, works as the development director at PHWFF National Headquarters. Their children volunteer at events wherever and whenever they can.

Don Lee's introduction to PHWFF came through a friend who was already involved in the program. That introduction, coupled with seeing a poster about fishing at the VA hospital in Long Beach, California, piqued his interest. He'd done a great deal of saltwater fishing as a youngster but hadn't been exposed to the fly-fishing world at all until finding the Long Beach program.

Don Lee's rod-wrapping skills are noteworthy. With rod in hand, here he displays his loom for thread weaving. Photo courtesy Don Lee.

Don, who is very quiet and prefers to be seen and not heard, graciously relayed to me some of the issues he's grappled with over the years. As a Vietnam veteran he knows firsthand what service members, and in particular Marines, have to deal with once they come home from combat. "I like being around other veterans, particularly combat veterans because I just can't talk and relate to other people as well." He credits PHWFF with helping him break out of his shell, get out of his house, and venture into the community more.

Don is honest about the fact that he still struggles, even with the help of PHWFF. "The truth is, after forty-two years I still have flashbacks

Like many veterans, Don learned to enjoy rod building and found it peaceful. Hours at the bench with rod jig and loom produce amazing results. Photo courtesy Don Lee.

Here's Don's take on the Marine Corps' nickname Devil Dog. Photo courtesy Don Lee.

from time to time, especially at night. There are still times I can see the scenes so clearly that I feel like I am still there, even to the point of being able to smell the same smells. There isn't a day that goes by that I don't think about what happened over there, and I still struggle with anger issues." These flashbacks often generate a great deal of emotion and are understandably hard to process.

One aspect of PHWW that resounded well with Don was rod building. Despite suffering from myopathy in his hands, he's become an avid rod builder. In fact, he's become so accomplished, he won first place in his area's rod-building program last year. As the first-place winner he received a fishing trip to Costa Rica. "Winning that trip was one of the best days of my life," he says. The trip was memorable to say the least, and Don really

Don fishing in Alaska, proving he knows how to use a fly rod as well as build one. Photo courtesy Don Lee.

whacked the fish. In total he landed multiple species, including tuna, barracuda, red snapper, and a sailfish estimated to be over seven feet long and weighing in at over 170 pounds.

Since his introduction to PHWFF Don has gone on to build several more rods in various weights and sizes, and his love of this undertaking continues to grow. Beyond the obvious benefits of creating his own rods to fish with, Don sees it more as therapy than anything else. "Rod building has really helped me, especially with my self-esteem, and even family can tell a change in my behavior since I got into rod building. My advice to other veterans is, you really need to try this program out. PHWFF really helps me keep my mind straight. When I'm concentrating on wrapping a rod or tying a fly, I'm focusing on that and nothing else."

Don Lee continues to support and be active in his local PHWFF program. He fishes as often as he can.

Carole and Jeff Katz taking a breather from fishing California's Owens River. Photo courtesy Carole Katz.

"We have to do this," murmured Carole Katz, clutching a copy of *Flyfisher*, the flagship publication of Fly Fishers International. "We simply have to do this."

Katz, who at the time served as president of the Long Beach Casting Club in Long Beach, California, read with growing excitement about retired Navy Captain Ed Nicholson and a fledgling program at Walter Reed Army Hospital to introduce wounded veterans to fly fishing and fly tying. "I knew right away," remembers Katz, "that this was a perfect fit for LBCC. We could make a real difference."

The venerable Long Beach Casting Club has a surprising and impressive pedigree. Chicago native and world-champion distance caster David Linder moved to Long Beach in 1923, often practicing his casts in the public park to the delight of curious onlookers. Just two years later the Long Beach Casting Club was born. Today the group's clubhouse features a casting pond and large classrooms suitable for fly tying, rod building, and other activities.

A certified nurse anesthetist married to an anesthesiologist, Katz began her career in anesthesia in 1969 and worked for nineteen years before leaving the field to stay home with her children. "When I went to nursing school at the Harrisburg Hospital School of Nursing in Pennsylvania," she says, "I opted to become a nurse anesthetist because of the challenge. You have to know a little bit about everything, from cardiology to obstetrics." To the suggestion that she was a pioneer as a female nurse anesthetist in a period before nurse practitioners and even physician assistants, Katz demurs and jokingly refers to herself as a former "gas passer."

Katz discussed the new fly-fishing project with her husband, who embraced it as quickly as she did. For the Katz family, veteran outreach was no academic exercise: Jeff Katz's father Charlie, a veteran of the war in the Pacific, had been taken prisoner by the Japanese on the Philippine island of Luzon. Countless prisoners of war died from dehydration, starvation, torture, merciless beatings for the smallest perceived infractions, inadequate or nonexistent medical care for diseases like malaria, or simply for the amusement of the prison guards.

By 1945, their resources spread thin, Japanese officials determined that it was too expensive to maintain the prison camps. Instead, they transferred prisoners to local caves, packed them in tightly, poured gasoline at the cave entrances, and set entire caves ablaze.

The elder Katz and his fellow prisoners escaped this horrific ordeal when they were liberated in a daring nighttime raid by Army Rangers and Filipino guerrillas operating behind enemy lines. The 2005 movie *The Great Raid* recounts the operation, which saved five hundred American lives.

"Jeff's father had been a physician in the Army," says Katz, "and he really struggled when he returned. He'd witnessed the terrible things human beings can do to each other. He thought he should have been

Carole with a whopping 7.5-pound rainbow caught on the Tasman River in New Zealand. Photo courtesy Carole Katz.

able to save more of his comrades' lives. This weighed on him heavily. I really don't think he ever totally got over it." Jeff Katz, aware of the high cost of military service that families have to pay, was as eager as Carole was to be a part of Project Healing Waters. He only wished something similar had been available to his father.

Carole Katz had assumed that starting a program would be a breeze: She knew Dr. Bill McMaster, chief of orthopedic surgery at the VA and an avid fly-fisherman, and assumed he could open doors for the program. LBCC, with its experienced instructors, was just half a mile from the VA. And the program wouldn't cost the VA or its veterans a dime. Piece of cake.

But penetrating the VA bureaucracy was much more difficult than Katz had anticipated, largely because at that time no one in the system had yet heard of PHWFF; Katz was asking them to take a chance on something new and different. The director of VA Voluntary Services, Rex Jennings, was interested because he'd always wanted to learn to fly fish and could envision it being beneficial. Eventually Jennings introduced

Katz to Joe Gonzalez, recreational therapist of the Day Treatment Center, who, to her good fortune, was also a fly-fisher. Finally, Katz had gotten the long-awaited green light.

Both were willing to walk out on a limb with Katz, inviting her to work with some of their patients with challenging mental health issues. They soon found the patients responded well to Katz and her cadre of volunteers. Focusing on and engaging the fine motor skills required to tie a fly brought participants a sense of peace. Beyond this, Katz watched as tentative friendships developed between volunteers and participants. During one local day of fishing, a patient who rarely talked caught a lot of fish. For weeks afterward he couldn't stop smiling and telling everyone about his experience. The VA's chief of psychiatry said, "Carole, I don't know what you gave him, but I want three hundred doses for my other patients!"

Project Healing Waters was essentially unknown when Katz began to put her program together. "We were the first PHWFF program on the West Coast," she says. "The only other VA in the entire country partnering with PHWFF was the Togus VA in Maine, and that was run by a recreational therapist." Standardized guidelines and policies were few and far between, so Katz learned everything the hard way: through trial and error. She made progress, but at a glacial pace.

By 2008, after a year with the Day Treatment Center patients, the program Katz and her faithful volunteers had built was officially on the map. Word of mouth brought new veterans almost every week, and therapists at the VA began referring patients to them as well. "Our welcoming volunteers attracted veterans and kept them engaged," Katz insists. "It didn't hurt that in the beginning I could communicate with the hospital staff in medicalese." Still, she says again, "Ultimately we succeeded because of the hard work of volunteers and veterans." Katz is especially grateful for the leadership and assistance of veterans like

Andy Anderson, Jesse Garza, Mike Escarcida, and Don Lee, all of whom served in Vietnam.

In the early days, Anderson recruited other patients from the Spinal Cord Injury Unit and later from the lapidary workshop. It was Anderson who pushed—vehemently pushed—for Katz to start a rod-building class that led to the creation of the national rod-building program and contest. "These vets were comfortable sharing how their service affected them both physically and mentally," says Katz, "and that made all the difference. They really care about their fellow veterans. Their willingness to be vulnerable and authentic is palpable."

More than 250 veterans have participated in the Long Beach program and Katz argues that their true success can be measured by those participants who've become leaders. One such returning participant is Iraq War veteran Lisa Ornelas, currently the assistant program lead, who credits older veterans like Garza, Escarcida, and Lee with helping her learn to live with herself and her war experiences and to acclimate to a group setting. "To be honest," says Ornelas, "when I first got here I thought perhaps because I was female—and quite young, compared to some of the Vietnam vets—they might treat me differently. I thought they might even look down on me a bit. The exact opposite was true: These guys couldn't have been any better to me. They've grown as close to me as family members now, and I can't imagine my life without them. You simply won't find a better group of folks to be around, who know how you feel and accept you where you are. They don't even have to say anything; they seem content to just be with you and be available. They've had a huge impact in my life, and I will forever be grateful to them."

In 2015, Carole Katz lost Jeff, her husband of forty-two years, to cancer. The program she launched to help others rallied around her. "There were times when I was just in a really bad place emotionally,"

Katz remembers, "and I was glad I had the program to focus on. The folks I've met during my time with PHWFF have meant the world to me. I got into this to give back to the local veterans, but I've gotten back so much more in return." Her eyes welling with tears, Katz says, "It's not easy to put into words," before pausing to regain her composure.

"It's so humbling when a veteran tells you what a difference the program has made," Katz continues. "I remember a vet asked me, 'Do you have any idea what you're doing here?' I braced for the worst, but instead he said, 'You guys saved my marriage and most likely my life. Before PHWFF my life consisted of clicking a TV remote and counting the moments until I could take my next pain pill. Now I have a reason to get out of bed because I look forward to coming to class and being with you guys. I've gone from wanting to kill myself to wanting to be a part of what you're doing here. I can't thank you enough.'

"I can't blame the Long Beach VA too much for doubting me or our program initially," Katz reflects. "Lots of people want to help veterans but just don't understand the challenges they're going to face in doing so." The key to a successful program, says Katz, is consistency and perseverance: "You have to convey that you're in it for the veterans—that you're not a 'one-trip wonder.' We're in it for the long haul. We show up every week and spend hours with these guys and gals. We really focus on the tiny steps. They might not look like much at the time, but those tiny steps build trust. They allow us to just *be there* for vets. If you take enough tiny steps—if you do that long enough—you'll be shocked at what you see."

Carole Katz previously served as both the program lead for PHWFF at the Long Beach VA and the Southwest regional coordinator. She continues to serve those in the veteran community whenever she can.

NAME: JONATHAN MOZINGO
RANK: STAFF SERGEANT E-6
BRANCH OF SERVICE: US MARINE CORPS
YEARS OF SERVICE: 12
HOME BASE: WEATHERFORD, TEXAS

Jonathan Mozingo at an outing with Pete Robertson, a longtime volunteer at the PHWFF Quantico program. Photo courtesy Jonathan Mozingo.

Jon Mozingo was done dreaming about military service; he was ready to live it. He wanted to be an integral part of an elite fighting force, the very best on earth: the United States Marine Corps. Only seventeen, Mozingo required his parents' permission to enlist. They gave it on the condition that he not go into the infantry. Mozingo agreed and worked toward being assigned to an aviation support unit until he turned eighteen, at which time he changed to infantry.

In 2007 Mozingo was patrolling hostile areas inside Iraq. "Looking back I understand just how immature I was—how little I really knew about life. One day on patrol I was talking smack back and forth with a fellow Marine. I said some really unkind and foul things to him, and less than a minute later he stepped on a landmine and lost both his legs. We began to take heavy fire from the enemy, and our Sergeant ordered us to fall back into a nearby house. It was over within minutes, but it was enough: That Marine didn't make it. And now I have to live with not ever being able to take back those words I wished I'd never uttered."

Like most combat veterans, Mozingo is reluctant to speak of his service; when pressed he'll admit to two combat tours in Iraq and one in Afghanistan. Most of what they did, he says, was try to win the hearts and minds of the locals, giving out water and stabilizing the community. At the time, he didn't fully understand how important that outreach really was. And although he now sees the value in the humanitarian aid he offered, Mozingo's deployments certainly weren't peacekeeping missions.

"I remember a pretty heated firefight that lasted just over six hours. We really couldn't move without being exposed. I called in an airstrike but was told to maneuver to a better position and continue fighting because they wanted to avoid collateral damage from an air assault or artillery. I directed one of my fire teams to move to a new position to flank the enemy, and they obeyed immediately. As a result of my orders," Mozingo says quietly, "one of my Marines took a round directly to the head. He died instantly. After he was killed they agreed to the airstrike—but by then it was too late. To this day I regret not arguing more with my command to send in that airstrike."

On April 1, 2010, Mozingo's platoon was on patrol in Afghanistan when he stepped on a landmine that blew off most of his lower left leg. "Two other guys nearby also stepped on mines. A firefight quickly ensued, and all I could think of was trying to keep my men safe. Honestly, I didn't realize how badly I was hurt until someone took my radio from me to prevent me from issuing any more orders." His men pulled Mozingo to safety, "dragging what was left of my left foot behind me."

Mozingo recovered amazingly well from his injuries, returning to active duty in record time and serving an additional seven years. He could no longer be deployed to combat zones, of course, which weighed

Jonathan saw multiple combat tours and was severely injured in Afghanistan. While he loved the Marine Corps, he believes they can do a far better job preparing Marines for life after leaving the service. Photo courtesy Jonathan Mozingo.

heavily on him. "I've got seven dog tags tattooed on my arm to help me remember fellow Marines I lost in combat," Mozingo says, "and this doesn't even count the ones who came home and then killed themselves. Make no mistake: those suicides were combat losses, too."

When he finally left the Marine Corps, Mozingo felt unmoored. The Corps, he believes, lacks vision for Marines who leave the service. "They do little to nothing to prepare you for life outside. Sure, you get a transition course for two weeks. But what is that compared to planning the rest of your life?" He had always defined himself as a warrior and a Marine; now, after separating because of his injury, Mozingo was neither. "Like so many others, I faced an identity crisis and decided drinking was the only way to deal with it. Eventually I had a choice to make: I could either have a great wife and a family who loved me, or I could keep drinking. I couldn't have both."

Mozingo knows only too well that the transition to civilian life can be a harrowing search for purpose. "What we need," he argues, "is to be grounded in something larger than ourselves. For me, that grounding is Jesus Christ, and I owe any recovery I have to Him and to my wife, Kelly." PHWFF has also played a pivotal role in helping Mozingo connect with other veterans and find a healthy outlet: fly fishing. "As far as I'm concerned," he says, "Bob Gartner's and Marty Laksbergs's programs are the gold standard. They're textbook examples of selfless leadership. They know how a program should be run. They took an interest in me as a person, and they enabled me to develop deep personal relationships with them. This made all the difference in the world."

In the final analysis, says Mozingo, veterans have a choice: live forever in yesterday or live in tomorrow. "I think Jesus made things clear: We're called to love Him with our whole hearts, and to love others as ourselves. I think if more people followed this principle, we'd be a lot farther along in healing one another and the country."

Jonathan Mozingo develops leadership courses for men across the country. Topics include what it means to be a man, what the characteristics of a good leader are, and how to understand yourself better through your experiences in the outdoors.

COMING HOME
TO HARMAN'S

Scattered along the South Branch of the Potomac River in aptly named Cabins, West Virginia, are twenty-one cozy dwellings owned by the Harman family since 1939. The river that runs right in front of the cabins is stocked regularly with large rainbow, brown, and brook trout, many of which look more like steelhead, weighing in at twenty inches long and upwards of six pounds. The Harman family's vision—to provide a place

The only thing that rivals the excellent trout fishing at Harman's Cabins is the outstanding scenery. Veterans from every branch of service visit here each year. Many will land their first trout on a fly rod along this river's bank.

for families to get away from it all together—has proven wildly popular; in fact, it's difficult to secure a reservation in the summer. Many families return to Harman's, booking the same cabins their grandparents rented when they first came as little children. Each cabin has a washer and dryer and outside grill (some include fireplaces and hot tubs), and what the property blessedly lacks in cell reception it more than makes up for in picnicking, fishing, hiking, horseback riding, and rock-climbing opportunities. This picturesque spot has even become a popular wedding venue.

Bob Gartner, the program lead for Project Healing Waters at Fort Belvoir, usually stays in the background. However, during the first week of December at the annual Project Healing Waters gathering here at Harman's, Gartner is front and center. He and Marty Laksbergs, the former program lead at Quantico, collaborate for months to prepare for the Harman's trip, sharing gear and working tirelessly for their vets.

Gartner, who worked for the National Park Service and then with the Bureau of Indian Affairs for thirty years, has an eye for logistics and planning. He's also a bit of an expert, having authored a number of books, including one on fishing in the national parks. Gartner couldn't believe his good fortune when in 2011, while fishing in West Virginia, he stumbled upon Harman's and its excellent fishing, comfortable lodging, and proximity to DC. "As soon as I got home," he remembers, "I called Marty and told him about it. That first year was tough, with nine veterans and eight volunteers. In one of the cabins, I did all the cooking with the help of Dr. Mike Cherwek, a retired cardiologist and founding member of the Fort Belvoir program. It's a good thing our faithful volunteer Jim Ottevaere did lunches, or Mike and I would have been cooking and cleaning nonstop for three days."

The Harman's weekend is a homecoming for many. "We've had guys return from as far away as Guatemala," says Gartner. "They want to relive their experiences here and reconnect." Today the annual event hosts as many as forty-five veterans and a comparable number of support staff. What began in a single cabin now takes the entire Harman's property.

The only job the nearly one hundred veterans and volunteers are responsible for is arriving at Harman's on time. Gartner and crew manage everything else, from meals and lodging to guiding, flies, and gear. Between the singular generosity of the Harman family and a grant from an anonymous foundation, no veteran or volunteer has ever paid anything to participate.

In 2015 Laksbergs decided to show his appreciation for the support the program has received by asking vets and volunteers to bring canned and dried food with them for the Interfaith Pantry in nearby Petersburg, West Virginia. To date the pantry has received more than five tons of donated food from grateful attendees. When a global pandemic canceled the 2020 Harman's trip, Laksbergs and Gartner gathered donated food and delivered it to the Interfaith Pantry anyway. The spirit of the event lived on even if the actual trip had to be put on hold.

After arriving on Friday and dropping off their food, veterans check in at Cabin 13. The road alongside the cabin is usually lined with small flags from each branch of the service, signifying that all are welcome. Vets are checked in and assigned a cabin. As a general rule, only veterans get beds; all others sleep on couches, on mobile cots, or in sleeping bags. Gartner sets up his weekend headquarters in Cabin 14, where he calls dibs on the couch.

The entire group assembles at dinnertime on Friday in a local church hall—large, clean, and complete with commercial kitchen—for introductions and an orientation. Laksbergs employs his "Marine voice" for the safety pitch, reminding participants that they should never fish alone because falling is a real hazard along much of the river.

Slippery rocks and swift, ice-cold water can be deadly for veterans with limited mobility, and the sound of the river will drown out many a cry for help. Bright orange whistles are issued to all along with this instruction: if you hear a whistle, drop whatever you're doing and investigate.

Gartner and Laksbergs have carefully selected the guides who participate in the event. Of course they're all great anglers who cast well, tie knots, and read fish behavior. But these guides also have to be able to read *people*, quickly determining the

Flags acknowledging their branches of the military welcome veterans.

best approach for a particular veteran. Some vets have balance issues or short-term memory problems, whereas others may become easily fatigued or even overheated. One veteran may want to fish from sunup to sundown; another is going to require a break after about forty-five minutes of fishing; yet another might opt for an afternoon off on the banks of the river to soak up the serenity.

Despite these challenges, Laksbergs and Gartner preside over a waiting list full of guides. What's their secret? In fact many of the guide staff were at Harman's not so long ago—as veterans. Where once there was a timid and self-conscious veteran who carefully watched every step, there is now a self-confident, determined guide eager to help a fellow vet along his or her own path to healing. The student has become the teacher.

Volunteers Bob Gartner and Marty Laksbergs check in the participants at Harman's Cabins.

After breakfast on Saturday morning, dozens of guides and veterans line up next to Cabin 14 for a group photo. Some are still a bit bleary-eyed, having stayed up late tying flies and reminiscing with old friends until the wee hours. All are eager to get on the water, and most of the guides meet informally to decide who is headed where. The vets with significant mobility issues are given prime spots, including areas with little to no grade that feature big pools of eager fish. Guides will take less experienced anglers to spots with little streamside brush to minimize back-casting snags. Novices may need extra help rigging up—or even casting lessons, in which case they've been paired with an excellent casting instructor like longtime volunteer Duber Winters, who guided professionally for years in Florida and elsewhere.

By lunchtime on Saturday the camaraderie is palpable, and a bystander could be forgiven for assuming that the vets and their guides have known each other for years. Marines are now comfortable enough to tell Army what they *really* think: that, let's be honest, they simply weren't tough enough to be Marines, as all reasonable Soldiers desire to be. At which point Navy remind Marine Corps that they're tolerated on board only because they perform essential custodial services. Air Force quip that all of them would've washed out of that branch, which after all requires its service members to be literate. Pranks and gallows humor proliferate. Prosthetics are brandished as weapons. And fish tales abound as cell phones are passed fervently—not to check texts and social media but as picture proof of the one that didn't get away.

While the vets jest and jeer, guides quietly confer on what flies and honey holes are working and who is and isn't catching fish. Vets having a particularly rough day will be shuffled to more reliably "fishy" spots. All of the guides want every veteran to have a great day, and sometimes that means spending hours, individually or even in a small guiding team, helping a single veteran catch his or her first fish on a fly rod.

The highlight of the weekend is an informal gathering on Saturday evening in Cabin 20, after dinner but before the late-night fly-tying sessions begin. Volunteers and vets eagerly cram into the cabin to find out who caught the largest fish, the smallest fish, and the most fish—and to regale each other with the best fish tales of the weekend. Laughter rocks the room, but so do heartfelt confessions of just how much the weekend has meant to one or another participant. Organizers cap the evening of camaraderie with giveaways, including rods, reels, fly lines, boxes filled with flies, rain jackets, artwork, fly-tying materials, vises, and more. These prizes are distributed with no strings attached except an admonishment to put them to good use.

The room's vibe is almost palpable now: Dozens of individual veterans have become a cohesive unit. Those first timers who, just one day ago, were unsure of themselves, have made lifelong friends; they're now a part of a community that includes veterans who've been coming to Harman's for years. This cohesion might not be rare at a PHWFF gathering, but the speed at which these bonds are formed at Harman's really is awe-inspiring. To the untrained eye it all looks so easy, perhaps even effortless. But the truth is that Bob Gartner and Marty Laksbergs have put in hundreds of hours of work behind the scenes. These veterans know it, and they love them for it.

Late in the evening a veteran shares that he hadn't believed what he'd been told about Harman's; it seemed too good to be true. After all, what kinds of people invest this much effort in strangers? No one, that's who. He was injured, he says, and he still experiences nightmares. His life revolves around medications and treatment. He misses the career he loved so much. "Normally I'm a pretty angry guy," he admits wryly. "But not today. Today was a really good day, and I will never forget it. Catching my first trout on a fly rod, the new friends I've made: I'll never forget. I just want to say thanks so much. This has meant the world to me."

Quiet just a moment before, the room erupts in a chorus of voices: "Thanks, Bob," "Thanks, Marty," "We love you guys!" Gartner and Laksbergs are already uncomfortable with the praise when the individual voices finally coalesce into a single chant: "Bob! Bob! Bob!"

Mark Pierce and Clem Danish stand alongside fellow veteran Cody Montelo. No matter the weather, the fishing must go on. Photo by Lally Laksbergs.

Veterans stomp their feet in time and continue chanting until Gartner, eyes filled with tears, implores them to quiet. "You know," he chokes, clearing his throat and soldiering on past the emotion, "Marty does all the real work." Pausing for the inevitable laughter, Gartner regains his composure. "Unfortunately for Marty," says Gartner with a grin, "I write the trip report, so no one will even know he's here this weekend." The room is a cacophony of voices and laughter once again, and Gartner resumes handing out gear.

Bob Gartner serves as a program lead at Fort Belvoir and can be found every Monday evening at the USO where his program meets.

Marty Laksbergs is the former program lead for Marine Corps Base Quantico. He's donated thousands of volunteer hours to the organization and is highly regarded for his selfless leadership. Laksbergs is best known for his "can do" attitude and his unceasing motto of reminding everyone to "put the participants first no matter what."

Mike Banaszewski served in the US Navy and is seen here fishing alongside an American flag in New York's Delaware River.